To Shane, with love
John + Mary.

MILESTONES IN MURDER

To the memory of my late parents,
Thomas John Jordan and Anne Cunningham Jordan.

MILESTONES IN MURDER

DEFINING MOMENTS IN ULSTER'S TERROR WAR

HUGH JORDAN

MAINSTREAM
PUBLISHING

EDINBURGH AND LONDON

First published in Great Britain 2002 by
MAINSTREAM PUBLISHING COMPANY (EDINBURGH) LTD
7 Albany Street
Edinburgh EH1 3UG

Reprinted 2002 (twice)

ISBN 1 84018 640 2

p. 15 Lyrics from 'Sean South' by Dominic Behan, reproduced
by kind permission of the Behan family.
p. 44 Poem reproduced by kind permission of Gusty Spence.
p. 100 Lines from 'The Volk', reproduced by kind
permission of Sean O'Callaghan.
p. 129 Song reproduced by kind permission of Jim McLean.

A catalogue record for this book is available from the British Library

Typeset in Badhouse and Van Dijick

Printed in Great Britain by
Mackays of Chatham PLC

Contents

Acknowledgements

In the course of researching this book I came across many people from a variety of backgrounds who gave freely of their time, which allowed me to explore the complexities of the Northern Ireland conflict. Some are actually named in the text and others, for reasons which should be apparent, have asked that their identities should be protected. This I am happy to do and I assure them that the confidential nature of our conversations will remain as such forever.

I wish to thank writer Martin Dillon for encouraging me to get on with actually writing the book instead of talking about it. Martin set the standard for writing about Northern Ireland in a way that gets behind the media headlines and I found him to be a source of inspiration and assistance at all times.

I thank everyone at Mainstream Publishing in Edinburgh and especially Ailsa Bathgate and Graeme Blaikie for being so understanding and patient in the face of a looming deadline. Some people who have been central to my life since I grew up in Glasgow have contributed by their support. I am indebted to my brothers Tommy and Peter for being themselves, and also to my sister Marie and her husband, Colonel Andrew Whiddett MBE, who, despite coming under intense pressure from me, refused point blank to divulge any of the Queen's secrets. Brian Wilson, British Cabinet Minister, Labour MP for Cunningham North and personal friend of Cuban leader Fidel Castro, provided assistance on various aspects of Irish history.

Thanks are due to Cathy Boyle for her help in the early days of this venture, to my lawyer, Ted Jones, of Jones & Co., Belfast and to my friend Mary McMahon.

Thanks also to Paddy Joe McClean from Beragh, Co. Tyrone, Joe Clark from the Falls Road, Belfast, and Mickey Donnelly from Derry, who were forced to endure a week of horrendous torture following the internment swoops of 1971. I am indebted to them for providing such an insight into this most shameful episode of British involvement in Irish affairs. Particular thanks are due to Paddy Joe for pointing me in the right direction when I was trying to discover the truth about Connie Green, the Second World War hero who survived the African and Italian campaigns only to lose his life on the Irish border fighting for a little-known nationalist army called Saor Ulaidh.

Sean Curry, Sean O'Hare and Sean McConnell, the three Seans, patiently explained the stresses and strains within the republican movement during the moratorium which took place following the failure of the 1950s border campaign.

In the world of the media, I found countless people who were willing to give of their time and expertise. My colleagues at the *Sunday World* in Belfast were helpful in providing background to some major events. The assistance of my friend Jim McDowell, the paper's Northern Editor, proved invaluable, because as a young reporter living and working in Belfast throughout the Troubles, Jim gained a superb insight into what motivated many of the main players. To him I extend a special thank you. In the *Sunday World* Dublin offices, Paul Williams and John Paul Thompson were a great help throughout this project and the paper's editor, Colm MacGinty, provided guidance on how to approach a number of sensitive subjects.

David Sharrock, formerly of the *Daily Telegraph*, now the *Times'* Madrid correspondent, and Henry McDonald, the *Observer's* Ireland editor, gave copious advice on a range of difficult matters. I thank Eoghan Harris for allowing me to freely tap into his superb insight into things Irish. At the *Belfast Telegraph* Lindi McDowell and Walter McAuley kept me right on a number of issues and their help was invaluable.

At Ulster Television, Chris Moore, Ken Reid and Darwin Templeton were always on hand to offer advice, as were my friends, Vincent Kearney and Kevin Magee on the BBC NI *Spotlight* team. Gerry Gregg – an extremely talented documentary filmmaker from Dublin – provided me with background material on the early life of Sean South. My friend David Ross, a former editor of BBC Radio Ulster's *Talkback* programme and now with Radio 4's *File On Four*, encouraged me all the way. I also wish to thank broadcasters David Dunseith, Stephen Walker and Jeremy Adams for their help and encouragement through the years.

Howard Foster and Clive Entwhistle, formerly of *The Cook Report*, have been great friends and colleagues who were always willing to lend a hand when they could.

To Donna Carton, News Editor at the *Sunday Mirror*, I extend a special thanks for taking the time to read the chapters and for suggesting necessary changes. And also to her sister Jane, for laughing at my jokes. In Holland, journalist Ed van de Kerkhoff and Pete Sneider of the *Eindhoven Dagblad* gave of their time and company. And in America, Matthew Cunningham in New York and Paul Matthews in San Francisco did the same.

Over the years I have enjoyed a great relationship with a number of press photographers and I have always admired the courage they have displayed in the face of danger. Conor McCaughley, Alwyn James, Kelvin Boyes and Alan Lewis are among the best.

Many police officers and former police officers gave freely of their time to talk me through some of the most horrendous crimes of the Ulster Troubles. Eric Anderson, Kevin Sheehy and Eamon John Canavan went out of their way to help whenever they could and I am deeply indebted to them. And former Detective Sergeant Johnston Brown led me by the hand through a dangerous web of intrigue and subterfuge. To Johnston and his wife Becky I extend my sincere thanks. My friend Colin Breen, a former officer, took time out of a hectic schedule to introduce me to many ex-policemen who provided help.

Other friends deserve a word of thanks for a variety of reasons, some of which are too complex to go into in the space available. They include Tim and Joyce McGregor, special friends whose company I always enjoy. Tim, a former Detective Superintendent with the RUC, managed to maintain a sense of humour throughout his 30 years of service and he was always available when I needed assistance. I'll never forget him for that.

A number of people who had been and in some cases still are involved with loyalist and republican paramilitary organisations were of tremendous assistance to me, but, for reasons which should be obvious, I have declined from naming them here.

And finally, I wish to thank Seamus and Helen McKendry for having had the courage to tell the world the dreadful story of the 'disappeared'. Helen was just 15 when her mother Jean McConville was abducted by the IRA, never to be seen again. The story was not unique, at least ten other families suffered similar heartache. For decades the issue was swept under the carpet until Helen, along with her husband Seamus, launched a campaign which embarrassed the IRA and gave the rest of the world an insight into the savagery of paramilitary organisations. Helen and her family were not allowed to give their mother a Christian burial, because her body was never returned and it probably never will be. It had been my intention to explain something of this story, but a lack of space prevented me from doing so.

Hugh Jordan
12 July 2002

Foreword

Writing about conflict while living in its midst, and not supporting the combatants, is a dangerous pursuit. Yet it is only through an understanding of the underlying causes of conflict that society can adequately address it. That understanding can only be achieved by writers prising open a window into the world of terror.

One has to get down there into the darkness to find out what it is about. From the first cave paintings about tribalism to the present day, humans have only been successful in dealing with internecine warfare when they have understood its causes. In so doing they have been able to avoid acting in a reflex manner that leaves them vulnerable.

Such understanding demands knowledge of the threat and those who represent it. The mainstream media rarely achieves the process of opening that window into communal strife or terrorism. It deals with the day-to-day events arising from violence and rarely peers behind the headlines to explain the seminal issues underpinning the thoughts, aspirations and actions of the participants to a conflict.

This is a book that will add to our knowledge of the Ireland conflict – one that continues to simmer. Hugh Jordan has painstakingly investigated murders which individually and collectively portray a secret world of callousness and barbarism. It is a world few journalists choose to enter, but one that offers us clarity of perception about the players, whether they are mass murderers, terrorist agents, agents of the State or committed ideologues.

Hugh Jordan first discussed writing this book while we sat in the Windows on the World restaurant in the World Trade Centre in Manhattan over two years ago. I remember telling him that what he proposed to write was a book that would fill a gap in our knowledge. It would shed light on events seminal to a conflict we had both lived with for many years.

I reminded him that it was critical to his book that he understood the fact that history was more important to people in Northern Ireland than their counterparts in other areas of Europe. In many respects that was one of the underlying causes of conflict. Catholics learned Irish history – not the history of Ireland. Protestants learned British history and not the history of Ireland. Both communities approached the conflict with a learned oral tradition of inherited prejudice. Anyone writing about conflict issues had to keep in mind those traditional thought processes in order to write with integrity and without embellishment about contemporary history.

I told him that when I wrote *The Shankill Butchers* and *Dirty War* I was castigated and threatened by people who felt I had not given myself to their agendas. Some warned that I had crossed the line in revealing aspects of the conflict that called into question their motives justifying the murder of innocents.

Like other journalists, I feared for my life. I kept a loaded shotgun by my bed and looked under my car each morning for fear it might be rigged with a bomb. I had been told by security sources that killers I had named by letters of the alphabet in *The Shankill Butchers* had met to discuss slitting my throat. Just as they had years earlier sat over drinks and planned the murder of innocents, they talked about my demise in a similar setting.

Mr A and Mr B were both alive at that time. Since then Mr B has died in a car accident but Mr A remains alive and well, living in west Belfast – probably walking the same streets where he butchered his victims.

As Hugh Jordan has discovered, many of those who killed in the name of a cause or deity are no longer in prison. That is one of the peculiarities of conflict. Life never means life for murderers when the politics of expediency require political solutions.

I found it admirable that Hugh Jordan continued to write this book in the wake of the killing of his colleague, the journalist, Martin O'Hagan. Martin's death illustrated the risks of writing about and living in the midst of conflict. Some observers commented that he was in the wrong place at the wrong time when he was shot dead. They failed to understand the nature of terrorism. By their standard so were the thousands of people in the World Trade Centre the day it was attacked.

On 11 September 2001, Martin O'Hagan phoned me in New York.

'I just wanted to make sure you were okay,' he said in his whimsical fashion.

I had been more concerned for his safety and had warned him on several occasions to be vigilant. When I had written *God and the Gun* he had set up interviews for me with people who shared the same prejudices as those who eventually murdered him. I wrote the following tribute to him:

> *To Martin O'Hagan*
> *(Murdered in Ireland on 28 September 2001)*
> We lived with conflict, you and I,
> wrapped in a war over space,
> clothed in a history made by others.
> We lifted stones and peered under them,
> knowing a Bishop left vipers,
> venomous and angry in ignorance.
> A firestorm was in Manhattan
> with another God in the mix,
> while ours was in bullets waiting for you.

Hugh Jordan is a journalist familiar with the terrain and has brought to this book a serious journalistic study of killings that illustrate the murky and horrific nature of conflict.

Enough time has passed to enable a detailed investigation of episodes like the Malvern Street shooting, which occurred at a critical time in the troubled history of Northern Ireland. That event symbolised a period when major fissures began to appear within the Unionist monolith and led to a form of unionism that remains fractured to this day.

Malvern Street brought the gun back into politics as well as the cult of the gunman. It also involved a conspiracy that was conveniently swept under the carpet when the political tapestry of the province was dramatically changing.

Within the Catholic community, disillusionment with republicanism had given way to demands for change within the system. All the variables were in there as far as the IRA was concerned, from traditional nationalism moving towards socialism, and republicanism seeking a new definition and British civil rights. The events in Malvern Street in 1966 changed all of that. In many respects it was one of the critical elements in history that propelled both communities into a tribal conflict and decades of violence and suffering.

This is a book that people should read and learn from.

Martin Dillon

– CHAPTER ONE –

Sean South of Garryowen

O have you been in Limerick Green . . .
From 'Sean South' by Dominic Behan

Shortly after teatime on New Year's Day 1957, Sergeant Kenneth Cordner was about to play the ace of clubs to win yet another game of pontoon, when he heard the unmistakable whine of a lorry making its way down the street outside.

Everyone in the room tensed. In an instant Cordner dropped the cards and ran down the single flight of stairs to take a closer look. His worst fears were confirmed. As he opened the door of the rural police station, a fusillade of gunfire splattered the front of the building.

It was the Irish Republican Army (IRA). Cordner, a sergeant in the Royal Ulster Constabulary (RUC), knew it was them. An RUC spy within the IRA had ensured he was expecting the visit.

He slammed the door shut, but swung it so hard the latch failed to secure and the door remained open. By the time Cordner was halfway up the stairs again, shouting a warning to his fellow officers, the battle had already commenced. Outside, an IRA flying column was frantically mounting what was supposed to be a surprise guerrilla attack, but it was all about to go dreadfully wrong, with tragic consequences.

The plan had been to drive into the mainly Protestant village of Brookeborough, Co. Fermanagh, a few miles inside the Northern Ireland border, position the lorry just past the small police station and, using the vehicle as cover, mount a landmine and grenade attack, which hopefully would result in the quick surrender of the police officers holed up inside.

A few minutes before the lorry, a quarry dump truck, pulled into the village, two local boys, Stanley Thompson and Ernest Duff, were still playing in the street. It was just before seven o'clock and the light had long gone, but the boys were determined to enjoy as much of their holidays as possible. The youngsters got the shock of their lives when two men wearing khaki-coloured army tunics jumped from the vehicle and ordered them home.

The men were IRA lookouts and the attack which was about to take place was part of the IRA's Operation Harvest – a border campaign aimed at reclaiming the six Irish counties of Antrim, Armagh, Down, Derry, Fermanagh and Tyrone, which had been annexed into the state of Northern Ireland within the United Kingdom when Ireland was partitioned in 1921.

The main problem for the IRA was that there was no one in its ranks with local knowledge and Brookeborough, which took its name from the nearby family estate of the Northern Ireland Prime Minister, Lord Brookeborough, was enemy territory.

Brookeborough's usually thriving main street was deserted that New Year's evening, apart from the schoolboys. The police station, which is situated at the northern end of the town, blends in perfectly with the pleasant architecture of the other two-storey buildings. Apart from the sandbags which had been placed around its windows and doors that very day, it was not easily recognisable as the barracks of the paramilitary RUC, which was viewed by many at that time, including the Northern Ireland government, as the armed wing of Ulster Unionism.

In the days following Partition, the RUC may have provided much of the muscle to ensure Unionism's survival in the ongoing siege it was forced to endure at the hands of Irish nationalism. But at a local level and on a day-to-day basis, its members were known to and enjoyed the support of the community, including some Catholics.

Brookeborough Barracks, with its mock-gothic doors and diamond-shaped iron and glass windows, gave more the impression of being an English country cottage, rather than the bolt-hole of the men who were ready to resist the firepower of the IRA with equally lethal force. This, coupled with the fact that no one in the 12-man raiding party had knowledge of the town's layout, probably accounted for why the IRA was unable to identify its target on entering the town. It later emerged that, apart from the plethora of military hardwear on board, the only pieces of equipment available to Sean Garland, the IRA's man in charge, were an Ordnance Survey map and a first-aid kit. Garland, a 22-year-old Dubliner from Belvedere Place in the inner city's north side, had little experience of rural Ireland apart from time spent on IRA training expeditions. Garland and his second-in-command, Dave O'Connell, would later play centre-stage roles in the developments which followed the calling off of the campaign five years later, but for the moment they were restricted to bit parts in a physical force drama which would secure a place in Irish republican folklore.

The man driving the lorry, Vincent Conlon from neighbouring Co. Monaghan, was the nearest thing the IRA had to a local man on the job. But so unsure was Conlon of where he was going that he drove past the barracks completely and was forced to reverse back up the main street after one of his colleagues spotted the target disappearing in the rear-view mirror. The altered tone of the gear change further alerted Sgt Cordner and his colleagues that something was wrong.

Positioned in the back of the truck, manning a tripod-mounted Bren gun, was Sean South from Limerick, a 28-year-old clerk who had left his native city a few weeks previously without telling his family where he was going. Next to South was Paddy O'Regan, whose job it was to thread the belt-fed magazine through South's deadly weapon. Both men were ready for business and their eyes were firmly trained on the assault team whose job it was to plant a mine at the front of the barracks. They were to provide fire cover.

The second his IRA colleagues were safely out of the firing line, South opened up as Sgt Cordner twisted open the door latch. The policeman's split-second appearance at the door went unnoticed as South and O'Regan continuously pounded the building. The electrical charge to detonate the mine was turned on, but nothing happened. As members of the assault team hastily prepared another mine, the rest deluged the building with machine gun fire. A second mine was put in place, but again it failed to go off when the charge was applied. The IRA knew that the RUC personnel would probably occupy the upper floor of the barracks and decided to concentrate their fire on that part of the building. But Sean South was experiencing great frustration, because the lorry was parked only a short distance of some 40 ft from the barracks and as a result he was unable to get the required elevation of gunfire. The presence of such a powerful machine gun was posing no serious threat to the occupants.

Inside, the RUC officers who had been forced to hit the deck at the first hail of bullets were frantically returning fire and wondering what other defensive action to take when Sgt Cordner switched on the light in the front upstairs room which housed the armoury. A fusillade of shots from the IRA men below sent a shower of broken glass across the room as Cordner knocked off the light and slid along the floor to where a Sten gun was bracketed into a wall.

In an instant, he released the weapon from its mounting and prepared it for use by inserting a magazine. Bravely, Cordner made his way slowly towards the window to where he hoped to assess the danger he and his men faced. IRA grenades aimed at the upper windows bounced off the iron casements and exploded in the street below, adding further confusion. As yet unable to size up the opposition, the sergeant glanced out the window. He spotted a large red open-topped lorry with armed men on its platform as well as in the street. The RUC man leaned forward and emptied the entire contents of his gun's magazine before jumping back inside. Below, Sean Garland and Dave O'Connell returned the fire. As Cordner struggled to replace his spent mag, Sean Garland, realising he was now not likely to achieve the quick surrender he had been looking for, decided to call off the raid. But as Garland and the rest of his men quickly made their way to the rear of the lorry before mounting the platform, Sgt Cordner stepped towards the window for a second look. His targets, he saw, were now concentrated in one small area at the back of the truck. With his Sten on fully automatic, he fired one continuous burst of 25 rounds at the IRA. Although he didn't know it at the time, Sgt Kenneth Cordner's action would, for a while at least, alter the course of Irish history and help create two more Irish republican martyrs whose memories are revered by IRA members to this day.

Feargal O'Hanlon, a 20-year-old draughtsman who worked for the council in his native Monaghan Town, slumped to the ground, badly hurt by two wounds to his legs. Sean Garland, the flying column leader, was also hit a number of times in his back and leg. As the bullets from Cordner's Sten continued to rain down on the escaping IRA, Garland and O'Hanlon's comrades dragged them onto the back of the lorry. Every bullet fired by Sgt Cordner hit either the lorry or an IRA man who was on its platform or inside the cab. Sean South, who lay slumped over his machine gun, looked finished and his Bren gun partner had been hit twice. In the cab, Vincie Conlon was shot in the foot, and a bullet struck the buckle of Phil O'Donaghue's belt. The bullet travelled right around his body leaving a bright red mark on the skin surface, but he was otherwise unhurt.

Despite his injuries, Vincie Conlon, following Garland's orders, started to drive the lorry in a southerly direction towards Roslea. But with two tyres punctured by bullets, and a tipping gear mechanism shot to pieces, he was unable to move the vehicle quickly enough to escape the fire of Cordner and his RUC colleagues, who were by now also concentrating fire on the lorry. Minutes later the two IRA lookouts, Mick Kelly and Mick O'Brien, reboarded the vehicle at the far end of the street. They were both completely shocked at what they saw. With nothing to secure it, the platform moved continuously up and down as the lorry trundled towards the border with the RUC in hot pursuit.

A few miles away, at Colebrooke House, the Prime Minister of Northern

Ireland, Lord Brookeborough, was listening to the story of the battle and the chase on the radio set of a police car outside his home. The police officers were at Colebrooke as part of a close-protection service provided for the man who was the leader of the Ulster Unionist Party. The police radio was tuned into Brookeborough Barracks and the officers had summoned the politician as soon as the attack began. Within an hour of the attack, Lord Brookeborough visited the barracks, where he congratulated Sgt Cordner and his men. 'The police behaved with great gallantry. They made a very brave show,' he told the press as he emerged from the badly damaged police station.

Five miles out of Brookeborough, the IRA flying column reached Altawark crossroads and the lorry, which was by now travelling at a snail's pace due to the amount of damage it had sustained in the crossfire, trundled to a halt. The men, or at least the ones who were able to do so, jumped out. The platform of the vehicle was covered in pools of blood. The IRA had taken a pounding. If he wasn't dead already, Sean South was at death's door, and Feargal O'Hanlon, a strongly built athlete who had played senior Gaelic football for his county, had also slipped into unconsciousness. Sean Garland was suffering badly from gunshot wounds. But despite this he pleaded with his comrades to be left beside South and O'Hanlon. He also demanded a machine gun to protect them during the inevitable RUC follow-up operation, which was already swinging into place. The IRA men persuaded the red-haired Dubliner of the folly of this approach and the bodies of South and O'Hanlon were placed in a nearby cow byre. One volunteer was ordered to call at a nearby house to raise the alarm, and it was hoped the men would receive medical attention as soon as possible. The IRA party, using an Ordnance Survey map and a compass, headed slowly for the Monaghan border. But they were stopped in their tracks after a while by the sound of sustained gunfire coming from the direction of the cow byre and the abandoned lorry at Altawark crossroads.

The retreating IRA men wrongly assumed that the RUC were administering a *coup de grâce* to South and O'Hanlon. But in fact two police search teams, including Sgt Ken Cordner, had just reached the crossroads, arriving from both directions in a pincer movement and, on discovering the abandoned lorry, had opened fire on it. Head Constable C.H. Rodgers was in charge of the operation and, after ordering a halt to the gunfire, approached the vehicle, which was riddled with holes. He found six army haversacks, live and spent ammunition, along with a Thompson sub-machine gun, the IRA's favoured weapon. The large quantity of blood on the platform shocked the police officer, who also discovered a well-stocked first aid kit. Despite the heavy casualties sustained by the lorry's occupants, the first aid kit remained untouched. A trail of blood led across the road to a nearby house. There were marks on the back door where obviously a blood-stained hand had earlier knocked. There was no one at home and the door was locked. A further trail of blood led to a cow byre 50 yards away. Accompanied by Sgt Cordner, Rodgers cautiously entered the building. There he found the bodies of Sean South and Feargal O'Hanlon. The policemen knew instantly that South was dead. O'Hanlon showed faint signs of life, but died within a matter of minutes.

At an inquest into the IRA men's deaths, held two days later at Fermanagh County Hospital, a police District Inspector (DI) said the raiders who carried out the attack on Brookeborough Barracks had left one of their comrades to die in the byre. DI Wolseley condemned the action of the IRA men. Immediate first aid would have saved the life of Feargal O'Hanlon, he insisted. The police officer's claims were backed up by the relief surgeon at Fermanagh County Hospital, Mr J.W. Wilson, who carried out a post-mortem on the young Monaghan man. Death was due, Mr Wilson told the inquest, to shock and haemorrhage following a gunshot wound and fracture of the left thigh. There was no evidence, he said, that either of the wounds had been caused by close-range shots, putting paid to the notion that the RUC had executed O'Hanlon on finding his body in the cow byre.

DI Wolseley said Sean South was dead when he found him, and he strongly criticised the actions of the IRA team in leaving one of their men to die in the byre. He said: 'These armed raids are made by these men, apparently in defiance of the elected representatives, of the people and against the advice of all sections of the community and church leaders.' And, referring to O'Hanlon, the policeman added: 'It would appear that, far from helping this unfortunate man, he was abandoned and left to die.' On the day of the inquest one of O'Hanlon's comrades told an Irish newspaper that the IRA had left South and O'Hanlon at the home of a Catholic family and had summoned a priest and a doctor, but evidence given to the coroner contradicted this.

Mr Wilson, who also carried out a post-mortem on Sean South, said that, like O'Hanlon, he too had died as a result of shock and haemorrhage from a gunshot wound, which had severed his femoral artery. The Limerick man had also sustained a number of superficial gunshot wounds, said the doctor. The jury returned a finding in compliance with the medical evidence. Feargal O'Hanlon's father and one of Sean South's brothers attended the inquest and gave evidence after formally identifying the bodies of their loved ones, which were kept in a nearby building. Eugene O'Hanlon from Park Street in Monaghan Town said his son left the family home on 29 December and that he was unaware of his whereabouts. Sean South's elder brother James, who had travelled from Limerick, told the inquest that he had last seen Sean alive on 7 December when he had left home without saying where he was going. He said his family was unaware that Sean was a member of the IRA, although he had at one time been a member of the Irish Territorial Army, but had severed all connections with the organisation. James South said his family were shocked when they learned of Sean's involvement in the Brookeborough raid. At the end of the inquest the coroner, Mr J.R. Hanna, complimented the police actions in defending the barracks at Brookeborough.

Militarily, the operation was a disaster for the IRA. Of the twelve men who took part in the raid, two had died and four others had been injured by gunfire, two of them seriously. Despite the outcome, the IRA was about to turn it into a huge propaganda coup.

A massive security operation swung into action following the Brookeborough attack. The Northern Ireland government used every available tool at its disposal as it desperately tried to catch the escaping IRA men. Four hundred men joined in the border manhunt and fifty square miles of mountainous country were scoured. British troops, RUC men and Special Constables were drafted in to track down the men. Two Royal Navy helicopters from the air station at Eglinton on the outskirts of Derry were scrambled and a detachment of recruits from the police training depot at Enniskillen were also used. For them it was their first taste of action in the fight against the secret army of the IRA.

The authorities believed a number of IRA gunmen were trapped in the bleak Cooneen Mountains area of south Fermanagh and concentrated the search there. Searchers using walkie-talkie sets and tracker dogs combed vast ranges of the desolate terrain. Flares went up all night long, but there was still no sign of the fleeing gunmen. Across the border in the Republic, Irish soldiers and police were also out in force.

Against all odds, the badly injured Sean Garland and his men, three of whom were also suffering from gunshot wounds, made it across the border. A five-hour march found them in the Slieve Beagh mountain range and it was now safe for them to come down and seek help for their injured personnel. By now their condition was deteriorating badly and they urgently required medical treatment. The injured men were left to rest at a house, while Dave O'Connell, the second-in-command, went for help. The others made off on foot and were arrested by the Irish Army later that morning.

Two Irish policemen who had been searching all night were dozing in their car on a remote mountain road, when they were suddenly woken by a loud bang. The officers were somewhat startled to see a young man lying sprawled across the car bonnet. It was Dave O'Connell. The exhausted IRA man had just pushed through a hedge and then slipped down a roadside banking onto the car. The game was up. There was no need for O'Connell to explain who he was. He was arrested and then took the policemen to the house where the injured men were hiding. Reinforcements and medical help were summoned immediately and the wounded men were rushed to Monaghan County Hospital.

Until now the IRA had been viewed on both sides of the border as a bit of a joke. Its members were seen as well-meaning fanatics with little relevance to the modern world. Fundamentalists like them certainly had little or nothing to contribute to modern Ireland, north or south. Both parts of Ireland were desperately trying to shake off the austerity of the post-war years, which were dominated by unemployment and emigration. But things were about to change and the IRA was about to snatch its greatest victory for decades from the jaws of defeat. The funerals of IRA volunteers Feargal O'Hanlon and Sean South were to have a profound effect on Irish life at home and abroad, and they also tapped into a deep vein of Irish nationalism most thought had long ago died out. As a result of the deaths of these two young men, who lost their lives after taking part in terrorist action, republicanism was about to enjoy its most fertile period for decades.

At his son's inquest two days earlier, Eugene O'Hanlon told the court he had received a number of messages of sympathy, but now they were arriving in torrents. Special post deliveries in Monaghan and Limerick were introduced to cope with the mail addressed to the families of the dead men. City corporations and town councils the length and breadth of the Republic passed votes of sympathy. In some cases politicians proposing the motions said the men should be honoured for their courage and dedication to the cause of Ireland.

Unionists were outraged and the government in Belfast ordered a clampdown on known republican sympathisers. Arrests were made and Sir Anthony Eden, the Tory Prime Minister, issued a statement condemning IRA attacks in the north. In Dublin, senior politicians were also concerned, because suddenly their country was in the middle of a week of unofficial national mourning for what, in the public perception, were two brave sons of Erin who had been gunned down by a Unionist police force at the behest of their political masters at Westminster.

Nothing could have been further from the truth, but the IRA was determined to milk this opportunity for all it was worth. The IRA's border campaign – Operation Harvest – had begun less than a month ago with a series of coordinated terrorist attacks which, despite the normal Unionist outrage, caused little more than a few raised eyebrows and a few heavy sighs.

But now the world was watching and the IRA had two more martyrs in the tradition of Pearse and Connolly, who had died at the hands of British firing squads in Kilmainham Prison only 40 years ago. IRA leaders felt sure the support was now there for a violent bid to end Partition and reunite Ireland.

People lined the streets as the bodies of South and O'Hanlon passed through the towns and villages of Fermanagh as they made their way home for burial. When the hearses crossed the border into the South, the crowds seemed to swell with every mile. At Feargal O'Hanlon's funeral in Monaghan, huge crowds watched as a guard of honour made up of young men dressed in trench coats accompanied the remains to the cemetery. The coffin was draped in the Irish Tricolour and there could be no doubt that this was an IRA funeral.

A photograph of O'Hanlon's grief-stricken mother appeared in every national newspaper the following day and the tortured image prompted Irish songwriter Dominic Behan to pen one of his most famous ballads, 'The Patriot Game'. The song became a worldwide hit. Behan, who had started out in life as an Irish republican, came to detest the elitism of nationalism and later changed some of the words for fear that it may have given the impression he supported the IRA and its campaign of violence.

By the time the hearse carrying Sean South's body reached his native Limerick the following Saturday, the crowds had swelled to staggering proportions. The dead IRA man's brothers told reporters they expected his comrades to stage some sort of military funeral in his honour. They also said they expected shots to be fired over his coffin and many with no interest in republicanism turned out to witness this dramatic display of defiance. One brother said that he had travelled north to identify Sean Smith with a heavy heart and filled with hatred of the IRA. It was his brother's membership of the terrorist organisation which had brought about his death, he explained. But as he began to realise how the people of Ireland felt about Sean, and the high regard in which they held him, his opinion had changed. He now felt immensely proud of his brother and soon converted to the republican ideals his brother Sean espoused.

As with the O'Hanlon funeral, an IRA guard of honour marched alongside the hearse as the coffin bearing Sean South's body made its final journey. An estimated 50,000 people turned out to pay their respects. As usual a rousing ballad was composed, and 'Sean South of Garryowen' was sung in Irish bars all the way from Gweedore in west Donegal to the Gorbals area of Glasgow, where the IRA commanded support among Irish immigrants. Mickey Joe Heraghty, a tunneller from the Fanad Peninsula, invested his savings in a pub at Gorbals Cross. The name of the bar, which was known locally as 'The

Coronation Bar', was promptly changed to the 'Garryowen' in memory of the young IRA man who lost his life on a bleak New Year's Day in Brookeborough.

By all accounts Sean South was a unique individual, but he was also a product of a city which was very conservatively Catholic and at times even reactionary. It was in Limerick at the turn of the century that anti-Semitism first reared its head in Ireland. From the 1880s onwards an influx of poor Jews, many escaping Tsarist Russia, began to arrive in Ireland, and the Jewish community swelled to an all-time high of over 3,500. Many of them settled in the cities of Dublin, Cork and Limerick, and it was there in 1904 that Jewish immigrants suffered attacks and a sustained period of persecution. Their homes and businesses were targeted by club-wielding mobs who attempted to burn them out, while inflammatory speeches by a Redemptorist priest, Father John Creagh, inspired a two-year boycott of Jewish shopkeepers and traders. Republicans were deeply involved in encouraging the anti-Semitic feelings in the city, which caused many of the Jews to flee to Cork and Dublin or quit Ireland altogether. Some years ago when journalist Simon Sebag Montefiore, a descendant of a Jew who had been driven from his Limerick home, made a television programme highlighting republican involvement in the persecution, he was severely criticised in the press.

At 28, Sean South remained unmarried and those who knew him said he had a priestly quality about him. He was also a very devout Catholic and one former IRA volunteer, who was on the Brookeborough raid along with him, told how he said the rosary before mounting his Bren gun on the back of the quarry dump truck which would take him to his death. He said: 'Sean was a very serious person and he believed that the action he was about to take was the only route open to him to bring about a united Ireland. He had a great interest in Ireland, but his knowledge of the North was extremely limited.'

South earned his living by working as a clerk. But he was also a painter, a gifted musician, and a Gaelic writer who published his own magazine, *An Gath*. On the face of it Sean South had much to contribute to the Ireland of his day. People his own age and younger were leaving Ireland in droves for the dubious attractions of Kilburn and the Bronx. Yet he chose the path of violence to advance the cause of the country that he dearly loved.

Sean South was born in 1929, just seven years after the foundation of the Irish Free State. He grew up in Limerick during the hungry '30s, when life in the west of Ireland was particularly hard. It was and still is in many ways a city of extremes. To some it may seem odd, but, as the rest of the world was erasing the memories and horrors of the Second World War to the strains of a new music called rock 'n' roll, a group of young Irishmen, with no political mandate, were preparing to finish the job which had been started on the steps of the General Post Office in Dublin when Padraig Pearse proclaimed the Irish Republic on Easter Monday 1916. South was only one of many young men from right across the island who believed deeply that it was time for Britain to leave Ireland for good. And, as far as they were concerned, the only way Britain was going to agree to this was by force of arms. It was the Irish way, it had been successful in past. As far as South and his comrades were concerned, it was time to finish the job and they were up for it.

A spy in the IRA ranks, however, brought a premature end to these plans. Details of the Brookeborough raid had been betrayed by the word of an informer. RUC agent George Poyntz's double-dealings would cast a long shadow over the IRA for the next 30 years. When his cover was blown in 1984, it created a major flap inside the Special Branch of the RUC, which was responsible for handling him. But that reaction was nothing to the rage it caused among members of the IRA and Sinn Fein who had dealings with him, particularly Gerry Adams.

Based in Castleblaney, Co. Monaghan, Poyntz established himself as a trusted IRA and Sinn Fein figure. In fact he became chairman of Sinn Fein in Monaghan. He ran a bar in 'Blaney, as it is known locally, which soon became a favourite watering hole of IRA men travelling north and south. By the time the Provisional Branch of the IRA, the Provos, emerged in the 1970s, Poyntz was so well connected that it became almost compulsory for senior IRA from the North making their way to Dublin to stay the night at his house.

George Poyntz ingratiated himself with the IRA even more when he married Mary McAuley. She was a woman who had family ties with leading members of the republican movement. For three decades Poyntz operated inside the IRA as an RUC and Garda informer.

Poyntz, at great danger to himself, worked diligently for three decades passing on valuable information to both the RUC and the Garda Siochana. A moment of madness, however, almost cost him his life. Poyntz made a cassette recording offering his services to the Ulster Defence Association (UDA). It has been suggested that he may have been put up to this by British Intelligence agents. On the tape, Poyntz said he was in a position to pass on detailed information about republicans. He was careful not to reveal his name, but he sent the tape to the then Supreme Commander of the UDA, Andy Tyrie. When he received the tape at the UDA's headquarters at Gawn Street, just off the staunchly loyalist Newtownards Road area of Belfast, Tyrie called a meeting of the terror organisation's top brass, which included the notorious racketeer James 'Jimmy' Pratt Craig from the Shankill Road. A number of copies were made of the cassette and Craig, ever the opportunist, spotted a chance to ingratiate himself with the Provos.

For some time now, Jimmy Craig had been under close scrutiny from within his own organisation. John McMichael, a senior UDA figure and founder member of the Ulster Loyalist Democratic Party (ULDP), had launched an investigation into Craig's dodgy dealings. Craig, a brute of a man, was well aware that time was running out for him, and, as the net closed in, he demonstrated a ruthless survival streak, which included setting up the murders of other loyalists. To do this he engaged the help of the Provisional IRA, which was only too glad to take advantage of Craig's treachery.

Craig was in the habit of having regular meetings with a senior IRA man who was known within the republican terror group by the nickname of 'Joe Buck'. The pair would meet in a city-centre bar where Craig passed on details regarding the movements of loyalists he wanted eliminated. Craig gave Joe Buck a copy of the George Poyntz cassette tape.

It was played a short time later to a gathering of senior Provos in another part of the city. Those present were shocked when it became obvious that the genial host who looked after them so well when they called at his Castleblaney home was a dangerous double agent who was prepared to sell them out to their sworn enemies in the UDA. But it was also clear that Poyntz had been an RUC and Gardai informer for many years.

A plan was put in place immediately. It was decided to lure Poyntz to Belfast on the pretext of attending a meeting. He was to be abducted, tortured and, after a tape-recorded confession was extracted from him, Poyntz was to be shot dead as a 'tout', the Ulster word for an informer. Touts are detested within all paramilitary organisations and, once uncovered, are shown no mercy.

Around the same time, early April 1984, the trial was taking place in Belfast of an RUC officer charged with the murder of two Irish National Liberation Army (INLA) men, Seamus Grew and Roddy Carroll. Poyntz wasn't named in the trial, but it emerged that, prior to losing their lives, Grew and Carroll and the INLA leader, Dominic McGlinchey, had visited Poyntz's home in the Republic. They told Poyntz they planned to travel back north together. McGlinchey changed his mind at the last minute, but it was made clear in court that the information on the terror team's movements could only have been passed on to the RUC by George Poyntz. His time was up.

Through another republican informer, the RUC Special Branch learned of the IRA's plans to execute George Poyntz. Poyntz had been an excellent Special Branch servant over the years and the race was now on to save him. His handlers made contact and asked Poyntz to rendezvous with them at an arranged spot in Keady, just inside the south Armagh border. They told him they knew of the Tyrie tape and warned him his life was now in danger.

Poyntz tried to assure the policemen he had the skills to successfully endure an IRA interrogation. He believed his connection with Gerry Adams would help. The police officers were not impressed. One placed a hand on Poyntz's shoulder and said: 'George, I'm arresting you for your own safety.'

In Gough Barracks in Armagh city, Poyntz, who was 57 years of age, agreed to go into protective custody and asked to see his family. They were contacted by Gardai at their Castleblaney home. In an emotional meeting in which Poyntz revealed his secret life, he told his family he would not be returning home to Castleblaney. It was the last time he saw them. Within minutes of his family's departure, plans were put in place to create a new identity for the man who, starting with the Brookeborough Barracks raid in 1957, had spent almost 30 years as an informant.

A short time later, Poyntz was lifted out of Gough Barracks in a helicopter and today lives a quiet life under an assumed name. His neighbours have no idea that the elderly Irishman living in their midst once topped an IRA hit list.

A month after the 20th anniversary of the Brookeborough Barracks raid, Sean Garland, the man who was the IRA commanding officer that day, approached the podium at the annual conference of Official Sinn Fein.

By now, Garland was National Organiser of the party and had rejected paramilitary activity in favour of Soviet-style Marxism. He urged delegates to vote to change the party name to 'Sinn Fein – The Workers' Party'. The suffix, he said, reflected the new socialist direction of the party. IRA men from the North who were also delegates were ordered to vote for the name change.

Later that night, at an after-conference social gathering, a spontaneous sing-song broke out in a club next to the party headquarters at 30 Gardiner Place. Someone struck up a rousing version of Sean South of Garryowen, but Kitty O'Kane, a veteran republican activist from Belfast, angrily shouted out: 'What are yous singing that for? Sure yous don't care about Sean South anymore and the next thing yous'll be doin' is dropping the Sinn Fein bit.' Five years later, delegates to the Sinn Fein – The Workers' Party conference (the conference of the Official wing of the republican movement) did indeed vote to drop Sinn Fein from the party title.

Kitty O'Kane left the party. Garland remained as General Secretary. Within a few years the Workers' Party enjoyed limited electoral success with seven TDs (Irish MPs) in the Irish Parliament and a Euro MP at Strasbourg.

Two of these TDs were Tomas Mac Goilla – a former Sinn Fein President – and Proinsias De Rossa. Both Mac Goilla and De Rossa had been interned in the Republic during the IRA Border Campaign of the 1950s. Following a split in the Workers' Party in 1992, over the thorny issue of whether a lingering paramilitary faction linked to the party was still active, De Rossa left Garland and Mac Goilla and formed the Democratic Left.

De Rossa later served as Minister for Social Welfare in a coalition government made up of Fine Gael, Labour and the Democratic Left. His party eventually amalgamated with Labour and De Rossa was elected party president. At least for some contemporaries of Sean South, the journey was complete.

– CHAPTER TWO –

The Border Campaign – From Volunteer Connie Green to Constable John Hunter

But dark indeed would be the Foyles waters,
And parched the land without ere leaf or sheen,
No bird to sing, no flower to bloom and cheer us
Should we break faith or bond with you, O Connie Green.
1950s nationalist ballad, writer unknown

From the moment Éamon de Valera chose to renounce paramilitarism and enter the Irish Parliament in 1927, militant republicanism entered a period of decline which grew more pronounced with each passing decade. As each 'physical force' group gradually accepted the reality of Partition and bought into the new political structures, violence as a means of achieving the holy grail of the 'Republic' seemed more and more meaningless. By the early 1950s, however, the IRA believed Ireland was once again ready to take up the struggle to remove the British presence from the six counties which made up Northern Ireland, and, as the story of Sean South demonstrates, the IRA wasn't widely off the mark. Although most of the population weren't prepared to take up the gun personally, many had a great deal of sympathy for those who were.

If there was to be a campaign, preparations had to be made. Sean Garland was asked by the IRA leadership to join the British Army with the sole purpose of stealing weaponry that would later be used against the ancient enemy.

Garland undertook the task with relish and travelled north to join the Royal Irish Fusiliers. It was a daring and imaginative plan. Garland was a dedicated volunteer and he possessed in abundance the one quality which would ensure the success of the venture. It was an attribute many others in the IRA at that particular time did not have, namely patience.

The Royal Irish Fusiliers were based at Gough Barracks, a formidable building in the centre of Armagh. An IRA volunteer passing the front of the barracks one day noticed that the soldier guarding the main gate was carrying a rifle, but it lacked the one part which transformed it into a deadly weapon – a magazine full of bullets.

The IRA was intrigued and felt it had nothing to lose by asking a volunteer to explore what went on behind the barrack wall. It wasn't uncommon at that time for young Dublin men to extricate themselves from a life of poverty by joining the British armed forces. In the years before the formation of the Free State, the Dublin Fusiliers played a major role in the British Army, having earned honours at Gallipoli and Murnmansk. Strong and fit, John Garland, as he was known at the time, made excellent soldier material and within a short period was promoted to the rank of colour sergeant. At one point he was actually employed as a sentry at Hillsborough Castle, the Ulster residence of Her Majesty, Queen Elizabeth II. He even managed to bring a couple of IRA members into the barracks at weekends under the guise of attending a dance. To his superior officers, Garland seemed a normal soldier, and they had no way of knowing that the red-haired squaddie in their midst was also a volunteer soldier in another army, whose sole purpose was to force the British out of Ireland forever.

Using a tiny Minnix camera, Garland photographed every inch of Gough Barracks in detail and relayed the information back to the IRA's General Headquarters in Dublin. He also made maps and diagrams and passed them to Tony Magan and Pat Murphy in Dublin. Magan was chief-of-staff and Murphy had recently been appointed adjutant general of the shadowy terrorist organisation. There were many within the ranks of the IRA who were desperate to see action and so, if the Gough Barracks arms raid was to prove successful, the IRA would be back in business and more than well positioned to commence another armed campaign.

Eventually, in early June 1954, Garland discovered that all weapons at the barracks were to be brought to the armoury where an inventory would be taken. These were ideal circumstances and plans were put in place to pull off the raid. The idea was to have a party of 20 volunteers who would drive into the barracks in a truck once the unarmed guard on the gate had been overpowered. After the weapons had been loaded on, the truck would be driven back out the main gate.

On 12 June a cattle truck was hijacked in Dundalk and the raiding party, made up of 20 volunteers from the Dublin unit, was briefed by Pat Murphy on the exact nature of the operation.

In Armagh the raiders held a last-minute briefing before an IRA volunteer walked up to the sentry on the gate and asked how to go about joining the army. The soldier said he could not recommend the military life to anyone, but he got the shock of his life when the pleasant stranger then pulled a revolver from under his jacket and ordered him to step inside. At that point three other IRA men brushed past and on into the guardroom. The sentry was tied up and his place on the gate was taken by an IRA volunteer. The IRA man was wearing full British Army uniform and he was carrying a Sten gun. The difference was that the new guard's gun had a full magazine in it.

Pat Murphy, who was taking part in the operation himself, overpowered two other soldiers and they too were bundled in the guardroom after being bound hand and foot. All army personnel were directed to the guardroom, where they were immediately set upon and tied up. At one stage there were nineteen soldiers and one civilian being held prisoner as the IRA cleaned out the entire contents of the armoury and stacked the weapons in the cattle truck. Half an hour after the raid began, the IRA piled back into the lorry and left the barracks after taking the trouble to lock the front gate. By the time the alarm was raised, the truck was heading safely for the border.

The weapons, which consisted of 250 rifles, 37 Sten guns, 9 Bren guns and 40 training rifles, were driven to a farmhouse in Co. Meath, where they were cleaned before being dumped. The raid had been a major military success, but it was also a tremendous propaganda boost in terms of its sheer audacity. The IRA was back in business and the British Army was deeply embarrassed after being made to look foolish in its own backyard.

The Gough Barracks raid and the publicity it attracted gave the IRA leadership the confidence it needed to try a repeat performance, therefore maintaining the momentum during the build-up to a campaign. This time it was Omagh Barracks the IRA had in mind, the home base of the Royal Inniskillen Fusiliers. However, after the embarrassment of the Armagh raid, the British Army had tightened up its security and the IRA's odds of success were much reduced. In the end, the operation turned into a fiasco and, following a confused gun battle inside the army base, eight men were arrested, including Tom Mitchell who would later make history by being elected three times to the Westminster Parliament on a Sinn Fein ticket while still a felon serving a jail sentence.

Despite this setback, the IRA continued to attract recruits and organise training camps where young fit men, who were mostly armed with nothing more than enthusiasm, were taken through the rudiments of weapons training. A final opportunity presented itself to pull off yet another daring arms raid, this time at an army base at Arborfield, in the English county of

Berkshire. Again, using information supplied by a 'sleeper' inside the British Army, an IRA team, which included Ruairi O Bradaigh, overpowered unsuspecting sentries and cleared out the contents of the armoury, which was by all accounts substantial. Two vans were brought into the base, the weaponry was then loaded on and driven off. But one van was stopped by the Berkshire police after it was clocked travelling at 75 mph, and after the officers made a quick check of its contents the driver and his pals were arrested. The other van managed to make it on into London as planned. However, a receipt found in the pocket of one of the IRA men in custody gave the police a clue as to the location of the terrorists' London base and a huge haul of arms and ammunition were recovered. The three IRA men arrested shortly after leaving Arborfield were all given life sentences after refusing to recognise the court when they appeared at Berkshire Assizes.

The IRA had been hoping for success on English soil because it had already lost three able men on an arms raid. In 1953, Cathal Goulding from Dublin, John Stephenson (who later changed his name to the Irish Gaelic version, Sean MacStiofain) from London and Manus Canning from Derry were caught after pulling off an arms raid at the Officers Training Corps in Felstead in Essex.

Despite the setbacks and what seemed to some volunteers as endless stalling, the now rejuvenated IRA, mainly as a result of the Gough Barracks success, was finally gearing itself up towards a border campaign aimed at breaking the British connection.

However, it had competition from at least two rival republican factions which also claimed to represent the true spirit of militant Irish Republicanism. One of these – Laochra Ulaidh – amounted to not much more than a one-man bombing machine in the form of Brendan O'Boyle. He had joined the IRA in 1940 and, after being jailed in Derry, was one of 21 men who successfully dug their way out of the place three years later. The IRA leadership procrastinated too much for O'Boyle's liking and, in spite of a brief flirtation with the IRA's other rival Saor Ulaidh, O'Boyle eventually went his own way. He met his death in 1955 while planting a bomb outside the building which housed the Stormont telephone exchange.

The leader and driving force behind Saor Ulaidh, the other paramilitary group vying with the IRA to win the hearts and minds of Irish nationalists, was, however, very different, and he posed a real problem for the IRA leadership. The organisation's founder and leader, Liam Kelly, was a legend in his native Tyrone. He was also a resourceful and charismatic figure. Apart from being physically courageous, Kelly displayed a political understanding which was unique as well as imaginative in its day.

Kelly was booted out of the IRA in 1951 for organising military action without the express permission of the leadership, which remained Dublin based – a situation many northern activists failed to accept. When he parted company with the IRA, which he saw as incapable of grasping the political realities of the day, Kelly immediately formed a new military organisation calling itself Saor Ulaidh (Free Ulster). The entire Tyrone Brigade followed him and he began to attract the interest of able-bodied recruits throughout the north. This was a situation the IRA GHQ found worrying, particularly when it emerged that activists in Belfast were debating whether to join the new organisation.

But Kelly was also a founding member of a political party which went by the name of Fianna Ulaidh (Soldiers of Ulster). Its programme included recognition of the Irish Parliament in Dublin – a position which was anathema to republicans who considered the IRA the true government of Ireland, north and south. In 1953, Kelly stood on an abstentionist ticket for the Stormont Parliament in his native Tyrone and even managed to get himself elected. But the Unionist government ordered the police to charge him with sedition and he was jailed for 12 months.

While in prison Kelly was nominated for and elected to the Senate, the upper house of the Irish Parliament in Dublin, on the same day that the IRA pulled off the Gough Barracks raid.

On his release from jail, Kelly concentrated on the military side of things, despite his limited resources. And in November 1955 – over a full year before the IRA finally started their border campaign – Kelly's men gave notice that they had no intention of disappearing.

The Saor Ulaidh chief-of-staff had a reputation which instilled enthusiasm and confidence in the men under his command. 'Never ask a man to do something you're not prepared to do yourself' was a maxim he was fond of quoting.

At 5.30 a.m. on 26 November, Kelly and his gang moved in on the RUC Barracks in the centre of Roslea, Co. Fermanagh. The police station, which was also home to an RUC man's family, was silent as the Saor Ulaidh men placed a mine at the front of the property before running round the back of the building to wait for the charge to detonate. A huge blast left a gaping hole in the front wall and Kelly's men riddled the building with gunfire before moving through the gap and shouting to the RUC personnel to surrender. But upstairs, Sergeant William Morrow, who a until few minutes before had been fast asleep along with his wife and two sons, looked down into the clouds of swirling smoke and dust. He knew roughly the position from where the voices had come and, pointing his Sten gun, opened fire. There was further scuffling and then silence. On descending the stairs, Morrow found a colleague who had been injured in the crossfire, but the raiders had gone. The IRA GHQ in Dublin issued a statement denying involvement.

It later emerged that Connie Green, a former British Paratrooper with a distinguished military record during the Second World War, who had been persuaded by Kelly to join Saor Ulaidh, had been seriously injured when Sgt Morrow returned fire. The Saor Ulaidh raiding party quickly retrieved Green from the rubble and retreated into the darkness.

Follow-up operations around the border produced nothing. Connie Green died the following day at a remote farmhouse south of the border. Kelly, with the assistance of his Clann na Poblachta colleague Sean MacBride and the cooperation of the Minister for Justice in Dublin, Michael Keyes, arranged to have him buried quietly so as to deny the enemy the opportunity of gloating. Before Green died, his comrades managed to bring a sympathetic priest to administer the last rites of the Roman Catholic Church and Kelly stayed with him as he died.

Green, from Derry, is buried in the quiet country cemetery of St Enda's at Carrickroe, near Emyvale, Co. Monaghan. As his body was lowered into the grave, a volley of shots rang out in the winter air. Kelly had wanted to have Green buried without any official acknowledgement. But when it was pointed out that a sudden death and burial without an inquest was impossible, a compromise was reached. A doctor in the company of a senior Gardai officer attended the inquest at the farmhouse and returned a verdict of death by shock haemorrhaging. But no name, address or occupation ever appeared on Connie Green's death certificate. In the column marked 'age', the doctor wrote 'about 30'. As details of this secret deal emerged, the British and Unionist governments were furious and expressed their disgust to the Irish government in a flurry of diplomatic activity.

In the aftermath of his funeral, Saor Ulaidh produced a collection of Irish nationalist ballads in honour of Connie Green. In it Liam Kelly recorded: 'It is with pride that we remember him.' Green was undoubtedly a remarkable soldier and, given all that he had been through, it is all the more remarkable that he died on the receiving end of RUC bullets in his native Ulster.

At the age of 16, Connie Green joined the British Army. He was every inch a soldier. During the Second World War he saw service on many military fronts. He served as a Commando Sergeant in North Africa and Italy and at the time of the Normandy landings he earned himself a reputation as one of the bravest Paratroopers in the Allied Forces. An army boxing champion, Green was also decorated with the Africa Star and the Italy Star in recognition of his contribution to the fight against fascism.

However, when he returned to his native Derry, Connie Green immersed himself in Saor Ulaidh, because he believed, wrongly as it turned out, that the IRA were a crowd of bluffers who were never going to mobilise against the Northern Ireland state. He was probably the finest republican training officer of all time, although it is highly unlikely that any current active serving member of the IRA has ever heard of him. Connie Green's dedication gave Liam Kelly confidence. He knew he was lucky to obtain the services of such a highly trained volunteer.

A plasterer by trade, Connie Green gave no hint to his workmates in Derry that he was involved in republican paramilitary activity. Said one man: 'I worked with Connie and liked him a lot. We all knew about his army background, although he didn't talk about it. But we had no idea he was in Saor Ulaidh or the IRA or anything. The first we knew was when one of his relatives told us what had happened. It came as a great shock.'

If Liam Kelly's presence on the border wasn't bad enough, the expulsion of Joe Christle was to prove a disaster as far as the IRA leadership was concerned. An able, well-educated and extremely popular volunteer, Christle had fallen out of favour with his IRA bosses, especially chief-of-staff Tony Magan. Like Kelly, Christle also refused to fade into obscurity and immediately formed his own terrorist organisation, taking half the Dublin IRA unit with him. When Christle joined forces with Kelly to carry out armed attacks on six customs posts on 11 November 1956, the IRA's bluff was called and a date for Operation Harvest was set. 'It was a case of "die dog or shite the license" as far as the IRA was concerned,' said one volunteer who had been anxious for action at that time.

In the build-up to the campaign, the IRA was boosted by the return to Ireland of Sean Cronin, a former Irish Army officer, who had spent a number of years in the United States. Cronin had indicated he wanted to join the IRA and, after a few initial problems, quickly rose through the ranks to a leadership position. Using his military experience, Cronin completely transformed the IRA. The IRA's battle plan, largely devised by him, relied mainly on four 'Flying Columns' operating in the western part of Northern Ireland. Once the counties of Derry, Fermanagh, Tyrone and Armagh had been secured, the IRA would, so the blueprint read, move towards the eastern seaboard, with the help of local units.

The IRA at this time was almost entirely controlled by Dublin, with little or no knowledge of the sectarian realities of the north. Nevertheless, it was decided that no military action would be taken in Belfast for fear of stirring up ancient tribal rivalries. With good reason, the leadership was also worried about the loose lips of a number of Belfast-based volunteers.

It was an ambitious declaration of war as far as the IRA was concerned, but the reality turned out to be very different. Wearing uniforms purchased from army surplus stores and black berets, to comply with the Geneva Convention, which stated that soldiers at war must be indentifiable as legitimate armies, the Flying Columns moved towards the border. The idea was to attack the infrastructure of the British-backed state in the North. Again there were last-minute hitches and the starting date of 10 December was put back 24 hours, but once it began there was no turning back.

An IRA unit in Derry, despite receiving only a few hours' notice of the start of the campaign, successfully destroyed a BBC transmitting station at Park Avenue, Rosemount. The action ensured headline publicity, but angered many in the local population who were just starting to enjoy the delights of television broadcasting.

Members of the Derry unit had previously pulled off a successful arms raid at Ebrington Barracks in the Waterside district of the city. A landmine attack destroyed a Territorial Army base at Enniskillen, and, in Magherafelt, Co. Derry, a team under the command of Seamus Costello set fire to a courthouse.

For the next 20 years, Costello was destined to play a contentious role in militant republican politics, which would culminate in his death at the hands of an Official IRA gunman, but for the time being he was earning himself hero status in the staunchly nationalist Sperrin Mountains.

The following day the IRA issued a statement justifying its actions, and, using grandiose language, promised more of the same.

That night, the IRA hit two RUC barracks in Fermanagh and partly blew up two bridges. Despite the years of tedious build-up, the authorities on both sides of the border were largely taken by surprise. The Special Branches of the Gardai and the RUC, which at that time enjoyed only limited cooperation, had believed wrongly that the Kelly–Christle split had paralysed the IRA.

An IRA Flying Column in north Antrim weren't as lucky as their friends along the border. The group was picked up by the police almost immediately, and the presence of volunteers from Cork alerted the authorities to the reality that they were facing a concerted military attempt to overthrow the state by force.

The IRA plan, compiled mostly by Sean Cronin, was for the Flying Columns to lay low in safe houses and remote farms during the day, and use the cover of darkness for military attacks at night. In south Derry, for instance, IRA men hid in specially constructed hides by day and only moved out at night. However, the deplorable conditions destroyed many a healthy man in a matter of weeks. Also, the ability of the notorious RUC B-Specials to collate intelligence on suspicious activity could never be underestimated. Many of these men, especially in rural areas, were, unlike their IRA counterparts, steeped in the local community and were capable of instantly spotting something untoward. A southern brogue or a strange cattle truck would draw attention immediately. The sudden disappearance of a Catholic farmer on a supposed cattle-buying trip down south would also be noted and, furthermore, be double-checked.

The Unionist government, with the support of their British Tory allies led by Sir Anthony Eden, gave notice that Northern Ireland had no intention of surrendering to the outrageous exploits of a terrorist organisation and almost immediately conducted swoops on the homes of known republican sympathisers. But it was not until the Irish government woke up to the latent support for the republican cause in the wake of the South and O'Hanlon killings that it chose to act.

The government's decision to impose internment in the Republic had a devastating effect on the IRA campaign, when many of those who were masterminding the military side of the operation suddenly found themselves locked up in the Curragh.

The following November, exactly a year since Connie Green was shot dead at Roslea, the IRA suffered its greatest blow for three decades. But it wasn't at the hands of the RUC or the British Army. In a small cottage off the main Newry to Dundalk road, just inside the Republic in the town of Edentubber, four IRA men were preparing bombs, probably for use that day as Armistice Day commemorations were taking place. A short circuit detonated the explosives and the cottage, which was owned by a local sympathiser, was demolished, killing him and the four IRA men who were with him. The IRA hotly denied that an Armistice Day attack was its intention, but the massacre at Enniskillen three decades later clearly demonstrated that events honouring dead British servicemen are not outside the IRA's list of legitimate targets.

A couple of bizarre incidents around this time showed that, although the IRA campaign had failed to fuel the imagination of the nationalist community, there were others who wished to continue the struggle against all odds. For some time, the IRA had been waiting for the arrival of a consignment of bazookas that were being smuggled into Ireland from America. Shortly before Christmas the weapons arrived.

On Christmas Eve, two IRA men, one of whom was the ill-fated Seamus Costello, removed two of the bazookas from an arms dump in the Dublin mountains with the intention of test firing them. Some IRA volunteers, still unable to read the writing which was by now clearly written on the cell walls of Crumlin Road jail and in the compound huts of the Curragh internment camp, genuinely believed the bazookas were going to change the nature of the campaign; that the RUC and the British would soon hold their hands up and surrender.

Costello was from Bray in Co. Wicklow and known as 'The Boy General'. He was anxious to assess the firepower of bazooka and so he told his companion to aim the weapon at a large rock and then engage the firing mechanism. The volunteer did as he was told. Nothing happened. Everything was checked and the process repeated. Again nothing happened.

An afternoon of failure turned into frustration and Costello and his companion decided to replace the weapons in the dump before heading home. As they made their way down a remote mountain track, the IRA men noticed the Christmas lights of Dublin starting to twinkle in the fading light. Costello said: 'I hope those people appreciate what we are doing for them.' The remark epitomised the arrogance which permeated and continues to permeate the ranks of the Irish Republican Army.

In the New Year a group of teenagers in Belfast approached a known republican activist. They wanted to join the IRA and help kickstart the campaign. The IRA man they spoke to told the youngsters there was no point in them joining the IRA at this stage. He said the IRA did not have enough weapons for its serving volunteers, never mind new recruits. Although bitterly disappointed, the boys, two of whom were still at school, were not put off. They decided to steal their own weapons and set about planning an arms raid. The idea was to break into an RAF Squadron depot at Edenmore, Whiteabbey, on the outskirts of Belfast and steal weapons that were being stored there. By forcing a ventilation screen, the boys were then able to open a window and gain access to the premises. They stole two Bren guns with full magazines, thirteen .303 rifles with magazines, and they also took explosives and other military equipment. The weapons were placed in cloth sacks and hidden in undergrowth nearby before being removed to hides in west Belfast.

The four-man teenage army consisted of 18-year-old Robert Murray, 17-year-old Tony Cosgrove, John Campbell who was also 17, and a 16-year-old youth who wasn't named in court. They were also assisted by two other schoolboys who played relatively minor roles in the operation.

Campbell was taken into custody after his father discovered the weapons in a garden shed, and he made a full confession. Murray and Cosgrove were arrested and all the others were interviewed. The case was heard at Belfast City Commission in front of Lord Justice Curran on 23 March 1960. It got off to a dramatic start when Murray and Cosgrove refused to enter a plea or even recognise the court. The judge had no hesitation in sentencing the two eldest boys to ten years each. Campbell, who had two previous convictions for arson, was bound over to keep the peace for three years and fined ten pounds. The 16-year-old was also bound over to keep the peace for a similar amount of time. Their more lenient sentences reflected the cooperation they gave the police during the investigation. The court heard that all the weapons taken in the Edenmore raid had been successfully recovered as a result of information the police received during interviews with the accused.

As sentence was passed, the temperature rose again sharply when Murray, in true republican tradition, made a defiant speech from the dock. He told the court: 'I merely did my duty as an Irishman. And I intend to continue to do my duty as an Irishman to stop the British occupation of our country.'

Justice Curran told Murray and Cosgrove: 'You think of yourselves as national heroes, but I have no sympathy for you and so you will go to prison.' He told Campbell and the younger lad: 'You are just a couple of mugs.'

The harshness of the sentences meted out to the two older boys reflected the tough stance adopted by the Northern Ireland authorities towards those willing to take up arms in pursuit of political demands.

Meanwhile, the mainstream IRA campaign was trundling along much as usual, but it impacted on the lives of ordinary people less and less. The RUC had the campaign boxed off and everybody else was getting on with their lives. The IRA was also riddled with internal difficulties. A number of factions in the Curragh internment camp were vying for supremacy. An IRA convention in June 1960 heard calls for renewed effort and determination in the north, but even a fool could see the show was over. It was only a matter of time before the curtain finally came down.

On 17 January 1961, however, the IRA killed an RUC constable near Roslea, Co. Fermanagh. He was accused by the republicans of spying inside the Irish Republic. The murder had the desired effect of getting the IRA back on the front pages again, but at a horrendous cost. It emerged that the young officer had merely crossed the border to visit his girlfriend and it left the IRA open to the charge that the killing of the policeman, who was off-duty, was merely a sectarian attack. The murder was widely condemned by all sides.

A number of sporadic attacks took place during the summer, but it was now obvious that any support the IRA had was reduced to an absolute minimum. An autumn election in the Republic revealed the true extent of the decline in support. Out of fifteen candidates, only one in Co. Kerry managed to save his deposit and Sinn Fein's support was reduced to just 3 per cent. The IRA army council was now forced to face the fact that it was time to call off the campaign. Some volunteers hoped against hope that something might happen to bring the Irish people to their senses and they would finally realise that their future lay in the plans laid down by the republican movement.

Constable John Hunter was a farmer's son from Macosquin, Co. Derry. Armed with not much more than a pleasant personality and an easy manner, he left home to join the police. The farm wasn't big enough to provide a living for the whole family and at least the police offered a steady if not great income. Constable Hunter was stationed at Forkhill, Co. Armagh, and on 12 November 1961, the 28-year-old officer set out with a number of RUC colleagues to set up a checkpoint at Flurry Bridge on the outskirts of Jonesborough, yards from the border.

A short distance away on the southern side, republicans were staging a commemoration at Edentubber in honour of the four IRA volunteers and a civilian supporter who had lost their lives there three years earlier, when the bomb they were preparing exploded prematurely. The police orders were to monitor those attending the rally by stopping cars arriving from south Armagh. But, unbeknown to Constable Hunter and his colleagues, the IRA was planning to use the cover of an event held to honour republican dead to spring a murderous attack on the police. The IRA leadership thought an attack like this was just what was needed to rekindle the campaign. The ambush had been planned a year earlier when the local IRA volunteers noted that the RUC had set up a checkpoint at exactly the same spot when the Edentubber commemoration was taking place.

A crowd had gathered to hear a series of speakers at the Celtic cross erected on the site of the cottage which had been demolished by the IRA bomb. The police chatted to each other and Constable Hunter remarked to a fellow officer that it wouldn't be long now before they could head back to base, as it was a cold day and people at the commemoration wouldn't want to hang about.

As the commemoration was about to get underway shortly after 2.30 p.m., a heavily armed four-man IRA team moved in through the grounds of Jonesborough Parish Church and glanced over its perimeter wall. The church wall had an elevated position near the main road. The IRA men had a clear view of the police who were a distance of just 50 yards away. Suddenly, shots rang out and, although confused, the police returned fire immediately. But the high wall and the church building gave the gunmen time and cover to escape.

The fleeing IRA assault party, wearing battle dress with black berets, ran across a field towards woodland on the southern side of the border, less than 40 yards away. Within seconds the weapons were dumped and the men mingled with those gathered at the commemoration. Shouts of celebration went up as the IRA volunteers dispersed into the crowd.

Back on Jonesborough main street, Constable John Hunter lay dead and three of his colleagues were wounded, two of them seriously. John Hunter was the fifth member of the RUC to be killed since the IRA border campaign began five years previously.

A large force of police officers led by County Inspector W.D. Wolseley swamped the area. He was an experienced officer who had also been on duty the night Brookeborough was attacked four years before. In a follow-up search, his men found a fully loaded magazine for a Thompson machine gun at the rear of the church. On the southern side of the border a large detachment of Gardai from Dundalk also searched, but nothing was found.

Father Stephen Teggart, the local parish priest, gave the injured RUC men comfort as they waited for help. One of the seriously injured officers, Special Constable Patrick Skehin of Bessbrook, Co. Armagh, who was a Catholic, was given the last rites as he lay bleeding on the road. The injured were rushed to Daisy Hill Hospital in Newry, where they were visited by the Minister of Home Affairs, Brian Faulkner, and the Inspector General of the RUC, Albert Kennedy.

At Constable Hunter's funeral three days later in his home village of Macosquin, near Coleraine, thousands turned out to pay their respects. Six pall bearers, all officers from Forkhill RUC Station, carried the young officer's coffin, which was draped in the Union Jack. The tiny hamlet was silent as the cortège made its way from Constable Hunter's family farm to Ringsend Presbyterian Churchyard.

In a short sermon the Reverend Dinsmore reflected on the young man who left Macosquin to make a career for himself in the police. He told a hushed congregation: 'Constable Hunter was a happy young man. In his heart and life, there was no malice against anyone, but rather he had a cheerful, helpful spirit which made him beloved by all.'

Students at University College Dublin chipped in money to send a wreath to Constable Hunter's grieving family. A card attached expressed the students' deepest sympathy for the policeman's heartbroken relatives. It read: 'For a young Irishman who died in the execution of his duty.'

If the leaders of the IRA ever really believed the Jonesborough attack would re-ignite its floundering campaign, they were badly mistaken. The papers the following morning screamed condemnation. 'MURDER MOST FOUL' shouted one front-page headline, while the *Irish Times* editorial read: 'Whatever the motives were, they cannot be held good enough to justify the foul murder of a young Irishman.' It went on to describe the IRA as criminals and urged the authorities to take drastic action to bring the policeman's killers to book.

The Taoiseach Sean Lemass, who had in the past been a committed IRA man himself, echoed the sentiments of the entire southern state (with the exception of the republican movement) when, condemning the murder, he said: 'No sane person could think that such murderous activities serve any national purpose.'

The murder of Constable Hunter and in particular its cruel and callous nature had backfired and the IRA knew it. In Belfast and London politicians demanded action. How could the Irish government allow a terrorist organisation to use its northern counties as a safe haven from where it could spring murderous attacks? Only a few months ago, the people of the Republic had firmly rejected Sinn Fein. It was time for action and everyone looked to Lemass to deliver.

Within days the Irish government reintroduced military tribunals, an effective method brought in during the 1940s when Éamon de Valera practically wiped out the IRA. The tribunals were conducted without juries and senior army officers acted as judges. Sentences were severe and the round-up of IRA activists was growing by the day.

Despite the growing forces lined up against it, the IRA pulled off yet another landmine attack on an RUC jeep at Whitecross, south Armagh, injuring three officers. Then, in the New Year of 1962, the IRA met to consider the way forward, but practically all those attending the army council meeting knew the campaign was over. It was now a question of – and they were not to be the last army council to ask themselves this – how to get out with a degree of dignity.

Typically, the IRA blamed the people of Ireland for the failure of the campaign. It was their fault things hadn't worked out. The Irish, according to the IRA, were far too interested in material gain to care about Partition, and as a result the IRA was going to dump its weapons until such times as the Irish people could see the error of their ways.

Calling off the campaign formally, the IRA issued the following statement:

> The leadership of the resistance movement has ordered the termination of the campaign of resistance to British Occupation launched on 12 December 1956. Instructions issued to volunteers of the active service units and of local units in the occupied area have now been carried out. All arms have been dumped and all full-time active service volunteers have been withdrawn.

The statement went on to chastise the public for not lending the campaign support and it said, the 'resistance movement' looked forward to the final and victorious phase of the struggle for the full freedom of Ireland.

It was greeted with sighs of weariness mixed with relief. Military analysts had predicted the failure of Operation Harvest within three months of the campaign starting. The groundswell of support from within the nationalist community it required to succeed just didn't materialise. It was only a matter of time before the IRA leadership admitted the reality of the odds it faced.

As the casualty figures show, the campaign was aimed largely at material targets. In the entire period six RUC officers lost their lives, as did eight IRA men. Two republican supporters and two members of rival republican groups were also killed, and in terms of manpower resources and compensation, it had cost around ten million pounds. This was largely met by the British Exchequer, although it also cost the Republic money it could ill afford.

In Crumlin Road Prison and in the jails of the Republic, IRA men reflected on the situation in which they now found themselves. Most wanted to go home to their wives and families. Others used their time in jail wisely and woke up to the fact that they had been on the wrong track from the beginning. These people realised it was now the 1960s and the world had changed. The Limerick of Sean South no longer existed and the Unionist monolith of Northern Ireland would be around for a long time to come. For them, there had to be another way – a political way – where Irishmen of all persuasions could live for Ireland, instead of dying in a remote rural village, a hundred miles from home like the two Derry men, Volunteer Connie Green and Constable John Hunter.

However, there were others still who thought the fight should have continued. 'Drive them into the sea' was the way they saw things. The only thing the Brits understood was force, they said, and despite the setbacks they were prepared to wait for their opportunity. In less than a decade that opportunity presented itself in an explosion of civic strife never seen before. But for the time being, the guns, or what was left of them, were silent.

– CHAPTER THREE –

Out of the Shadows . . . Stepped the UVF

When Ulster is in danger, the extremist will take a hand,
Because they have an extreme love, towards their native land,
A faith, a crown, a way of life, they will never sacrifice,
But fight like loyal Ulstermen, and not like . . . Ulster mice!
A poem by Gusty Spence

Peter Ward just couldn't resist the temptation of having a late-night pint with his pals. The lads had been working hard all night serving drinks in the bars of Belfast's International Hotel and another couple of relaxing beers would be a nice way to finish the night off.

'I know a pub on the Shankill which serves late, but we'd better hurry,' said one of the boys.

'Lead the way,' said another.

The Malvern Arms was typical of the many local bars at that time which enjoyed corner sites in working-class areas of Belfast during the 1960s. Known locally as Watson's, the pub was the hub of the close-knit community which lived in that part of the lower Shankill Road. Its owner, Joe Watson, knew most of his customers and, like many other publicans, wasn't averse to turning a blind eye to the licensing laws and serving after-hours drinks to locals at weekends. The local police knew it went on and only occasionally clamped down. In fact, one or two officers at Brown Square Barracks, which served the lower Shankill area, were known to enjoy the odd bottle of stout themselves. Some bars even had small snug areas, called family departments, which were sectioned off from the main public bar by a small curtain. It wasn't uncommon to see the shiny black skip of a Peeler's helmet peeking through the bottom from time to time.

When Peter Ward and his three workmates reached the side door of the

Malvern Arms, it was nearly 1.00 a.m. on 26 June 1966. Andy Kelly knew the secret knock so as not to alarm the late-night revellers or the publican inside, who might have thought they were a police raiding party. 'I'm only staying an hour and then I'm heading home,' said Peter, anxious to get back to his widowed mum, Mary, who was waiting for him in the family home at Beechmount Parade, off the Falls Road.

Before that hour was out, however, he would be lying dead on the pavement outside, cut down when a single bullet pierced his heart. Two of his companions, Andrew Kelly, his boss at the hotel, and Liam Doyle would also be shot, and Richard Leppington, the fourth member of the group, would miraculously escape the hail of bullets fired at them by self-styled assassins belonging to a shadowy loyalist group calling itself the Ulster Volunteer Force (UVF).

A few years before the Ward murder, a bible-thumping fundamentalist preacher by the name of Ian Paisley had burst onto the Ulster religious scene. Since forming his own Free Presbyterian Church in Ulster 15 years previously, Paisley had been a thorn in the flesh of the straitlaced clergy of both the Presbyterian Church and the Church of Ireland. Using his booming powers of oratory, Paisley lambasted other Protestant church leaders, often accusing them of rejecting Bible-based religion in favour of ecumenism. This, of course, in Paisley's view, meant dialogue with the anti-Christ himself – the Pope. But by the 1960s, Paisley also had another target for abuse – the Unionist establishment which had governed Northern Ireland since the state was set up in 1921.

Born in Armagh in 1926, Paisley, the son of an Independent Baptist minister and a Scottish mother, was brought up in a strictly religious household. The family then moved to Ballymena, Co. Antrim, and it was there in the heart of Ulster's well-known bible belt that the young Paisley's religious convictions were formed. He preached his first sermon when he was just 16 and he was very impressed with the rigid religious views of the Free Presbyterians in neighbouring Scotland. Paisley formed his own Ulster version of the Free Presbyterian Church in 1951 after he successfully exploited a split in a Presbyterian church in Crossgar, Co. Down. But it wasn't until 1963 that he began to show an interest in gaining power through politics.

Following Partition, the Unionist establishment battened down the hatches and cut itself off, not only from the rest of the world, but also the rest of the United Kingdom, of which it was a junior partner. The foundations of the northern state were built on the certainty that Unionism had been right to stand up to the might of Irish nationalism, and that the way Unionists could ensure survival from the encroaching interests of a hostile neighbouring state was to treat every Catholic as a potential traitor and subversive. In the 1960s, Unionist domination and power was still in the hands of 'big house' politicians who practised a kind of 'we know what's best' paternal politics. All who believed in the Union would enjoy the benefits provided they didn't rock the boat.

Poorer Protestants were led to believe that, despite their lowly status and prospects, at least they were a little higher up the ladder than the Catholics. And, of course, gerrymandering of election boundaries and the denial of votes to non-property holders during local council elections meant there was little Catholics could do about it. It was a case of 'croppies lie down'.

One thing, however, had a devastating effect on the way Unionism had planned the Province's future – the 1947 Education Act, which ensured free third-level education to all. The same act had been introduced in the rest of the UK three years earlier, but through a series of stalling tactics the Unionist government had managed to avoid implementing it in the North for three more years. By the 1960s, Catholic pupils from poor backgrounds were attending university as a matter of course, and Europe generally was starting to enjoy a more prosperous time.

However, Paisley and his followers continued to preach hostility to any advancing Catholicism or nationalism. Paisley was horrified when he learned that Belfast City Council planned to lower the Union flag which flew over Belfast City Hall to half-mast as a mark of respect following the death of Pope John XXIII in 1963.

He organised a protest march that was subsequently banned under the notorious Special Powers Act, introduced in 1922 to cover the government in the event of any form of dissent. Despite the ban, Paisley went ahead anyway and was arrested and fined ten pounds. He said he would go to prison rather than pay the money, but was denied martyrdom when the fine was paid anonymously. The following year, Paisley's outpourings helped spark three days of rioting when the RUC removed an Irish tricolour from the window of a shop in Divis Street – the Republican HQ during the general election of 1964, which saw a Labour government returned to Westminster for the first time in 13 years.

Paisley developed a skill for publicity stunts and when Northern Ireland Prime Minister Captain Terence O'Neill invited Irish Taoiseach Sean Lemass to Stormont to discuss topics of mutual interests, he was once again to the fore, claiming a united Ireland was just around the corner as a result of O'Neill's double dealings. Lemass had fought in the General Post Office alongside James Connolly and Padraig Pearse during the Easter Rising of 1916 that eventually led to the formation of the Irish Free State. He was also a member of the IRA section which stood up to Michael Collins' Free State Army by occupying the Four Courts during the Irish Civil War. In short, Lemass was everything Paisley despised. Irish, republican, Catholic and, most important of all, prepared to do business with Terence O'Neill. For Paisley, if any more evidence had been necessary to prove that Ulster was about to be sold out, then this was it.

Paisley began to target O'Neill and his colleagues in mainstream unionism more frequently, accusing them of 'going soft'. He developed an 'O'Neill Must Go' campaign and consistently warned the loyal Protestants of Ulster that their birthright was about to be sold to an Irish Republic run by a mixture of gunmen and priests. To help him in his quest to topple O'Neill, Paisley formed a couple of support groups in areas that were traditionally seen as being 'hardline Protestant'. He set up the Ulster Constitution Defence Committee (UCDC) and the Ulster Protestant Volunteers (UPV). A number of those involved were also members of Paisley's church, although membership was not by any means restricted to the congregation of the Free Presbyterian Church, because, despite the vocal presence of their moderator, Free Presbyterians even today only number 12,500 in the whole of Ireland.

Also around this time, a far more sinister loyalist organisation was formed to 'defend Ulster'. At a series of meetings in various parts of the North, hardline loyalists were sworn into the Ulster Volunteer Force (UVF). The name was taken from the organisation which was set up in Ulster to oppose Home Rule during the 1912 crisis. Again there was an overlap of membership with Paisley's UCDC and the Protestant Action Volunteers (PAV), but the difference was that the new UVF was a paramilitary group committed to the use of violence as part of its opposition to O'Neill. The group soon engaged in a series of sabotage terrorist attacks across the Province, blaming the IRA for the attacks.

The RUC Special Branch quickly became aware of the existence of the UVF through its network of informants and set about compiling a dossier on the shadowy terror group.

In the Irish Republic, the government was gearing itself up for the 50th anniversary of the 1916 Easter Rising and UVF leaders believed that, if it laid the blame for terrorist attacks in the North at the door of the IRA, the apathetic public might wake up to the fact that O'Neill's 'sell out' plan was about to be implemented.

In reality, the IRA was in no position to carry out attacks, although some in the organisation felt it should make some sort of display of defiance in the name of the Republic. In 1963, an IRA volunteer was killed and his comrade injured while they were attempting to blow up a republican monument in Cork where the Irish President Éamon de Valera was due to speak. In other parts of the country occasional terrorist acts were committed by disaffected IRA men, but these were all 'freelance' operations which were not sanctioned by the IRA leadership.

On the evening of 1 March 1966, a petrol bomb was thrown into the Dublin home of the British Military Attaché. A week later, on 7 March, an explosion rocked the centre of Dublin when republicans blew up Nelson's Pillar on O'Connell Street.

The monument was a hangover from the days when Dublin was the second city of the empire and anything honouring an admiral from Britain's Imperial past was largely seen as having little relevance to modern Ireland. No one was killed or injured by the bomb and there was a quiet admiration for those behind the attack. 'Some people seemed glad that there were still people about who believed in the dream of a republic and were prepared to do something about it, even if the government wasn't,' said a republican who was active during this period.

However, while Dubliners sniggered, the reverberations of the blast were felt on the Shankill in Belfast. News of Nelson's demise was greeted with outrage. Paisley went into overdrive as loyalists were told the IRA was planning to use the 50th anniversary of the Easter rebellion to launch yet another campaign of violence against the North.

The Shankill Road section of the UVF was led by Augustus 'Gusty' Spence, a former soldier. He had served with the Royal Ulster Rifles in Cyprus, but by 1966 he was working as a stager in the shipyard. Spence was a member of the Prince Albert Temperance LOL 1892 – a local Orange lodge – and was very popular in the hardline loyalist district where he had grown up. He had also been in prison after being convicted of deception and enjoyed a reputation as a 'hardman'. Like many of his peers, Spence was convinced by the rhetoric of Paisley and others and decided to do something about it by joining the UVF in his own area.

On 18 February 1966, UVF members petrol-bombed the Glengall Street HQ of the Ulster Unionist Party while its Westminster MPs sat in session. Two days later a Catholic school in west Belfast was also fire-bombed. On 6 April, two days before Prime Minister Terence O'Neill was due to address an ecumenical conference on reconciliation at Holy Cross Girls' School in Ardoyne, a UVF team petrol-bombed it.

The police were well aware of the existence of the Shankill UVF, although Special Branch detectives were still unsure about who was pulling the strings of the secretive group. O'Neill accused Paisley of having associations with the UVF and of supporting its aims in his speeches. Paisley angrily denied the accusation. It was nevertheless obvious to the police that the UVF was now on a course which could only end in murder, and it wouldn't be long until their fears were confirmed. Before the end of June, three people would be dead and another two shot and seriously wounded as a result of the actions of the Shankill UVF.

Probably through contacts in the Ulster Special Constabulary (the notorious B Specials), the fledgling UVF managed to learn the name and address of a man it believed was a member of the IRA. Leo Martin lived in Baden Powell Street, in the nearby Oldpark district, and later went on to play a leading role during the formation of the Provisional IRA. But in 1966, the IRA was inactive and still involved in a period of reassessment and discussion following its failed border campaign. Despite this, the UVF were determined to hit out at what they saw as the rising tide of republicanism and Leo Martin was as good a target as any, not least because he lived close by.

Spence was determined to get him. The plan was simple. A team of UVF men would drive to Martin's house, knock on the door, and if he answered he would be shot. However, Spence had only one problem. Martin never seemed to be at home any time the UVF called.

On 27 May, John Scullion, a 28-year-old single man from the Clonard area of Belfast, was drinking in the Conway Bar off the city's Falls Road. Around 11.00 p.m. he decided to head back to his aunt's house where he lived along with his widowed father. When he reached the door of the house he began looking for his key. As he stood searching his pockets, a car containing four members of the Shankill UVF pulled up. Minutes earlier, the UVF had been on a mission to assassinate Leo Martin but John Scullion had accidentally stumbled across their path.

The murder gang had earlier spotted Martin standing with a group of men outside a pub, but when they returned he had gone. They drove back to the Falls area and then into the narrow warren of streets around Clonard Cathedral. When they spotted John Scullion standing at his door the driver of the UVF car pulled up opposite him and the gunman shot him at close range. John Scullion managed to get inside the house and reached the top of the stairs before collapsing on the floor.

In the mid-'60s sectarian shootings were thought to be a thing of the past and not surprisingly doctors assumed John Scullion was the victim of a stabbing incident, although neighbours and a number of eyewitnesses said they had heard the sound of shots. A bullet was even found near the scene.

In hospital he received emergency treatment and it was thought he would recover. But, after suffering a series of heart attacks, he died two weeks later on 11 June. A statement issued by the UVF to the *Belfast Telegraph* admitted responsibility for Scullion's death and promised more would follow. The police insisted he had been stabbed, but when his body was exhumed from Milltown Cemetery on 21 June, an autopsy the same day showed John Scullion had indeed been shot. The UVF murder gang had claimed its first victim and was keen to claim more.

Even a cursory examination of the paramilitary activities of the UVF on the Shankill Road in June 1966 reveals that the biggest single factor in all incidents was alcohol. Fired up by bottles of stout and whiskey, UVF men went out with murder in mind. Their excuse was that they were striking a blow for Ulster and that their actions would ensure the continuity of the Union with the United Kingdom. As a result, their Protestant heritage would also be safe from the scourge of Irish Nationalists, who wanted to end Partition by bringing Northern Ireland into the Republic. So the rhetoric went. UVF violence, its volunteers were told, would also destabilise the O'Neill regime which had gone soft on everything Ulster loyalists held dear.

Around this time, the RUC Special Branch learned through its wide network of informants that Gusty Spence and other UVF men were engaged in weapons-training classes, which were held in a locked room at Spence's Orange lodge.

The police had been told that a guard was placed outside the door while firearms practice was taking place and it was becoming clear to the police that there was a growing group of men on the Shankill Road who were prepared to use violence to further loyalist interests. It was also clear that there was some overlap of membership between Paisley's UCDC, the Protestant Action Volunteers and the UVF.

The Special Branch was anxious to uncover links between the UVF and any so-called respectable politicians opposed to the O'Neill government. They had suspicions regarding a number of well-known figures within unionism.

One of those was Jim Kilfedder, the Unionist MP for West Belfast. Originally from Kinlough in Co. Leitrim, he had studied law at Trinity College, Dublin, with Desmond Boal, an up-and-coming Belfast barrister who was also a confidante and advisor to Paisley. At university, Jim Kilfedder had shown some interest in the Fine Gael Party – a fact which Paisley would later use against him – but, for the time being, they were allies in the opposition to O'Neill.

Kilfedder quit a very successful barrister's practice in London to enter Northern Ireland politics. But he was also a promiscuous, although discreet, homosexual. Kilfedder stood for the Unionist Party in the 1964 election and, because of his strident anti-O'Neill views, received the full support of Ian Paisley and his followers in the UCDC and PAV. Paisley's antics prior to the Divis Street riots, when he threatened to personally remove a tricolour from the Republican candidates' HQ, are thought to have played a crucial role in getting Kilfedder elected.

As time went on, Special Branch officers were actively examining intelligence which indicated that Kilfedder had tutored Spence and others about how to handle police interrogation in the event of arrest. It has also been suggested that armed UVF men helped campaign for Kilfedder during the 1964 election when Gusty Spence's brother Eddie had been Kilfedder's election agent.

Police also believed Gusty Spence had been the gunman who had fired two shots at the home of Stormont MP for Woodvale, John McQuade. It was, they said, a bogus attack aimed at frightening loyalists into believing it was the work of the IRA, and that McQuade had himself been part and parcel of the ruse. The links between sections of the Ulster Unionist Party and the emerging paramilitary group, the UVF, were very real indeed and the police were worried about an escalation of violence.

Saturday, 25 June was a big day on the Shankill Road. Traditionally it was the day when the local Orange lodges, accompanied by loyalist bands, marched across the city to the Whiterock Orange Hall on the Springfield Road. Gusty Spence's plans were to enjoy the day out and, after the parade was over, to share a few drinks with his fellow Orangemen before attending a meeting of the UVF held in a room of the Standard Bar, which was known locally as McDowell's.

During the afternoon and evening, copious amounts of alcohol were consumed, and by the time the UVF met in the Standard Bar many of those attending were very drunk. Gusty Spence chaired the meeting and once again Leo Martin was identified as 'the target for the evening'. Two men were dispatched to carry out the assassination attempt on Martin and others were ordered to go and collect members of the organisation who lived some distance outside Belfast.

The UVF hit team ordered to assassinate Leo Martin had no better luck than their comrades who carried out the earlier murder bid. Once again there was no reply when the man detailed to shoot him arrived at his Baden Powell Street home. But this time the UVF men were determined they weren't going to return to the Shankill without striking a blow for Ulster. They smashed a window, forced the door, splashed petrol around the house and set it ablaze.

Back on the Shankill, the UVF were reasonably pleased with the night's work, although a bit disappointed that no IRA men had been taken out.

After more drinks in the Standard Bar it was decided the UVF team would retire to the Malvern Arms, a pub where drinks were served after closing time.

Most of the UVF men who had earlier attended the Standard Bar meeting congregated in the pub. Among them were Gusty Spence, Hugh 'Dandy' McClean, Robert Williamson and Dessie Reid, who would subsequently play a major role in the police investigation. They were also joined by Spence's brother-in-law, Frankie Curry.

Shortly before 1.00 a.m., Andrew Kelly, bar manager at the International Hotel in Belfast's city centre, gently knocked on the side door of the bar. He was known to the publican Joe Watson and had convinced his barmen work colleagues, Peter Ward, Liam Doyle and Richard Leppington, that the Malvern was the ideal spot for a couple of drinks before heading home. As they waited for Joe Watson to open the door, Peter Ward, without saying a word, pointed to graffiti scrawled on the brick wall of a house across the road. In large white letters, someone had painted the initials UVF. Local newspapers had recently carried reports on the shadowy loyalist group and the barmen, all Catholics, were well aware of the violent threat the UVF posed, but tonight they thought they had nothing to fear.

Within minutes of their arrival, however, the young barmen's presence was noted by the UVF men, who were by now well into a 12-hour drinking session.

Dandy McClean, probably on the instructions of Spence, spoke to Andy Kelly, claiming he thought he knew his face. Later one of the UVF group approached Peter Ward and asked: 'Where do you work?' Without the slightest hesitation, Ward replied: 'The International Hotel.'

Within minutes Spence stepped up to the bar to buy another round of drinks and on his return to his UVF friends said: 'I've been listening to their conversation, they're IRA men and they'll have to go.'

None of the barmen had any connection with the IRA, but they did work in a hotel where, earlier that year, republicans had attended a function to commemorate the 50th anniversary of the Easter Rising in Dublin.

Spence and some of his group immediately left the bar.

Augustus Andrew Spence, a married man who worked as a shipyard stager, and who lived in nearby Hertford Street with his wife and family, was 33 years old. His ally, Robert James Williamson, also 33, a fitter from Dagmar Street in the Shankill, was unmarried, while Hugh 'Dandy' Arnold McClean, a bricklayer from Larne Road, Carrickfergus, was 46 years old.

Police believe that what happened next was that Spence took Dandy McClean and Robert Williamson to a house in nearby Belgrave Street, where a number of handguns were distributed. The men then walked back and took up positions outside the Malvern Arms. Around 2.00 a.m., Andrew Kelly and his fellow barmen emerged from the side door of the bar.

Suddenly, one of the men standing at the street corner came rushing towards them. There was a series of loud bangs and the flash of sustained gunfire could be seen through the still night air. Andy Kelly and Peter Ward fell to the ground simultaneously. A single bullet pierced 18-year-old Peter Ward's heart and he died almost instantly. Liam Doyle was hit in the leg, but somehow managed to run onto the road. Miraculously, the hail of bullets missed Richard Leppington and the youngster, in a state of confused panic, was able to bolt down a nearby side street. He was eventually taken into a house where the residents gave him refuge.

At the trial of Spence, McClean and Williamson, who appeared in court four months later charged with the murder of Peter Ward, Liam Doyle, who was still recovering from gunshot wounds, described what happened when he and his friends left the bar and heard the first shots.

Said Doyle: 'I did not know what it was and just stood there. I saw Andy and Peter falling and I felt a pain in my leg. I ran onto the street. The men moved in on us.'

Doyle said he managed to run as far as a lamppost on the other side of Ariel Street before collapsing with his head next to the wall and his feet at the pavement. He continued: 'I saw this man running after me. I saw flashes coming from him and he started to shoot into me. He fired five or six shots into me. I was hit six times.'

Doyle said that as he lay on the ground he pleaded with the gunman not to shoot.

'I shouted "please don't" or something like that, but the man made no reply and did not stop shooting.'

Asked by Mr Reid QC for the prosecution if he could see the man in court, he pointed to Gusty Spence. Liam Doyle said the gunman only stopped shooting when another man shouted: 'Come on, leave him there.'

Police sources who worked on the murder investigation say they believe that, following the shootings, Spence, Williamson and McClean ran back to the house in Belgrave Street, where the weapons used in the attack were placed in a canvas sack before being placed in an arms dump. Years later, Spence's nephew Frankie Curry Jnr, who was a teenage schoolboy at the time – and who was destined to become one of the most notorious loyalist killers of the Troubles – claimed he spirited the guns out of the street. Frankie Curry Jnr was himself shot dead on St Patrick's Day 1999 as a result of a feud among quarrelling loyalist factions.

Gusty Spence has consistently denied murdering Peter Ward, although he has admitted being in the vicinity at the time Ward was killed. There is no doubt, however, that Liam Doyle's eyewitness evidence proved crucial in identifying Spence and the other men police believe carried out the attack.

Within hours of the Malvern Street shootings the police incident room at Brown Square was awash with intelligence about the activities of the Shankill UVF the previous night. It wasn't long, therefore, before Spence, McClean and Williamson were in custody. Police knocked on Gusty Spence's door at number 3 Hertford Street at 6.15 a.m. At first he refused to open it, demanding to know if the officers were in possession of a warrant. They said they weren't, but if he didn't open the door they would force it open. Spence let the officers in. The police conducted a search of the house and one detective, on noticing the proliferation of loyalist paraphernalia around the house, commented: 'This is a right loyal house.'

To which Spence replied 'Yes it is', before asking: 'Is that why this house is being searched?'

The policeman said: 'Partly.'

Spence then remarked: 'That's what you get for being a Protestant.'

At Brown Square, the police concentrated on the weakest link, who was without a doubt Dandy McClean. According to police, when asked to explain during an interview why he joined the UVF, McClean replied: 'I was asked did I agree with Paisley and was I prepared to follow him. I said that I was.'

The police also allege that when charged with the murder of Peter Ward, McClean said: 'I am terribly sorry I ever heard of that man Paisley or decided to follow him.'

All three – Spence, McClean and Williamson – tried to distance themselves from the events outside the Malvern Arms and gave a number of contradictory accounts of their movements. Gusty Spence stubbornly refused to give a written statement – behaviour that caused detectives to think he had indeed received tutoring from Jim Kilfedder. Well-placed loyalist sources have recently claimed, however, that Spence would have had a working knowledge of interrogation techniques through his experience in the Military Police section of the Royal Ulster Rifles. At one point Spence offered to give a statement, but only concerning the events that followed the police arrival at his house.

Teams of detectives worked on the suspects and the tenacious work of Det. Sgt Leo McBrien is thought to have been a vital ingredient in the police decision to bring murder charges against all three. Spence was also charged with the murder of John Scullion, the unfortunate drunk who became a victim in place of Leo Martin.

A series of police swoops at the homes of suspected UVF members produced a number of firearms and explosives and by the time the case was called at Belfast Magistrates Court a total of eight men stood in the dock facing a variety of charges linked to loyalist terrorism.

The charge of murdering John Scullion was eventually dropped against Spence, although two other men who named Spence in their police statements were convicted on reduced charges. Apart from the strong evidence of victims Liam Doyle and Andy Kelly, the Crown also had another star witness in its case against Spence's UVF.

Desmond 'Dessie' Reid, a 31-year-old tyre inspector of Movilla Park, Rathcoole, Newtownabbey, was charged at the same court with possessing explosives with intent to endanger lives. The police searched Reid's home after receiving information as part of the follow-up investigations into the Malvern Arms shootings. There they discovered gelignite, which had been supplied to the UVF through a quarryman from the staunchly loyalist village of Loughgall, where the Orange Order had been founded.

Earlier the same year Ian Paisley had driven a man called Noel Doherty – who was a close associate of Paisley's and the printer of his weekly paper the *Protestant Telegraph* – to a meeting in Loughgall. In the car with them was Billy Mitchell, who would later be convicted of two loyalist assassinations. After dropping the men off, Paisley carried on to another meeting and picked up Doherty and Mitchell later that night. Doherty and Mitchell had travelled to the Co. Armagh village because some locals had expressed interest in setting up a branch of the UCDC. In the course of the Loughgall meeting, a man who worked in a local quarry said he was in a position to supply gelignite. It was from the same source that the explosives found in Reid's home had come after finding its way into the hands of the Shankill UVF through Billy Mitchell.

Dessie Reid gave the police a statement saying he had been present when Spence chaired the Standard Bar UVF meeting prior to the Malvern Street shootings. He agreed to give evidence against Spence in return for the explosives charge against him being dropped. In his police statement he said he had been present when Spence, McClean and Williamson returned to Spence's sister Cassie's home in Belgrave Street in the early hours of 26 June. He said all three went into the tiny scullery and he heard one of them say: 'That was not a bad job.'

Because Ian Paisley had driven Noel Doherty and Billy Mitchell to the Armagh meeting where gelignite for the Shankill UVF had first been discussed, some police officers believed they had enough evidence to bring charges of conspiracy against Paisley himself. But senior Counsel from the Crown Prosecution Service told them that they were wasting their time and that any charges brought would later be withdrawn. In fact, a charge against Paisley, Crown lawyers argued, might even look trumped up because he was a political opponent of the Prime Minister.

It should be noted that Paisley is on record condemning the Malvern Street shootings and his public statements were backed up in writing days later, when his newspaper, the *Protestant Telegraph*, also condemned the shootings.

After an 11-day trial – the longest in Ulster legal history at that time – all three accused were found guilty by an all-male jury of the simple murder of Peter Ward. They were found not guilty of capital murder, which carried a death sentence. The trial judge Lord McDevitt told the UVF men they had been found guilty of the brutal, cowardly and cold-blooded murder of Ward and that it only remained for him to pass sentence ordained by law which was that 'each of you will go to prison for life'. The judge added that he was imposing a minimum sentence of 20 years in each case.

The judge also paid tribute to the police officers involved in the investigation. Earlier, before the jury retired, he said his summing up of four hours and forty minutes reflected the seriousness of the UVF conspiracy before the court.

As sentence was passed, Spence, McClean and Williamson stood rigidly to attention in the dock, but the scenes in the public gallery at Crumlin Road Court House were much more emotional. Relatives of the men began weeping and one woman had to be assisted out of court. Police threw a tight security cordon around the court precincts, fearing a possible attack. Nothing materialised and the area was quickly cleared as shocked relatives of the guilty men made their way home.

Barman Peter Ward was also an ex-soldier. But he was so unhappy being away from home he had written to his widowed mother Mary asking her to scrape together £20 – which in 1966 was well above the average weekly wage – to buy him out of the army.

Peter was Mary Ward's pride and joy and she sent the cash immediately. She later told how pleased she was when she opened the door to discover her son was home from the army for good. Peter threw his arms round his mother and said: 'I'm home for good, Mom, I'm finished with all my roamin'.'

In less than six months, he lay dead in a Belfast back street, shot by two former soldiers and an ex-Royal Naval seaman. As the UVF team accused of his murder awaited trial, Peter Ward's sister Belle gave birth to a baby boy. In honour of her loving brother, she called the baby Peter Ward Sheppard.

In an almost forgotten footnote to the Malvern Street murders, another casualty of UVF violence met her death. This time the victim wasn't even a Catholic. Matilda Gould, a 77-year-old Protestant, died of serious burns on the very day Gusty Spence, Dandy McClean and Robert Williamson were arrested in the police round-up.

Mrs Gould, a widow with one child, lived next door to a Catholic-owned pub and off-sales at Upper Charleville Street in the Shankill district. At that time quite a number of Catholic publicans owned businesses in Protestant areas. Mrs Gould's house was attached to the licensed premises and to a stranger's eye may even have looked as if it was part of the pub.

On 7 May 1966, a petrol bomber belonging to the UVF hurled a device into her home in the mistaken belief that it was part of the pub next door. A few days before the attack, someone had daubed an anti-Catholic slogan on the wall of the pub. Printed in large yellow painted letters it read: 'This house is owned by a Taig – a Popehead – remember 1690.'

Like the Malvern Street killings, eyewitness evidence emerged during the inquest into Matilda Gould's death which suggested the person responsible for throwing the petrol bomb into her home was drunk.

The UVF conspiracy on the Shankill Road during the summer of 1966 may seem to many to have predated what we have come to call 'the Troubles', but as the policemen involved in the Peter Ward murder trial went for a celebratory drink, the sparks that lit the bonfire which would erupt in bloody conflagration on the streets of Belfast in August 1969 were well and truly beginning to crackle.

Five years later, in a statement to the Scarman Tribunal into the street disturbances of 1969, Ian Paisley angrily denied a suggestion that he had once employed Gusty Spence as a driver and 'minder'. Paisley admitted that he knew Spence, but insisted he had come to know him through a matter which was totally unconnected to the UVF.

With Spence, McClean and Williamson safely behind bars, the RUC Special Branch set about the task of bringing the rest of the UVF conspirators to book. Within days of the end of the Peter Ward murder trial, Noel Doherty, Ian Paisley's aide and the printer of Paisley's propaganda sheet the *Protestant Telegraph*, was sentenced to two years for possession of explosives.

The brutality of the Malvern Arms shootings shocked both communities and most Protestant people on the Shankill were disgusted at what the UVF had done in their name. There were others, however, who were anxious to continue with the anti-O'Neill campaign.

In a dingy back room on the Shankill, a hardline loyalist by the name of Frankie Miller arranged to meet Ian Paisley. Known as 'Pootsy', Miller enjoyed a reputation in the tough streets of the Shankill as a 'hardman'. In the 1950s he was involved in a famous street fight with a merchant seaman in Glasgow which was spoken about in both cities for decades after the event. A shipyard worker by occupation, Miller, along with Paisley and others, had been a founding member of the Protestant Action Volunteers. He was proud to be known as a Protestant bigot and Paisley was keen to find out what was going to happen in the wake of the recent loyalist trials.

Miller told Paisley he had been approached to take over the leadership of the Shankill UVF, but had turned it down. Paisley was intrigued and pushed Miller to explain why a man with his reputation would reject such an offer. 'Because as far as I'm concerned, the UVF are just a bunch of drunken bums. They are only interested in where their next drink is coming from and they can't be trusted,' he told the clergyman firmly.

However, it wouldn't be long before others filled the shoes of Spence and company in the campaign to discredit Terence O'Neill as his programme of reform continued.

Less than a mile away from the Shankill, on the Falls Road, Billy McMillen and Jim Sullivan, who controlled the IRA in the city, were committed to directing the small membership of the organisation towards political activity and at local level this meant IRA men got involved in housing action groups and the civil rights movement.

Both men were veterans of the border campaign and had been persuaded by Cathal Goulding, who became the IRA's chief-of-staff following the ending of the campaign, that political agitation was the way forward. McMillen was one of 180 northerners rounded up and interned by the Unionist government as part of the 1950s security clampdown, and when he emerged from Belfast's Crumlin Road jail in 1962 the organisation to which he belonged was practically non-existent.

The IRA had taken the conscious decision not to carry out military operations in Belfast during the border campaign for fear of stirring up the deep sectarian divisions which remained just below the surface in many communities.

Along with a small band of dedicated followers, McMillen and Sullivan became convinced of the merits of the new political direction advocated by Goulding. But the tradition they came from was one of physical force and many of their contemporaries looked upon republicans who turned their back on armed struggle with derision.

Unionist fears that the IRA planned to use the 50th anniversary of the Easter Rising as a platform to launch another campaign of violence were groundless. But behind the scenes there were still those within unionism who believed that the easiest way to stir up anti-O'Neill sentiment, which could then be channelled into opposition to change, was to lead the Protestant community to believe that the IRA was secretly reorganising.

– CHAPTER FOUR –

Tom Williams – Keeping the Dream Alive

Brave Tom Williams we salute you,
And we never shall forget,
Those who planned your brutal murder,
We vow we'll make them all regret.
Republican ballad, writer unknown

For decades northern republicans harboured grudges, believing, and not without some justification, that their forebears had been let down by their southern comrades after Ireland was partitioned. Michael Collins became a historical hate figure, particularly in Belfast, because it was he who went to London and signed the Treaty with the British which led to Partition. De Valera was also detested because, after voicing opposition to the Treaty and lining up against Collins in the Civil War, he eventually accepted the reality of Partition. Also, when his Fianna Fail party gained power for the first time in 1927, he set about ruthlessly smashing the republican movement by interning, and in some cases executing, members of the IRA.

But, as often is the case, the reality of the situation was somewhat different from popular perception. IRA volunteers from the North were amongst Collins' strongest supporters. It was because of this almost blind faith in his judgement that Collins was able to convince the IRA in Ulster to agree to a truce during the Downing Street negotiations and, amazingly, he also got them to agree to Partition. He argued that Partition wouldn't last and even continued to pay wages to IRA men in the North after the Treaty was signed. Collins managed to pull this off because he revealed plans to continue a terror campaign in the North aimed at breaking Unionist resolve. He argued that the Treaty was a 'stepping stone' to the Republic. However, he failed to convince many of his old comrades and a short, bloody and bitter

Civil War ensued. The pro-Treaty forces won out in the end and formed a government, but when Collins was cut down by an assassin's bullet at Beal na mBlath in his native Co. Cork in August 1922, many IRA members in the North felt trapped on the wrong side of the border. They believed few others in the republican leadership shared Collins' passion for the eventual reunification of the country and some IRA members cut their losses and moved south.

A Boundary Commission set up under the terms of the Treaty recommended no changes to the border which annexed six of the Ulster counties into the new Northern Ireland. A number of republicans even managed to secure jobs in the newly formed Free State Army and the Civic Guards, which was the forerunner police force to the Garda Siochana.

Others, who had given their all in the fight for Irish independence, retreated into themselves and, filled with bitterness and regret – much of it directed against their former comrades-in-arms south of the border – settled down to life as second-class citizens in Northern Ireland. The Unionist establishment considered most Catholics to be at best disloyal and at worst subversive, and the Unionist government employed the services of gunmen to strike terror into the hearts of the Catholic community.

One of these hired assassins was Alec Robinson from Belfast, known throughout the city as 'Buck Alec'. Robinson became famous for keeping a lion in his back garden and he regularly walked the animal round the narrow streets of the docks and Shore Road areas of the city.

The effect of this official terror campaign was that Catholics, although disappointed, began to accept that the dream of a 32-county socialist republic wasn't going to happen and the border was going to be a reality for many years to come.

The Unionists were determined not to be duped into a united Ireland and demands by the Free State government to end Partition only served to increase their resolve. Hundreds of IRA activists were rounded up and interned and, as a result, IRA action in the North became increasingly futile. By early 1923, it was obvious that support for the IRA was decreasing rapidly. Ireland north and south was war weary and most people wanted to get back to at least some semblance of normality. Despite this, the IRA chief-of-staff Liam Lynch was determined to fight on. He even spurned approaches from Éamon de Valera – who had also initially rejected the Treaty – to negotiate terms for a ceasefire.

On 10 April, Lynch was killed by Free State troops in Tipperary. He was succeeded by Frank Aiken, a legendary IRA figure from south Armagh. Aiken had been in charge of the Northern Command during the War of

Independence. Although opposed to the Treaty, Aiken was aware of the political limitations of his position and, after forming an alliance with de Valera, he signed an order to 'cease fire and dump arms'.

This was to prove a defining moment in militant Irish republicanism and Frank Aiken went on to become a major figure in southern politics. De Valera formed Fianna Fail (Soldiers of Destiny) and guided it towards full participation in constitutional politics.

In reality, however, Ireland was divided. It had endured the horror and bitterness of civil war, where fathers fell out with sons and brothers faced brothers down the barrels of guns, and yet despite de Valera's simple explanation of the political realities there were still some who wanted to fight on.

In an Irish drama that was to be repeated countless times over in the coming decades, these republicans accused de Valera of selling out and vowed to continue the struggle. Hardline IRA members claimed legitimacy from the men who signed the Proclamation of Independence read out on the steps of the General Post Office in 1916 and viewed themselves as the 'real' army of the Irish Republic.

In the years following de Valera's move away from militarism into what he described as the 'slightly constitutional' party politics of Fianna Fail, however, the IRA all but disappeared.

Support for Sinn Fein, which had won a landslide election victory in 1918, also collapsed and when de Valera formed his first Fianna Fail government in 1927, the party held only seven seats. For obvious reasons, de Valera had a degree of sympathy for his former comrades in the IRA and gradually many of them followed him into constitutional politics.

But the crunch came for republicans in 1936 when de Valera declared the IRA illegal. In that year, the IRA north and south was dealt a number of crushing blows. In Belfast, almost the entire Northern Command was arrested by the RUC and, in the South, de Valera ordered a major clampdown on republicans dedicated to overthrowing the state. A number of left-wing republicans joined the International Brigades and left to fight for the survival of the Spanish Republic against Franco's fascist rebels. The future looked bleak for the IRA, but some of its depleted membership still clung on to the dream of the republic.

As war clouds formed over Europe, the IRA, believing the old republican maxim 'England's difficulty is Ireland's opportunity', embarked on a bombing campaign of English cities.

The 'S' plan, as it was known, was the brainchild of the new IRA chief-of-staff, Sean Russell, who had fought in the Post Office in 1916. Within a short space of time over 120 explosions had gone off, incredibly leaving only one man dead, although dozens were injured in the attacks.

But then, on Friday, 25 August 1939, the IRA detonated a bomb in Coventry, killing five people and injuring sixty more. The device had been left in the basket of a bicycle and went off at 2.30 p.m. The man who planted the bomb made it safely back to Ireland but the Coventry police picked up two members of the IRA unit responsible and charged them. Peter Barnes and James McCormack were subsequently hanged.

A full 30 years after the atrocity, the volunteer who placed the Coventry bomb gave an anonymous interview to a newspaper reporter in Dublin in which he said he was delayed in traffic and took the decision to leave the bomb in a crowded street as a panic measure. However, this account has been dismissed as nonsense by another reliable republican source who insists that an order had been given to switch the detonation time from 2.30 a.m., when the street would have been deserted, to 2.30 p.m. on a busy Friday afternoon when the area was packed with shoppers.

This source claims the man who gave that order was Dominic Adams, an uncle of the Sinn Fein President and MP for West Belfast, Gerry Adams. He also claims that in justification of his actions Adams was heard to say: 'The gloves are off now!' Originally from Belfast, Dominic Adams spent the rest of his life in Dublin where he worked as a coal merchant.

London, Belfast and Dublin took action against the IRA independently, but the combined result pushed the IRA to the limits. Under Russell's leadership the IRA refused to see how the coming war in Europe would have spin-offs for Ireland. The Irish government's determination to preserve the country's neutrality angered many British politicians, but thousands of Irishmen nonetheless travelled to England to enlist in the armed forces to play their part in the fight against fascism, and when Belfast was bombed by the *Luftwaffe* in 1941, fire engines from Dundalk and Dublin rushed to the aide of the beleaguered city.

However, IRA links with the Nazis were a major cause for concern and were in danger of damaging any trust which existed between Britain and Ireland. Again in an attempt to take advantage of the war situation, the republicans had established links with the Nazis. A number of Nazi agents who were sent to Ireland to see how things could be progressed were arrested by the Gardai. The IRA even asked Hitler to supply them with money and weapons and Sean Russell travelled to Germany to discuss arrangements with the German High Command. As far as the Unionists in Belfast were concerned, the IRA friendship with the Nazis simply confirmed the treacherous nature of Irish republicanism.

In a fascinating twist, Sean Russell, the IRA chief-of-staff, actually died on board a German U-boat off the coast of Ireland while the Nazis were helping him return to Ireland after a money-raising trip to the US. After his death a period of rapid internal reorganisation ensued and a Derry man, Hugh McAtear, was appointed chief-of-staff.

In Belfast, a young man by the name of Tom Williams graduated from Fianna Eireann – the IRA's junior wing – into the IRA proper. Williams was born in the Beechmount area off Belfast's Falls Road in 1923. Previously the Williams family had lived in a Catholic enclave in the loyalist Shore Road district and had been subjected to violent sectarian attack.

The young Tom Williams was well aware of the divisive nature of the northern state under the Unionist regime and he passionately believed that the only way to change things for the better was for Ireland to be reunited. Williams also believed the only way to achieve this was by force.

The Unionist establishment was well aware that many in the Catholic community were bitterly opposed to the sectarian statelet of Northern Ireland and some were even prepared to use force to bring it down. To counteract this threat, the Unionists introduced the notorious Special Powers Act, which allowed Ministers in the devolved government at Stormont to do anything they deemed necessary to ensure the survival of the state. This included internment without trial and even the death penalty.

Following the death of his mother, Tom Williams and the remainder of his family moved in with his grandmother at 46 Bombay Street, in the shadow of Clonard Monastery, home to the Redemptorist Order of the Catholic Church. The Clonard district was made up of a small number of terraced streets that were home to Catholic workers who were employed in the local linen mills. It was also adjacent to the staunchly loyalist Shankill district and Catholics living in the area were ever mindful of their precarious position in times of tension. Under his grandmother's guidance, Tom Williams developed a deep devotion to Catholicism and regularly attended mass and Novena at Clonard Monastery, which attracted worshippers from all over the city.

Tom, however, did not enjoy good health – a fact that may have had some bearing on how his life was eventually to end. He suffered from chronic asthma and some say that in the months before he died he displayed symptoms of tuberculosis, a disease that was rife in the overcrowded working-class districts of his native Belfast.

After leaving school in his early teens, Williams worked at a variety of unskilled jobs, but by all accounts he was a willing worker who was extremely popular with all who came in contact with him. He also developed a fondness for Irish history and was an avid reader of anything which allowed him to learn more about his country's troubled past.

In 1940, at the age of 17, Tom Williams was sworn in as a volunteer in the Irish Republican Army, which was still trying to steal advantage while Britain was fully committed to fighting the Second World War in Europe. The IRA campaign lacked the support of the Irish people as a whole, but this did not deter the young Williams, who was soon promoted to Officer Commanding 'C' Company of the secret republican grouping. He became proficient in the use of arms and often held classes in weapons training, where he instructed other IRA volunteers about the tools of death.

Neither the war in Europe nor the hundreds of Belfast deaths caused by a wave of *Luftwaffe* attacks in April 1941 deterred the IRA from continuing its campaign, which was trundling on in a haphazard fashion on both sides of the Irish Sea. So, on Easter Sunday 1942, Tom Williams' 'C' Company embarked on a military operation which would result in the death of an RUC Constable.

Easter is one of the most important dates in the republican calendar, when the rebel leaders who were executed by the British following the 1916 Easter Rising are remembered and IRA volunteers vow to continue the struggle for freedom on their behalf. The IRA leadership decided that a token operation would be staged in Belfast as republicans gathered to honour their dead at Milltown Cemetery. Williams hand-picked his team which would fire a volley of shots over an RUC patrol car as it made its way through the Clonard district.

The firing party, which was led by Williams himself, also included Jimmy Perry, Henry 'Dixie' Cordner, John Oliver and Joe Cahill. Cahill would go on to play a crucial role in the formation of the Provisional IRA.

Four Webley revolvers and a semi-automatic Luger parabellum were distributed along with ammunition. The plan was to fire over the RUC car and then quickly make their way to an agreed place where another volunteer, Pat Simpson, would be waiting with two young women who had agreed to take possession of the weapons prior to returning them to an arms dump.

At 3.20 p.m., a police car turned into Clonard Street. The patrol consisted of a sergeant and three constables, one of whom was Patrick Murphy, a Catholic officer who lived nearby and was a popular figure in the area. He knew many local people personally, including Williams and other members of his IRA unit. All four police officers were armed. As the car moved on, a series of shots rang out. One bullet smashed a window of the car, but missed the occupants. The car sped away, but suddenly stopped to allow the sergeant and two officers to get out. The men drew their weapons and raced back towards the scene of the shooting. This action sent the IRA team into a blind panic. The entire unit raced into a small house, number 53 Cawnpore Street. Outside, Constable Murphy spotted Pat Simpson and a young girl enter the house from a back alley.

The policeman informed his superior officer, who began searching houses at the end of the street. Murphy returned to the lane to prevent the suspects escaping. Believing he could persuade the IRA gang to surrender, Constable Murphy slowly and silently approached the back door of number 53, which was accessed through a tiny yard where the outside toilet was situated.

Suddenly a hail of gunfire broke the silence as the IRA men opened up on the police officer. Constable Murphy was hit five times. Three bullets ripped into his stomach and two hit his chest, one of them piercing his heart. Remarkably, Murphy was able to return fire before he died and all three bullets fired by him struck their target.

Tom Williams was hit twice in the thigh and once on his left forearm. His comrades lifted the wounded IRA man and took him upstairs where he was laid on a bed. Other police officers converged on the house and entered through the front and rear entrances. The two who came through the back door found Constable Murphy lying dead at the entrance to the kitchen with his service revolver still clasped in his hand. As the RUC men made their way cautiously up the stairs, Tom Williams ordered Joe Cahill and the others to surrender. The men placed four weapons on a dresser a split second before the first policeman burst into the bedroom. Despite the IRA gunmen announcing their intention to surrender, the RUC officers, enraged by the death of their colleague, proceeded to beat them up. They were then arrested and taken to a city-centre police station, with the exception of the injured Tom Williams who was rushed to the nearby Royal Victoria Hospital where he was treated for gunshot wounds.

When he was well enough, Tom Williams was transferred to Belfast Prison on Crumlin Road, where he once again met up with his IRA comrades. All six had been charged with the murder of Constable Patrick Murphy and were remanded in prison to await trial. A few days after his arrival in 'The Crum', Tom Williams confessed to the other IRA men that while in hospital he had cracked under RUC interrogation and had made and signed a lengthy statement admitting his guilt in the murder of the police officer.

Contrary to the facts, Williams had claimed in his statement that he was the only IRA member to discharge his weapons in the direction of Constable Murphy. He insisted no one else had fired a shot and that the death of the policeman was solely his responsibility.

As Belfast returned to work following the annual summer holidays, the trial of Tom Williams and his five comrades opened in the Crown Court situated just across the road from the jail. The buildings were connected by a tunnel and the prisoners were required to enter the dock from a stairway below the courtroom. The Unionist establishment, political as well as legal, was determined to make an example of the IRA men and from the outset it was obvious that the prosecution was determined that all of the accused should receive the death penalty, as provided for under Northern Ireland's legislation.

The prosecution was able to prove that three of the IRA weapons had been discharged at Constable Murphy. Under oath, RUC men who had been present when the IRA men were arrested denied assaulting any of the accused and this was accepted by the trial judge. The defence team argued that the IRA men had acted in self-defence and that there had never been any premeditated plan to murder.

After three days, the trial ended and the jury retired to consider its verdict. Within hours the jury was back in court, where the foreman announced that, by a unanimous decision, the jury found that all six were guilty of murder, although in the case of Pat Simpson they were recommending leniency on account of his age and reduced role in the incident.

After listening to a short statement from all of the men in the dock, where in turn they all once again denied premeditated murder, the atmosphere in the courtroom was electric as the trial judge, Edward Murphy, donned a black cap and passed sentence:

> The jury have found each and every one of you guilty of the wilful murder of Constable Patrick Murphy . . . On Tuesday, the 18th of August, in the year of Our Lord, one thousand, nine hundred and forty two, you will be taken to a place of execution in the jail in which you are confined, and there be hanged by the neck until you are dead. And that your bodies be buried within the confines of the prison, within which the aforesaid judgment of death be executed upon you, and pray the Lord Almighty have mercy on your souls.

Amid scenes of chaos, police and court officials struggled to clear the premises while shouts of outrage rang across the courtroom as relatives and supporters of the IRA men voiced their feelings at the severity of the sentences. As was the norm in such cases, the execution date was postponed pending the outcome of an appeal which was immediately lodged by the defence team.

In Dublin, de Valera had already demonstrated his determination to smash the republican movement by executing republicans found guilty by special Military Tribunals introduced to protect the sovereignty of the Free State. But despite this, nationalist Ireland united behind the reprieve campaign.

The sentences were viewed as vindictive and support for the condemned men was sought in both Britain and America.

Back in Crumlin Road Prison, Tom Williams passed his time by writing letters to friends and family which displayed a deep commitment to the IRA and the methods by which it sought to unite Ireland. In one lengthy letter to Hugh McAtear, the IRA chief-of-staff, Williams expressed not a single word of regret about the death of Constable Murphy, but using extremely flowery language wrote about the righteousness of the republican cause, which was in his view certain to succeed because 'God and his Holy Mother' were supporting it.

Williams concluded the letter by asking McAtear to communicate a special message to other members of the IRA. He urged his comrades to:

> Carry on, no matter what the odds are against you, to carry on no matter what torments are inflicted on you. The road to freedom is paved with suffering, hardships and torture, carry on my gallant and brave comrades, until that certain day.

In August the appeal was heard in court, but the three Appeal Court judges upheld the previous sentence and a new date of 2 September was set for the executions to be carried out. The judges' decision gave the reprieve campaign a renewed vigour and a number of public figures offered support. The call for clemency became international as messages of support flooded in from all over the world. De Valera himself lent his support, ignoring the fact that earlier that year, George Plant, a Protestant member of the IRA had been hanged in Dublin.

All sorts of diplomatic activity was underway, but despite this the Unionists refused to yield to outside pressure. The Northern Ireland government was determined to make an example of the IRA men and it believed that, because Britain was in the middle of a desperate fight against Nazi Germany, most right-thinking people would understand why 'treasonous' acts by IRA men should be punishable by death.

However, towards the end of August the Stormont cabinet met to consider the case. There is no definite proof, but many believed at the time that it was the personal intervention of Winston Churchill, who understood well the complexities of the Irish Question, which resulted in the governor of Northern Ireland issuing a statement which commuted the sentences of all but one of the condemned men.

In the case of Tom Williams, the governor insisted: 'The Law must take its course'. But in the cases of Joe Cahill, Jimmy Perry, Henry Cordner and John

Oliver, they would now serve penal servitude for life. Patrick Simpson's death sentence was commuted to 15 years' penal servitude.

Some republicans, however, believe Tom Williams did a death deal with his co-accused, whereby he agreed to go to the gallows alone in order to save the lives of his comrades. Williams had been plagued by ill health most of his life and the conditions he was forced to endure in Belfast Prison did nothing to improve his state.

Joe Quinn, a republican from west Belfast whose father had been incarcerated along with Henry 'Dixie' Cordner, said:

> The way it was told to me was that Tom volunteered to die. The evidence against him was very flimsy and it is almost a certainty that he did not fire the fatal shot, if he even fired a shot at all. But Tom Williams was the senior man on the operation and he felt responsible for the predicament of the others.

Quinn also explained how he believed there was a religious dimension to Williams' decision. He said:

> You have to remember Tom Williams was a deeply committed Catholic who had been brought up on a diet of Catholic persecution. He saw dying as a principled thing to do, in the same way that Padraig Pearse did in 1916 and the Provo hunger strikers did in 1981. He believed in the blood sacrifice.

Supporters of the reprieve campaign were stunned by the governor's announcement and vowed to continue until the death sentence over Williams was also commuted. The campaign received an added boost as the initial shock turned to anger and thousands of people all over Ireland and beyond lent their support. All sorts of representations were made to the Unionists, but to no avail, and arrangements were put in place for the execution to go ahead as planned.

As expected, Ulster split into two religious camps over the issue, and, as the hour of execution approached, the Catholic community was shrouded in a deep sense of sadness and mourning. In contrast, the Protestant community and in particular the hardline loyalists of the Shankill Road, who lived in the shadow of the jail where Williams' hanging would take place, saw it as a case of 'a rebel' getting his comeuppance.

On the morning of 2 September, loyalists gathered at the corners of the narrow streets which linked the Shankill Road to the Crumlin Road. There was menace in the air as they sang the usual repertoire of loyalist party songs. It is a certainty that, as Tom Williams prepared to meet his maker, his thoughts were diverted by the strains of 'The Sash', 'Dolly's Brae' and 'The Lily-O'.

Williams attended mass and spent time with his spiritual advisers. It is said he remained completely calm and composed throughout. The execution was carried out by the notorious English execution team of Thomas and Albert Pierrepoint.

The evening before, Albert Pierrepoint had viewed Williams in the condemned cell and had commented that, due to his frail condition, it would require only a short drop to effect the execution.

Williams declined breakfast, stating that the last thing he wanted on his lips was the Holy Communion wafer. Shortly before 8.00 a.m., the execution team and the prison official entered the condemned cell. The cell was adjoined by the execution chamber and, after he was bound, Tom Williams was led to the gallows.

It is said he uttered a short prayer as Thomas Pierrepoint placed the noose around his neck. The trap doors were sprung and the young IRA man fell to his death. He was buried inside the prison. Another Irish martyr had been created and the tale of how 'Brave Tom Williams' lived and died would be told in the Catholic ghettos of Belfast for decades to come.

Two days before the execution, Gerard O'Callaghan, an IRA member who was also a friend of Williams, was shot dead by the RUC during an ambush at an IRA arms dump. This killing helped fuel anger in the Catholic community and Tom Williams' death marked a signal for a renewal of the IRA campaign which had been suspended during the fight to save his life. Throughout September dozens of IRA attacks took place throughout the North.

Although he had thrown his weight behind the reprieve campaign, Éamon de Valera had no intention of allowing renewed IRA activity to continue and moved quickly to quash it with repressive measures. The Stormont administration followed suit and, a week after Tom Williams' execution, the RUC raided the HQ of the IRA's Northern Command. Following a shoot-out many arrests were made, including that of David Fleming who had been sent north from his native Kerry to reorganise the units. When he appeared in court charged with the attempted murder of police officers, he shouted at the judge: 'Stormont was ballot proof, not bullet proof.' After he was sentenced, Fleming refused to conform to the regime in Crumlin Road, and embarked on a series of prolonged hunger strikes. When he left the prison he weighed just six stone and was regarded by republicans as a man to be looked up to because of his willingness to endure suffering for the cause.

Gradually, the IRA campaign ground to a halt due to lack of resources. Tom Williams' comrades who had managed to evade the hangman's noose were eventually released as the IRA threat subsided. Joe Cahill rejoined the IRA, but then quit as the organisation gradually began to reject violence in favour of political activity. The Stormont government rejected dozens of requests to release Williams' remains, but as the 50th anniversary of his execution approached it appeared a change of mind had taken place.

Once again people lobbied for Williams' remains to be released and a special place was reserved within the republican plot at Milltown Cemetery. In 1998, the authorities allowed a commemoration ceremony to take place at the spot where Tom Williams was buried and three years later Tom Williams' remains were released to members of his family, who insisted in burying him in a private family grave despite coming under intense pressure to have him interred in the republican plot.

His old comrade from that fateful day in 1942, Joe Cahill, spread an Irish tricolour on the coffin. On the Sunday following the funeral, 100,000 people from all over Ireland lined the streets of west Belfast in honour of Tom Williams as a commemoration ceremony attended by leading republicans took place at the cemetery where he is buried.

Following the abolition of the death penalty, Albert Pierrepoint, the executioner who placed the hangman's noose around Tom Williams' neck, opened a pub with the rather bizarre name of 'The Good St Christopher Sees Us Across The Road', in the Lancashire town of Oldham. One day he received a visit from the Irish writer Dominic Behan. Behan, whose brother Brendan had been sent to borstal in England after getting himself caught on a botched bombing mission, was working for Tyne-Tees Television at the time and had arranged to meet Pierrepoint with a view to interviewing him about his life as an executioner.

The Pierrepoints had been hangmen in Britain as well as both parts of Ireland and there was still great public interest in capital punishment. Dominic Behan asked Pierrepoint if he remembered travelling to Belfast to hang a young IRA man by the name of Tom Williams on 2 September 1942.

Albert Pierrepoint claimed he had full recollection of every execution he was commissioned to perform and said he remembered the Tom Williams execution well. He said Williams was probably the most composed condemned prisoner he had ever come across. He added that he still failed to comprehend why the Unionist government did not grant clemency to the young IRA man. Pierrepoint also told Behan he had come to the conclusion that the death penalty was pointless as a deterrent and that he was now opposed to it.

- CHAPTER FIVE -

From Civil Rights to Civil War

One man, one vote.
Civil rights marching chant

In Belfast, the spirit of the republican tradition was largely kept alive in the narrow streets of the Lower Falls, Clonard and the Pound Loney. It was there, in the small terraced houses and in the pubs which were on every corner that the tales of daring IRA exploits were told and the rights and wrongs of the settlement which annexed six Ulster counties into a Northern Ireland under British rule were discussed.

Every household had at least one family member who had been 'involved' and the IRA enjoyed a degree of tolerance which guaranteed its continued existence. Memories of the sporadic sectarian attacks endured by Catholics since the formation of the state were fresh in the folk memory of a community which never fully accepted the reality of Partition and in many ways managed to exist as a members of a state within a state.

Catholics had their own schools, their own sporting clubs, music and dance groups, thanks to organisations like the Gaelic Athletic Association and Comhaltas Ceoltoiri Eireann. And, much to the annoyance of the Unionists, they had their own exclusive language in the form of Irish Gaelic. Few in the North had any fluency in the language, but religious teaching organisations like the Irish Christian Brothers liked to batter at least a '*culpa focal*' (couple of words) into their charges before releasing them into the world of the Sassenach. This, coupled with their religion, gave republicans a feeling of martyrdom as well as victimhood. As Unionist discrimination denied Catholics entry to industries like shipbuilding, engineering, finance and the Civil Service, educated members of that community who chose not to emigrate went into education, while others ran pubs and bookmaker's shops.

Republicans were encouraged to develop a sense of national identity through exclusively 'Irish' organisations. They were constantly reminded that it was in Belfast that the Society of United Irishmen had been formed in 1791 by radical Protestants like Theobald Wolfe Tone, who had been deeply impressed by the egalitarian principles of the French Revolution. Tone in his day had called for the unity of Catholic, Protestant and Dissenter, but his latter day co-religionists were not impressed by this philosophy and they were not at all shy about letting the minority community in the North know it. Every 12 July, thousands of Orangemen took to the streets to proclaim their loyalty to the British Crown.

There was a sense of self-righteousness among republicans and many of them looked down on other Catholics who were prepared to accept the existence, even in a small way, of the state in which they resided and which quite clearly discriminated against them. This, of course, had a negative effect on IRA membership and by the time Cathal Goulding took over the role of chief-of-staff, following the abject failure of the Border Campaign of the late '50s and early '60s, the organisation was once again on its uppers.

Republicans tended to sit in clubs and pubs lamenting the lost opportunities of the past and secretly hoping for another chance to grease the gun for yet another campaign. Goulding had emerged from jail in England to find an IRA which had disappeared in all but name. However, despite the seeming hopelessness of the task he faced, the tenacious Dubliner, who was a house painter by trade, agreed to give things a go.

His first decision was to order a cessation of the Irish republican tradition of physical force dating back to the time of Wolfe Tone, whose own attempt at bringing freedom to Ireland ended with his death in a Dublin prison cell following the end of the failed rebellion of 1798.

Goulding was intrigued as to why so many Irishmen were attracted to join revolutionary organisations and give their lives for a cause which had little or no chance of success. This period of reassessment did not go down well with the little remaining membership the IRA had and, as the 1960s rolled on, many, including the likes of Joe Cahill, left, believing the dream of a united Ireland was well and truly over.

Cathal Goulding was a charismatic character who enjoyed the company of writers and intellectuals. He persuaded one such radical, a committed Marxist by the name of Roy Johnston, to join a 'think tank' with a view to developing draft policies which could be presented for internal discussion. Two years later, a nine-point document was prepared and Goulding called a special Army Convention where the proposals would be put before the rank and file.

Roy Johnston was a computer expert 20 years before the general public understood even the most basic workings of the machine which would come to dominate almost every facet of life. But he was also an ideal political confidante for Cathal Goulding, who was still struggling with new ideas himself.

The Dublin-based leadership of the IRA, which at that time was still the dominant partner to Sinn Fein in the somewhat casual marriage arrangement of the republican movement, was in awe of Johnston. One Dublin-based ex-volunteer said: 'It was almost as if we had discovered scientific socialism ourselves. Some people began sporting beards like the ones worn by Karl Marx and Lenin and the wearing of James Connolly badges was practically compulsory. It was like a new religion to us and we made excellent converts.'

Outside Dublin, however, the new thrust was not so popular and many viewed the concept of socialism as alien to the Irish way of life. As far as most of the rank and file were concerned, there was only one problem, and that was the border. The quicker new guns were acquired, the quicker the British would leave. Many of the men who espoused these beliefs had never set foot inside Northern Ireland and had little or no grasp of the life-threatening dangers of sectarianism, particularly in the ghetto areas of cities like Belfast.

Roy Johnston told the IRA leadership that armed force was not necessary in the circumstances facing the republican movement in the 1960s. It was a useful tool to have lying dormant, he said, but for now Irish revolutionaries should content themselves with joining organisations like credit unions, housing associations and land agitation groups. Johnston advanced a 'stages theory' of Irish history and, according to him, the gun played little or no part in the current stage.

Johnston visited IRA training camps and gave political lectures to men who were being given lessons on how to handle weapons. His views were regarded as heresy by many of the 1940s men and gradually the remaining few who were still wedded to military force left in disgust but, as events were to prove, it was not the last that would be seen of them.

Their loss was more than adequately compensated for by an influx of young and well-educated people attending colleges and universities in all Irish cities, including Belfast. The new direction of the Goulding-led leadership made much more sense to them than the shadow of the gunman mentality or the whiff of cordite which had sustained the IRA since the Civil War. Also, this approach was in keeping with other radical student and workers' movements now making their presence felt throughout Europe and also in the United States in the form of the civil rights movement.

In Belfast, Billy McMillen and his able assistant Jim 'Solo' Sullivan were committed followers of Goulding. McMillen had replaced the IRA veteran Billy McKee in 1964 and he and Sullivan firmly believed that the traditional strategy of the IRA – a strategy in which both of them were once willing participants – was always going to be doomed to failure. Building a radical political organisation in Northern Ireland with strong roots in the working class and links to Protestant workers made much more sense and they set about the task with relish.

One of the young men attracted to the republican movement at this time was a barman by the name of Gerry Adams. He came from committed republican stock on both sides of his family. Gerry Adams' father had been jailed after being caught red-handed carrying out an IRA gun attack in the wake of Tom Williams' execution. His uncle, Dominic Adams, had played a prominent role in the bombing campaign in England during the Second World War.

Gerry Adams worked in the Duke of York Bar in Belfast city centre. The place was a favourite watering hole for a variety of opinionated people, including lawyers and barristers, but also journalists, trade unionists and political activists from the Communist Party of Ireland and the Northern Ireland Labour Party. People who frequented the bar around this time remember Adams as a pleasant individual who was keen on political debate and regularly took part in the frequent discussions.

With the rallies to commemorate the Easter Rising of 1916 finally out of the way, the IRA leadership was anxious to get on with the mundane but much more politically challenging work of building a radical left-wing organisation with links to other groups which held broadly similar views.

The IRA had one major problem: Sinn Fein was banned by law from operating in the North and so the IRA was represented by a series of republican clubs. Short-term alliances were perfectly acceptable, although a far cry from traditional republican thinking.

In 1966, Cathal Goulding was invited to attend a meeting in Maghera, Co. Derry, where a number of liberal-minded people were hoping to thrash out ideas which could possibly force the Unionist government to accelerate its programme of reform, bringing the North into line with the other parts of the United Kingdom.

Goulding was sceptical about their chances of success, but agreed to attend and out of this meeting grew the Northern Ireland Civil Rights Association (NICRA) in January 1967. Also in 1967, the IRA started moves to dump the sacred cow of abstentionism – the refusal to take part in the political institutions of both parts of Ireland as a matter of principal. The IRA was about to dump a fundamental tenet of Republicanism in favour of reform in Northern Ireland. Internal opposition to this move was substantial and it was only a matter of time before the IRA split.

The majority of the Dublin leadership agreed to continue on the path towards politics and its commitment to the rapidly growing civil rights movement was reinforced. Civil rights rallies were attracting widespread support and the ferocity with which the RUC harassed those who took part shocked right-thinking people across the globe. The sight of RUC Inspector Ross McGimpsey lashing out with his baton at peaceful protesters in Derry gave many observers the impression that the Unionist government wished to run Northern Ireland as the white minority ran South Africa.

As the political storm clouds continued to grow, two incidents happened which convinced the Catholic community in Derry it could no longer rely on the RUC to afford it any protection whatsoever.

On New Year's Day 1969, a few dozen students marching under the banner of Peoples' Democracy set out from Belfast to Derry. They were demanding immediate reform and the RUC had agreed to accompany the protesters throughout the 75-mile route. Cathal Goulding, the IRA chief-of-staff, had refused to support the march on the grounds that it might be provocative.

As the demonstration passed through the nationalist village of Toomebridge, Co. Antrim, a young law student unfurled a republican banner but was quickly admonished by his peers. By the time the march reached the outskirts of Derry on 4 January, the number of marchers had swelled to several hundred and police officers protecting them from loyalist intimidation numbered around 80. At Burntollet Bridge, about five miles from Derry city centre, the marchers were attacked by a 200-strong loyalist mob wielding nail-studded cudgels and hurling missiles. The ambush was well-planned and relentless and most observers are agreed it was a miracle no one was killed.

Some police officers did try to prevent the attack, but others were clearly pleased that the students had 'got what they deserved'. Against all odds, the marchers regrouped further up the road and continued into Derry to rapturous applause when they reached Guildhall Square. But the disgraceful behaviour of some police officers sparked serious rioting and the police moved into the Catholic Bogside area in large numbers and proceeded to attack civilians and smash up their homes.

The Peoples' Democracy group agreed to quit protest marching as a result of its experience and socialist student leader Eamonn McCann acknowledged that the civil rights movement's hope of uniting the Catholic and Protestant communities had failed miserably. 'We have alienated the Catholics from their Protestant neighbours more than ever before,' he said.

As the fateful year of 1969 wore on, street rioting became a daily occurrence in many parts of the North, particularly in west Belfast and in Derry, where the Bogside area bordered the city centre. Law and order had virtually collapsed and the British Labour government in London, under Prime Minister Harold Wilson, was becoming increasingly frustrated at the Unionists' failure to govern Northern Ireland. More political reform was required. But the Unionist Prime Minister, Captain Terence O'Neill, was constantly looking over his shoulder at the right-wingers in his own party, as Ian Paisley, whose support was increasing by the day, continued to bay for his resignation from the sidelines.

On 19 April, Sammy Devenney, a 42-year-old Catholic father of nine children, stood outside his home at William Street, Derry, chatting to a neighbour and watching the spectacle of the local rioters engaging the police.

Suddenly, as baton-wielding cops rushed forward in a snatch squad movement, some of the rioters brushed past Mr Devenney and escaped through the back door of the house. Mr Devenney stepped back inside his home and closed the door. But seconds later, no fewer than nine police officers using shovels smashed their way inside and proceeded to violently attack Mr Devenney and other members of his family. The Devenney children looked on in horror as police officers proceeded to beat their father unconscious with batons and the shovels which had been used to gain entry to the house.

Sammy Devenney sustained multiple internal and external injuries, as well as a fractured skull. But he also suffered a massive heart attack and was rushed to hospital. Despite being released, then rushed back to hospital and then released again, Sammy Devenney remained seriously ill and died on 16 July as a result of his injuries.

A senior police officer from London was appointed to look into the case after an RUC inquiry failed to apprehend or even identify any of the men who entered the Devenney home. He complained a 'conspiracy of silence' among RUC officers had led to a lack of evidence.

In recent years there have been calls for an inquiry into the case. A number of people with knowledge of the circumstances surrounding the death of Sammy Devenney believe that a former RUC officer, now living in London, may be in a position to help clarify some aspects should the case be reopened.

The treatment meted out to Sammy Devenney, and the failure to track down the men directly responsible for his death, meant the RUC could no longer command any respect among Catholics in Derry. The stage was now well and truly set for what turned out to be a 25-year campaign of loyalist and republican paramilitary violence.

Terence O'Neill finally bowed to internal party pressure and resigned as Prime Minister of Northern Ireland. He was succeeded on 1 May by his cousin Major James Chichester-Clarke. Many hoped the new Prime Minister would be capable of papering over the cracks in unionism, but there was still no let up in the civil unrest.

Rumour and counter-rumour helped fuel fear and turn it into violence. In working-class districts, especially ones which doubled as interface areas where opposing tribes lived cheek by jowl, people on both sides of the divide believed they were about to be invaded by the other.

The Protestants were convinced that the civil rights campaign had just been a front for the IRA all along. They were led to believe – because Ian Paisley was telling them so – that they were now facing a renewed IRA campaign to smash Northern Ireland and force them into a 'priest-ridden' Republic. Nothing could have been further from the truth. But by now the violence had taken on an unstoppable momentum.

Catholics, on the other hand, thought that hordes of Protestants were about to invade Catholic areas and burn them out of their homes. The tension was palpable.

Finally, on 12 August, as an Apprentice Boys of Derry parade was making its way around the city's ancient walls, a number of marchers threw pennies down into the Catholic Bogside district which lies just below the old walled city centre. Local youths responded with stones.

Rioting on an unprecedented scale ensued, but worse was to come. In the early evening around a thousand heavily armed police officers moved into the area to clear out the rioters. Canister after canister of CS gas was lobbed into the narrow streets, causing tremendous suffering among elderly residents and children as it seeped under front doors into family homes.

What became known as the Battle of the Bogside had well and truly begun and the local community were determined to resist this naked aggression at all costs. The police were driven back and, as hurriedly built barricades were made even higher, John 'Caker' Casey painted on a gable wall the immortal words: 'You Are Now Entering Free Derry'.

His friend Eamonn McCann, journalist and left-wing activist, who was present, insists that before undertaking the sign-writing task, Casey double-checked to inquire if there were one or two Rs in the word 'Entering'. He was assured there was only one and in a few brush strokes the soon to be world famous 'no-go' area was born. The Queen's writ was no longer valid in this part of the United Kingdom and more areas like it would soon follow.

The Bogside was surrounded and the over-stretched police force was put under severe pressure. Calls were made to every available member of the part-time reserve – the notorious B Specials – to report for duty.

On 13 August, Jack Lynch, the Irish Taoiseach, and leader of the Fianna

Fail party – the largest republican party in Ireland – appeared on television. He lambasted the Unionists for operating a discriminatory system for nearly half a century. He said it was clear they were no longer in control and that the situation could not continue.

Then he uttered the sentence which sent shivers down the spines of Unionists who feared Northern Ireland was about to cease to exist. Lynch told an international TV audience: 'It is clear that the Irish government can no longer stand by and see innocent people injured and perhaps worse.'

To the Unionists, this appeared to indicate that the Irish Army was about to invade Northern Ireland. Indeed, some members of Lynch's cabinet, the likes of Neil Blaney from Donegal, just across the border from Derry, wanted Irish soldiers to proceed to the Bogside immediately. Blaney believed this action would internationalise the issue and lead to a United Nations force being sent in prior to the reunification of the entire island. The government of Northern Ireland made a hurried representation to their British counterparts requesting that British troops be sent to help restore law and order. The British agreed to the request.

In Belfast the republican movement was in turmoil as events spiralled out of control. But it was decided that some action be taken to take pressure off the beleaguered Catholic community of the Bogside. On the streets linking the Catholic Falls Road to the Protestant Shankill district, tension had risen considerably. Billy McMillen, the IRA commander in the city, ordered a number of volunteers to make their way to Springfield Road RUC Barracks to hurl petrol bombs at it.

The handful of IRA men in the city knew they were in no position to defend the Catholic community. Nevertheless, the IRA intention was to give the police the impression that a similar situation to the one which existed in Derry was about to develop in Belfast. The IRA unit took up positions at Colligan Street near Springfield Road police barracks. A number of petrol bombs were hurled at the front of the police station and officers inside responded, firing live rounds. A young man, Patsy Carberry from Gibson Street, was shot in the neck. An IRA volunteer was also shot by police as he was running away from the scene.

Throughout the evening, the streets around the Divis Street area further down the Falls Road were packed with people and hand-to-hand fighting broke out between Catholics and Protestants on the streets connecting the Shankill and Falls Road areas. A number of IRA gunmen had taken up position in St Comgall's School and opened fire on rampaging mobs of Protestants that had arrived in the area from the Shankill Road, while Catholic homes in Conway Street were burnt.

The IRA men were armed with a Thompson sub-machine gun and a revolver. Around midnight on 14 August, an IRA sniper shot 26-year-old father of one Herbert Roy in the chest, killing him almost immediately. He was the first person to die in an outbreak of violence which was to last for a quarter of a century. One of the IRA gunmen who fired the fatal shots was Charlie Hughes who, a few years later, was shot dead himself after he was caught up in a feud between the Official and Provisional IRA factions.

After the killing of Herby Roy, as he was known, the police knew the situation was getting more serious by the minute. Senior officers took the decision to send three Shorland armoured cars out onto the streets of the Falls district. Their presence there attracted further fire from the IRA and petrol bombs were thrown at them. The vehicles were fitted with powerful Browning machine guns and policemen manning the weapons opened fire in an indiscriminate and reckless manner as they drove up and down the Falls Road.

Nine-year-old Patrick Rooney had gone to bed early in his parents flat at St Brendan's Path in the Divis flats complex near the bottom of the Falls Road. His father, Cornelius, woke the child from his sleep, because he wanted to move the family into another room for safety. Patrick was to serve mass in nearby St Peter's Catholic Church the following day. But less than an hour after the IRA murder of Herby Roy, young Patrick Rooney was also dead after a bullet fired from a Shorland armoured car pierced the wall of a bedroom at his home and hit him on the back of the head.

A split second before, his father had been grazed by another bullet and when Alice Rooney saw her son slide down the wall, she thought he had just fainted at the sight of blood. The youngster was rushed to hospital and died there a short time later. He was the first of 68 children to lose their lives in the Troubles.

The Rooney family home was struck by a total of four high-velocity shots fired from the police vehicle and over a dozen other properties in the flats were also hit in what has to be one of the most disastrous actions ever carried out by police personnel in Northern Ireland.

A report on the civil disturbances by the British Judge Lord Scarman said there was no justification for the police decision to fire the weapons in the manner that they did. The police crew members who were on the Shorlands all denied firing at all, but eyewitnesses said they saw officers discharging weapons in the direction of the flats. Cornelius Rooney was granted just three hundred and ten pounds in damages when the case was called at the Recorder's Court in Belfast.

Thirty years after the event, Patrick Rooney's father said he blamed himself for his son's death because he didn't stick to plans he and his wife Alice had made to emigrate to Australia after he quit the British Army following a seven-year stint. Instead, the Rooneys came back home to Belfast after young Patrick was born. He was the eldest of five children. Mr Rooney described the night his son died. He said:

> Everyone was told on TV to stay indoors. The RUC were in armoured cars firing heavy-calibre tracer rounds. It was indiscriminate. We were terrified and not just the children. The walls were like cardboard and a bullet came flying in. Patrick slipped down the wall. His mother thought he had fainted. But when I went to him, Jesus, the back of his head was blown clean away.
>
> I had to creep out the back to avoid the shooting and crawl to the road where we flagged down a car to take us to the hospital. The RUC stopped us. They weren't going to let us through, then they did, calling us Fenian scum. I went to pieces for six months, but Alice was worse. She has never been the same since. There was no counselling and all the compensation we got was for Patrick's funeral. The RUC said that they had been firing but only over the flats. We lived on the ground floor so how come we were raked with bullets?

Following the shooting, Assistant Chief Constable Sam Bradley told the Scarman Tribunal that the police had been unable to investigate the killing of Patrick Rooney because the government sent in the British Army later the same day and the area was declared a no-go zone for police. The RUC crew who fired the fatal shot which killed Patrick Rooney were identified, but no one was ever charged in connection with the youngster's death. The Scarman report said that it was possible, but highly unlikely, that the police decision to fire the machine gun was in response to the sound of shooting a few moments before at the Whitewell block of Divis Flats where Hugh McCabe, a British soldier who was home on leave, was shot dead by police in suspicious circumstances.

Trooper McCabe, a 20-year-old married man and father of two children, was shot dead on one of the many balconies at the flats complex. The police said he was armed at the time, but local people denied this. The soldier's father said his son was trying to pull a wounded man from one of the balconies when he was hit.

Trooper McCabe served with the Queen's Royal Irish Hussars and was home on leave from a posting in Germany when he was killed. The following year the Ministry for Home Affairs at Stormont paid the soldier's widow eight thousand pounds in compensation, but insisted that the police action was lawful and justified. At a Coroner's Court Inquiry into Hugh McCabe's death, confusion arose about where the shot which killed the off-duty soldier had been fired from. It had been claimed that he was hit by fire from RUC men shooting from the roof of the nearby Hastings Street police station. However, McCabe's father insisted he saw men firing from a 'Whippet' police car. The Coroner rejected a claim that Trooper McCabe had been murdered and instructed the jury to return a finding of an open verdict.

Fighting continued throughout the night and into the next morning. Clonard Monastery in the Clonard District had always been a source of annoyance to hardline Protestant bigots from the Shankill Road and in late afternoon of 15 August a bunch of bully boys from that district decided to invade the Clonard area and systematically remove the Catholic residents from their homes. They also hoped to burn down the large church and Parochial House which was, and is to this day, home to an Order of Redemptorist priests who are deeply involved in community affairs. One of the order's members, Father Alex Reid, eventually played a crucial role in helping to persuade the IRA to call a ceasefire after 25 years of violence.

As fighting intensified, Father McLaughlin, who was acting superior at the monastery, became worried about a possible attack on church property by hundreds of Protestant thugs who were by now streaming into the area, burning Catholic homes at random. A local lad, Gerald McAuley, who was a member of the IRA's youth wing, Fianna Eireann, was detailed with others to offer whatever resistance possible in the wake of an attack on the church. Father McLaughlin gave two local men who were armed permission to patrol the church and keep watch for any possible attacks.

A short time later Father McLaughlin heard gunfire coming from nearby Waterville Street and rushed out to find a number of local people lying on the pavement after being hit in a wave of gunshot blasts. One of the victims was 15-year-old Gerald McAuley. Blood was pouring from a wound and the boy was ashen-faced and obviously in agony. The priest administered the last rites of the church to all of the injured before they were rushed to the nearby Royal Victoria Hospital, where Gerald McAuley died a short time later.

He was the first republican to lose his life in the Troubles and he is acknowledged as such in republican literature. The Scarman Tribunal concluded that the teenager was killed by a Protestant gunman who had fired at him from close range using a shotgun.

Gerald McAuley is viewed locally as a hero, because of the role he played in defending his community, but the IRA was castigated for failing to protect the community from loyalist attack. The following day graffiti appeared on walls around west Belfast which read, 'IRA – I RAN AWAY.'

It was as a direct result of the events of this period that the IRA split into two factions. The IRA leadership in Dublin was accused of doing little or nothing while the nationalist community was under attack. Thirty years to the day after her son died, Gerald McAuley's mother Ellen attended a commemoration ceremony in the Clonard area that was also attended by Cornelius and Alice Rooney.

In total eight people lost their lives as a result of the violence which erupted over 14 and 15 August.

Later that evening the first soldiers under the command of Lieutenant-General Sir Ian Freeland began appearing on the streets of Northern Ireland. The government in London had agreed to a request by the Unionist government for troops to help restore law and order. A company of the Prince of Wales's Own Regiment arrived in Derry, where they were well received by the local Catholic community, who at first saw them as protectors against the hated RUC, whose credibility had reached an all-time low.

Two and a quarter million pounds' worth of damage had been caused during the summer rioting of 1969. The Scarman Tribunal estimated that, in addition to the deaths, seven hundred and forty-five people were injured and out of that figure one hundred and fifty-four of them had been shot. One thousand five hundred Catholic families and three hundred Protestant families had moved home as a result of the Troubles. So-called 'peace lines' were hurriedly erected to keep warring communities apart. Even as the Troubles recently subsided, none of the peace lines were removed and in fact, in May 2002, a new one was built at Madrid Street in the Short Strand district of east Belfast. A short distance away at Cluan Place, the height of another 'peace line' where a number of people had been shot was raised from four meters to seven.

In October 1969, the Government-sponsored Hunt Report recommended the disbandment of the B Specials police reserve and also the disarming of the RUC to bring it into line with police forces throughout the rest of the United Kingdom and indeed the officers of the Garda Siochana south of the border. Predictably, working-class Protestant districts in Belfast erupted in violence, as local people took to the streets to vent their anger at what they saw as British interference in the domestic affairs of Northern Ireland. The British didn't understand the nature of the threat posed by Catholics, said the loyalists, and they shouldn't be poking their noses in where they weren't wanted. During the protests George Dickie and Herbert Hawe, Protestant cousins aged 25 and 32, were shot dead by soldiers in disputed, but separate, incidents. The army claimed they were petrol-bombers but this was strenuously denied by their relatives.

RUC Constable Victor Arbuckle, a 29-year-old married father of two, was on duty in the loyalist Shankill Road that night. The army had assumed a frontline role during street disturbances and Constable Arbuckle was standing with other police officers behind a line of soldiers who were doing their best to control a riot situation.

Constable Arbuckle was chatting to a colleague about sitting the police sergeant's exam when suddenly a shot rang out. Against all odds, the bullet, which had been fired by a UVF sniper, managed to completely miss the soldiers who were spread across the road and hit Constable Arbuckle. One of his colleagues, who was standing next to him when the gunman struck and who went on to retire with the rank of police superintendent, recalled the incident: 'I heard the crack and I saw Victor fall. As I stepped forward to lift him he gave a deep sigh and I knew he was dead. I just helped pick him up, but I couldn't help but think that it could just as easily have been me.'

Constable Arbuckle was the first of 302 RUC officers to die at the hands of terrorists in Northern Ireland. He died within two months of the outbreak of the Troubles and many found it ironic that he lost his life as a result of military action by the UVF – a loyalist paramilitary group which purported to defend the state of Northern Ireland, a state in which Constable Arbuckle was a serving police officer.

Three men were charged with the policeman's murder – an offence which still carried the death penalty – but were acquitted. However, a week later they were all handed down heavy sentences after being convicted of serious arms offences on the night the police officer was killed.

Eight days after Victor Arbuckle's murder, another death, this time across the border in Co. Donegal, left irrefutable proof, if any was now needed, that some of Ian Paisley's followers were involved in a terrorist campaign of political sabotage. However, these loyalist terrorists hoped the blame for their actions would be laid firmly at the door of republicans.

Thomas McDowell, a 45-year-old quarry foreman from Kilkeel, Co. Down, was found suffering from horrendous burns at a power station, at Ballyshannon, Co. Donegal. He had been injured when a bomb he was planting exploded prematurely.

McDowell's body was still on fire when it was found. Engineers who rushed to the scene following the explosion at first believed a swan had flown into a high-tension cable, but when the figure hanging on the wire fell to the ground they realised it was the body of a man. On the ground nearby, they found a massive amount of explosives and a loaded revolver. A UVF armband had been sewn into his coat. McDowell died in hospital two days later without giving a statement to Gardai investigating the incident. Nearly 6,000 volts had passed through his body.

McDowell was a member of the Ulster Volunteer Force, a member of Ian Paisley's Free Presbyterian Church of Ulster and the Ulster Protestant Volunteers, the militant religious organisation Paisley helped found.

Some months previously McDowell had been involved in the theft of gelignite that was subsequently used to bomb Castlereagh electricity sub-station, causing five hundred thousand pound's worth of damage. The general public wrongly assumed the bombing was the work of the IRA. The *Protestant Telegraph* told its readers the bombing was the first explosion carried out by the IRA since the failure of its border campaign. The explosions undermined the authority of the Northern Ireland Prime Minister Terence O'Neill, who later conceded that the bombings 'blew me out of office'.

Ian Paisley has consistently denied all knowledge that some members of the UPV were involved in terrorism. But it was Thomas McDowell's death which directly led to the police arresting other UPV conspirators and securing convictions for terrorist offences against them.

Thomas McDowell is buried in the cemetery at Ian Paisley's Mourne Free Presbyterian Church, in his native Kilkeel, Co. Down, and his name heads the officially sanctioned UVF Roll of Honour.

- CHAPTER SIX -

Say Hello to the Provos

Then rally to the call men, come let the Saxons know,
That hearts still beat for Ireland, where the Foyle and Lagan flow,
That the North again has Northmen, to raise the red right hand,
And never lag, till Ireland's flag, flies free throughout the land.
Nationalist ballad, writer unknown

As autumn turned to winter in 1970, the IRA, in Belfast at least, was close to mutiny. Few in the Belfast Brigade had faith in Cathal Goulding and the majority of the membership had even less in the Army Council's ability or willingness to address the age-old problem of lack of weapons in the North.

In particular, it was felt, the leadership had little or no understanding of the sectarian interface areas of Belfast, where the Catholic communities were under threat on a daily basis. Goulding's position, whilst principled, was typical of someone who had never personally experienced the naked aggression of a society divided on religious and cultural grounds, as was the reality of life in the North.

Old IRA men, who had previously quit the organisation in disgust at the new 'Communist-inspired' departure of Goulding and his friends, began to flock back.

Suddenly, Billy McMillen, Jim Sullivan and Bobby McKnight, who had remained faithful to Cathal Goulding throughout, were under pressure. An attempted 'military coup' took place, but the ever-shrewd McMillen, who was unarmed at the time, was able to persuade the gunmen that moves were afoot which might satisfy them. A compromise was reached. McMillen was warned that, in order to avoid a split, he would have to cut all ties with the 'Commies' in Dublin and concentrate on the issue in hand – defence of the Catholic areas of Belfast. Mick Ryan, a Dubliner from the inner-city North

Wall district, was told he was one of the few southerners who were still welcome in the city.

McMillen and his supporters were decidedly uncomfortable with this situation, but, in the interests of physical survival, agreed to reach an arrangement.

No one in the growing army of dissidents wanted to seriously cross swords with McMillen, because, after all, it was he who had carried the torch of republicanism in Belfast whilst they had deserted the cause; nevertheless, the tribe needed defending, and McMillen and his mates weren't up to it as far as they were concerned. A stand had to be taken and they were prepared to take it.

At the same time, however, Irish government agents were busy working in a covert manner trying to establish the real aims of the IRA leadership. The government did not like what it heard.

Captain John Kelly, an Intelligence Officer in the Irish Army, had spent a lot of time travelling round the North with the full authorisation of his government. He let it be known that the government in Dublin was prepared to donate 'aid' which could help relieve hardship among the nationalists of the North.

Northerners had streamed over the border in their hundreds to escape the sectarian strife which had engulfed the region and the government was beginning to panic.

Captain Kelly filed a report that revealed that Cathal Goulding's IRA had no intention of getting itself boxed into the role of defenders of the northern Catholics. He went on to say that the IRA leadership believed that the real battlefield was south of the border.

If the northern Protestants saw that the republican movement had been able to effect real change in the South, then maybe they would be more willing to dump the Union with Britain in favour of a new 32-county republic.

Furthermore, Captain Kelly informed his bosses that the current leadership of the IRA was heavily influenced by Soviet Communism, but he also added that there was a growing band of nationalists who wanted the IRA to return to its traditional role – defending the Catholic communities in the North.

The internal political dynamics of the IRA, however, continued to rumble towards conflict. Things came to a head when an IRA Army Convention was held a few days before Christmas at Knockvicar House, a rambling mansion on the outskirts of Boyle, Co. Rosscommon. Decisions made at this crucial time were to determine the course of Irish history – in the North at least – for the next quarter of a century.

Ostensibly, the main convention debate was to be about 'abstentionism' south of the border. Republican participation in politics and government would mean the acceptance by the IRA of the 26-county Republic of Ireland as opposed to the 32-county republic as envisaged by the leaders of the Easter Rising of 1916. This was heresy as far as 'traditional' republicans were concerned but the internal structure of the republican movement, then and now, meant it was impossible for the IRA leadership not to get its way.

The Convention would not have been called if there was even the slightest chance of a decision going against one previously taken by the leadership in secret. Soldiers don't vote. Soldiers do what their senior officers tell them.

As expected, a majority of those attending backed the proposals of the Goulding leadership. They were: 1) the de facto recognition of the governments in Dublin, Belfast and London by dropping the hallowed IRA policy of abstentionism, i.e. republican candidates would now take up their seats and participate in government if elected; 2) the forging of a National Liberation Front, i.e. linking up with various progressive elements for short-term advancement of the cause.

The losing faction withdrew, held their own Convention and formed a Provisional IRA. Two days later, the new group swore allegiance to the men and women behind the 1916 Proclamation of an Irish Republic and set about the task of building an IRA geared towards fighting Ireland's traditional enemy – the Brits. It also urged Sinn Fein members, due to hold an Ard Fheis (annual conference) within a few days, to reject the watering down of republican values.

The Provisional IRA's first chief-of-staff was Ruairi O Bradaigh, who quickly gave way to Sean MacStiofain, the London-born activist who had been jailed along with Cathal Goulding for the botched arms raid at Felstead Barracks.

The organisation quickly became known as 'the Provos'. The new group was made up mostly of IRA men who had been active during the 1940s and '50s, but they were well aware of the organisation's potential for growth. Cathal Goulding also knew that when it came to attracting recruits, his organisation could not compete and he conceded that MacStiofain's group was far in front. This would happen, he said, because 'Every Catholic youth in the North was a Provo at heart.'

Unlike IRA Conventions, Sinn Fein Ardfheiseanna (annual conferences) are, in part at least, public affairs and when the event took place at Dublin's Intercontinental Hotel on 10–11 January 1970, it attracted a massive amount of press interest.

The main issue centred on a resolution seeking to end abstentionism, which required constitutional change. The proposal, which had the backing of the leadership, failed narrowly. Immediately a call was made, again with leadership backing, to support the policies of the IRA Army Council – which of course had already dropped its policy of abstentionism. The ruse was anticipated and MacStiofain grabbed the microphone and asked delegates to back the policies of the newly formed Provisional Army Council. The meeting descended into chaos and the traditionalists left to meet at another city centre venue where Provisional Sinn Fein was born.

Three months after the conference, an incident took place in Dublin which attracted little publicity north of the border. Garda Richard Fallon, a 43-year-old member of the Irish police, was shot dead on duty by a rival republican terrorist organisation. The officer, who was married with five children, became the first serving member of An Garda Siochana to lose his life during the Troubles. He had 23 years' service in the force.

On the morning of 3 January, Garda Fallon, who was a member of a mobile patrol, received word to attend the Royal Bank of Ireland at Arran Quay on the banks of the River Liffey. The police had been told that the burglar alarm was ringing and were asked to investigate. On arrival at the bank, the unarmed officers (to this day ordinary members of the Gardai do not carry weapons on duty) were confronted by three men carrying revolvers who were escaping with the proceeds of a robbery. Bravely the officers gave chase, but members of the gang opened fire. Garda Fallon was hit in the head and was pronounced dead when he arrived at the nearby Jervis Street Hospital. He was posthumously decorated for his bravery.

The gunmen who murdered Garda Fallon were members of a self-styled revolutionary sect calling itself Saor Eire. The group were followers of the early Russian Communist leader Leon Trotsky, who was executed by an assassin in the Soviet secret police. Saor Eire had been formed in the late 1960s and was mostly made up of radical student types who saw physical force as a legitimate political tactic. Taking its name from an earlier republican political party set up by the IRA in 1931 in response to Éamon de Valera's Fianna Fail, Saor Eire distinguished itself in 1970 mostly because its members pulled off a series of bank and Post Office raids and then lived fairly lavish lifestyles for a few weeks on the proceeds.

The Garda Special Branch was stretched to the limits during this period, largely due to the growing turmoil in the North. Intelligence on Saor Eire and its stated aims and intention were limited. But then suddenly the Branch was given a handout in this regard from a most unusual source – the newly appointed chief-of-staff of the Provisional IRA, Sean MacStiofain. The IRA leader was compromised because a Garda Special Branch officer told him he had evidence to connect him to a murder in the Republic.

The IRA had killed a man and then secretly reburied the body in a grave belonging to someone else. MacStiofain was devastated at the prospect of going back to jail for a long period. After all, his big moment as chief-of-staff had come and he did not want to lose the opportunity of going down in history as the IRA leader who managed to bring about Irish unity. He especially did not want to be connected to such a distasteful thing as being part of a gang that had desecrated a man's grave by placing a murdered body in it. A deal was worked out where MacStiofain agreed to work for the Garda Special Branch and he regularly passed on information to his handler regarding the activities of Saor Eire. It is now accepted that MacStiofain's knowledge helped the Garda Special Branch gradually freeze the organisation out of existence. Saor Eire has since disappeared without trace.

In the first few months of its existence, the Provisional IRA was in no position to launch an offensive of any kind. For a start, its only weapons were a collection of odds and ends it had managed to scrape up from sympathetic people around the country. It had big plans, however, and trusted volunteers were dispatched to America to set up arms supply routes. Volunteers were joining in their droves, but a programme of training was necessary and IRA training camps were set up at various venues in the Republic. These were mainly week-long camps in the mountains of Donegal, Dublin or Kerry, where volunteers received basic arms instruction.

Around this time, money from the Irish government began to flow north. The Officials managed to get their hands on some of the cash, but the vast bulk of it ended up with the Provos. Fianna Fail was relieved it didn't have to provoke an international incident by invading the North, but instead sent cash to buy arms and allowed members of the public to travel to Dunree Fort, outside Buncrana, Co. Donegal, where basic arms instruction was given by serving Irish soldiers.

In May 1970, Taoiseach Jack Lynch sacked two of his ministers, Neil Blaney from Donegal and a man who would later become a legend in his own lifetime, Charles J. Haughey, following a sensational weapons importation scandal.

A case against Blaney was dropped, but Justice Minister Charles Haughey was charged, along with Irish Army Intelligence Officer Captain John Kelly and a Belfast IRA man also called John Kelly, with illegally importing arms into Ireland. They were all acquitted in the High Court, but the issue convinced unionists that the government of the Republic still had designs on the North.

In the North, relations between the British Army and the Catholic community continued to decline and a general election at the beginning of June saw a change of government at Westminster. The Tories, who had close ties with the Ulster Unionists, were back in power.

In June, the Provisional IRA in Derry was planning to go on the offensive, but a mixture of poor planning, naiveté and inexperience resulted in one of the most tragic incidents of the early Troubles.

Tom McCool, a 40-year-old father of five, had been appointed as Officer Commanding the Provisional IRA in the city. McCool had served a prison term for possessing guns during the IRA's ill-fated border campaign. His adjutant and second-in-command in the city was his trusted friend and comrade, Joe Coyle, another 40-year-old married man and father of two children. Both men had been involved with the Republican movement for some time, and when the split came they had sided with the Provisionals.

Tom McCool and his wife and family lived at Dunree Gardens in Derry's Creggan district overlooking the River Foyle. The estate was built in the 1950s to house the burgeoning Catholic population of the city.

Derry suffered the most blatant Unionist discrimination in the North at that time. The city had a two-thirds Catholic and very nationalist majority, but, thanks to a crude system of gerrymandering, the city council remained permanently under Unionist control. The feeling of alienation among Catholics was at its keenest in Derry, where years of unemployment among the male population had taken its toll.

Both wings of the IRA reaped the benefit of youthful frustration following the outbreak of the Troubles. The Provos were still the smaller of the two organisations, but Tom McCool and Joe Coyle wanted to lead by example.

The Provos clearly identified the British as the problem and the manifestation of this domination was in the thousands of khaki-clad soldiers – with English and Scottish accents – who seemed to roam the city harassing the Catholic residents. It was time to strike back and at the same time show the Brits that the IRA was back in business. It was time to let everyone know that the IRA regarded the British Army as the enemy.

In the early hours of Saturday morning, 26 June, Joe Coyle together with Tommy Carlin, another IRA man, called at Tommy McCool's house. Bomb-making materials had been gathered and the three IRA men set about making an explosive device that would mark the start of a Provo offensive. Tom McCool's family, his wife and five children, slept upstairs while the men worked in the kitchen. One of the men, probably McCool himself, was using a garden spade to blend the highly explosive ingredients together. A downward movement of the spade struck the concrete floor creating a tiny spark invisible to the eye. Suddenly a huge explosion ripped through the house, sending a huge fireball upwards. The entire house was engulfed in flames but, miraculously, Mrs Coyle and three of her children – two boys and a girl – managed to escape uninjured. The spark had ignited a huge bomb and the family home took the full force of the explosion and the blaze which followed. Three military policemen, who were on the scene within minutes, tried to enter the house, but the intensity of the heat prevented them. One soldier who was attempting to climb through an upstairs window from a ladder was blown to the ground when a second smaller explosion occurred.

Tom McCool and his two young daughters, Bernadette aged nine and Carol aged just four, were burnt to death in the blaze. Joe Coyle, who lived at Rathkeale Way, also on the Creggan estate, died as result of his injuries in hospital the following day. Tommy Carlin, who lived at Central Drive, was rushed to hospital suffering from horrendous burns. Somehow he managed to hang on to life for 11 days before his badly charred body gave up the fight. The cause of Tommy Carlin's death was given as pneumonia. The deaths sent shock waves through the Catholic community as local people and shocked relatives struggled to come to terms with their grief. In the years to come, the IRA were responsible for the deaths of 67 children, but the deaths of the McCool girls in such tragic circumstances became known as the first of many so-called 'own goals'.

At an inquest into the five deaths, which was held in Derry on 10 December, the Coroners Court heard that the tragedy was probably caused by highly inflammable material being ignited. The jury was told that Tom McCool and Joe Coyle were found dead in the kitchen by firemen, and that the two young girls were in an upstairs bedroom. One was dead on arrival at hospital and the other dead a few hours later. Divisional fire officer James Harvey said the seat of the fire was in the kitchen of the house and was consistent with a fire involving a highly volatile substance. He said he found the remains of a wooden crate containing the base of bottles which had smashed in the explosion. These bottles had contained chemicals used in the making of the bomb. A forensic science expert from Belfast, Dr W.H.D. Morgan, said he found no trace of petrol on the broken glass. A brown paper bag found in a cupboard at the rear of the house contained one and a quarter pounds of sodium chlorate, another essential bomb-making ingredient. Dr Morgan said it was obvious that a highly inflammable material had been ignited and that the occupants of the house had no chance of escape. The jury returned a verdict of death by misadventure.

Within days of the fire tragedy in Creggan, two incidents happened in Belfast which went a long way towards convincing the Catholic community that the army, which a year ago it had welcomed onto the streets with tea and sandwiches, was now the enemy.

On the evening of 26 June, stone-throwing between Protestant and Catholic mobs began in the lower Newtownards Road area of Ballymacarrett, which includes part of the small Catholic area of Short Strand. The Strand, as it is known locally, is situated just across the River Lagan in industrial east Belfast and is entirely surrounded by a large Protestant population. Since the formation of Northern Ireland, residents of the district had become used to sectarian fighting during times of tension. Short Strand residents had been reared on stories of how some of their forebears, who had been lucky enough to find work in the nearby shipyard, had been expelled when Protestant workers forced them to dive into the river and swim for their lives as a hail of nuts and bolts rained down on them.

The heartbeat of the Catholic community's continued existence in the area was St Matthew's Catholic Church, a solid sandstone building with an impressive steeple sited at the corner of Newtownards Road and Bryson Street. Behind the church was a primary school that was partly staffed by nuns and, over the years, the property occasionally became a focus for Protestant anger. Arson attacks and broken windows were a fairly frequent occurrence and, during the summer marching season, Orange 'kick-the-Pope' bandsmen making their way to the annual 12 July celebrations would pause outside, increasing the volume of their fifes and drums as a means of letting the Catholics know their place.

As the stone-throwing around St Matthew's intensified, both wings of the IRA, which were practically non-existent in the area, anticipated correctly that things were getting worse by the minute, and, as the Protestant stone-throwers swelled in numbers, reinforcements from other parts of the city were sent for.

The Provos were anxious to play the traditional role of the IRA by appearing on the streets as 'defenders' of the Catholic community and they were assisted by a group of former soldiers from the Catholic Ex-Servicemen's Association (CESA) who had loosely formed themselves into a defence force. A secret and almost laughable coded language was developed to warn members of imminent Protestant attack. CESA volunteers with phones in their houses played an important role in warning others in times of danger. 'The pigeons are out!' was a coded message which meant the area was under attack.

Inevitably the stone-throwing around St Matthew's turned to an exchange of gunfire and quickly developed into a major gun battle. British soldiers dispatched to the area found their route blocked by thousands of Protestants surrounding the area and the Catholic community took this as a clear signal that the authorities had no intention of protecting them. The gun battle raged all night and by the time morning broke two Protestants, 38-year-old Robert Neil and 34-year-old Robert James McCurrie, and one Catholic, Henry McIlhone, a 32-year-old father of five, were dead.

McIlhone had been assisting members of the Provisional IRA gunmen in the grounds of St Matthew's Church when he was cut down in a hail of bullets. Billy McKee, a founder member of the Provisional IRA who had travelled across town from the west to help defend the district, was also shot and injured. The image of McKee, wounded in the grounds of St Matthew's Catholic Church with a Thompson sub-machine gun in his hand – the traditional weapon of the IRA – was just the propaganda the Provos needed. The Provos had demonstrated they were willing to defend the beleaguered Catholics against Protestant mobs and even the British Army if necessary. All the Provos needed was the necessary equipment. During the 30 days of June, 7 people lost their lives as a result of the street unrest and 200 civilians were injured, 54 of them by shooting. Although the figures were alarming, the violence of that month was merely a dress rehearsal for what was to come.

On Friday afternoon, 3 July, British soldiers moved through the narrow streets of the Lower Falls towards a house in Balkan Street. They were acting on a tip-off and intended to search the property in the hope of uncovering a cache of stolen weapons belonging to the Official IRA. The Lower Falls in the west and Markets on the edge of the city centre were the two parts of the city where the Officials were the dominant republican grouping. The occupant of the house, Sean Maguire, wasn't at home when the soldiers called, but the search party appeared to know exactly where to look and before long a total of 19 weapons, consisting of rifles, machine guns and a quantity of handguns, had been recovered. The consignment had been smuggled into the area some months previously and had been stored in industrial gas bottles.

The IRA had developed a number of ingenious ways of hiding weapons and this was one of the best. Large gas cylinders used in industrial welding were hacksawed into two sections. Rifles were placed inside and the canister was then joined again by a series of tack welds. To the untrained eye, the canister was an innocent piece of industrial equipment but to the IRA volunteer it was a prefect weapons dump, which could be accessed in seconds by simply tapping the base with a heavy hammer.

News of the arms raid spread quickly and Joe McCann, a senior IRA man in the Markets area, was informed. Twenty-three-year-old McCann was a native of the Falls, but had been sent a mile across town by the Official IRA commander, Billy McMillen, to organise republican resistance in the Markets district.

The Lower Falls was the engine room of the Officials in Belfast and McCann was anxious to assess the extent of the arms loss. He slipped into the area unnoticed and met with other Official IRA members who explained that 19 weapons had been lost. The behaviour of the soldiers who entered the house in Balkan Street where the weapons had been found clearly indicated the army was acting on information received. The search party had gone straight to the spot where the arms were hidden. It was obvious that the Officials either had an informant in their camp or that a volunteer couldn't keep his mouth shut. The local IRA leadership, under the control of McMillen and his adjutant Jim Sullivan, had resigned itself to the loss the weapons and just wanted the Brits – as the army became known – out of the district as quickly as possible.

However, the IRA commanders' wishes were to be thwarted – by the Provisional IRA. Local youths began to hurl stones at the soldiers and the Provisionals decided this was an opportunity they weren't going to miss – especially on the Officials' home turf.

Suddenly some members of the Provos hurled nail bombs at the 'Brits' as they pulled out. The soldiers tried to retreat back to Balkan Street from where they had just left, but found their route blocked by hundreds of stone-throwing youngsters. The officer in charge took the decision to dig in and wait for reinforcements but the rioting escalated out of control. Lieutenant-General Sir Ian Freeland, the most senior army officer in Northern Ireland, decided it was time to take a stand and sent in 3,000 more troops, backed by helicopters and armoured cars. In a move which was completely illegal, he also announced a total curfew of the area while more house-to-house searches took place.

The Officials could see the possibility of their wing of the IRA being wiped out in their own true heartland. The Falls and the Pound Loney was where the flame of Irish republicanism in the North had been kept alight when most of the Catholic community had turned its back. McMillen established an HQ base in a drill hall run by the Knights of Malta ambulance corps in nearby Sultan Street. From there he organised the removal of a large amount of weaponry from the district by recruiting a small army of women. The idea was to stack weapons into the bases of children's prams and place babies on top before smuggling the deadly cargo out of the district unnoticed. The ploy worked, although McMillen did retain enough hardware to make a military stance if the situation arose, and it wasn't very long until it did.

Freeland's men threw a cordon round the district. British troops were placed on the Grosvenor Road, as well as along the Falls Road to its junction with Albert Street. Soldiers were also positioned along the entire length of Albert Street to where it reached Cullingtree Road and back round to the corner of the Grosvenor. The area, which is roughly the size of an inner-city park, was saturated with heavily armed soldiers. As the order to continue with house-to-house searches was given, plans for what was to become known as the 'Battle of the Lower Falls' were well underway.

Billy McMillen lined up his men, including Joe McCann, and explained to them the seriousness of the situation. This was not a confrontation they had sought, explained McMillen, but rather one which had been forced upon them. They had to take a stance because the Provos were watching from the wings and whatever happened now would determine how that organisation would view the Officials in the future, he said. Every available man was asked to play a role, including a group of auxiliaries – sympathetic helpers who were not actually IRA volunteers. As British troops booted their way into Catholic homes, smashing religious artefacts as well as furniture and the skull of anyone who got in their way, the Official IRA made its presence felt.

Although its ranks numbered just 80 men, the Officials threw everything they had at the army. The soldiers were bombarded with bricks, bottles, petrol bombs, ball bearings and live bullets. In Dublin, Cathal Goulding, the Official IRA's chief-of-staff issued a statement claiming it was the first time the IRA had engaged the British Army since the War of Independence, which had ended when the truce was called on 11 July 1921, paving the way for the Treaty which led to the partition of Ireland.

The exchange of gunfire between the IRA and the British was intense and prolonged. The Brits – who were made up of the Black Watch Regiment from Scotland and the Life Guards from England – reacted to the IRA offensive with renewed vigour and as the evening wore on the sickening smell of CS gas filled the air. Old people and children were the worst affected as locals struggled to find ways of counteracting the gas. Some of the Scottish squaddies, in particular, seemed to relish the opportunity of smashing up the homes of Catholic families. The soldiers traded insults with Catholic women, calling them 'Fenian whores' and 'Papish bitches'. Senior officers did nothing to restrain the excesses of their men.

William Burns, a 54-year-old Catholic shopkeeper, was the first to die. He was struck by a ricochet bullet fired by a British soldier shortly after he closed his business for the day. The incident happened as the troops moved into the area at the start of the British offensive. A short distance away in Linden Street, Charles O'Neill, a 36-year-old unemployed man, stepped out onto the road to warn the driver of an advancing troop carrier that easy access to the area could prove difficult as the entire district was up in arms. Mr O'Neill had served ten years with the RAF before being invalided out and bore no malice towards the army. As he tried to wave the army driver down, the Saracen vehicle appeared to speed up before striking him. The impact killed him instantly.

Around 11.30 p.m., Zbigniew Uglik, a 24-year-old London-born postman who had a longing to work as a freelance photographer, approached a house in Albert Street and asked the man living there if he could take shelter in his doorway as the gunfire was intensifying. He was invited inside and explained that he was trying to make his way back to the Wellington Park Hotel because he had no film for his camera. A short time later he made his way out over a yard wall at the rear of the house but was shot dead by soldiers within minutes. At an inquest into Uglik's death, the soldier who fired the fatal shot said he saw a man dressed in black making his way along a yard way and assumed he was a gunman. It also emerged the victim was not employed by any newspaper, but had travelled to Belfast of his own volition to take 'war pictures'.

Patrick Elliman, a 62-year-old local man who lived in Marchioness Street, was preparing to go to bed, but suddenly decided to take a walk to the end of the street to see if things had calmed down. As he walked along in his slippers and open-necked shirt, he was struck in the head by a bullet fired by a British soldier.

As well as the four civilian deaths, another sixty were injured. Apart from a short break to allow essential groceries to be delivered in to the area, the curfew remained in place until Sunday morning. By this time the district was quiet, but it had the appearance of a film set for a war zone region of Berlin at the end of the Second World War instead of a part of the United Kingdom. The stench of CS gas still hung over the area and the streets were littered with rocks and half bricks. There was hardly a house which did not bear the scars of gunfire.

At the end of the siege, the army had recovered a total of 52 pistols, 35 rifles, 14 shotguns and 6 varied automatic weapons. Large quantities of ammunition, explosives and bomb-making equipment were also found.

The army, or at least the officer class, was delighted. They had seen off a serious terrorist threat and taken control. The Unionists too were delighted and secretly wished for more of the same. Two Unionist ministers, William Long and John Brooke, who would later inherit the title of Lord Brookeborough, were driven around the Falls courtesy of the army to view the defeated rebel area.

The army had succeeded in its task of recovering illegal weapons, but it had also succeeded in alienating almost the entire Catholic community. Before the Falls curfew, Catholic soldiers had been able to attend mass at St Peter's Pro-Cathedral, but they were no longer welcome. Catholics viewed the army's actions as part of a plan introduced by the new Tory government at Westminster to prop up the discredited Unionist regime at Stormont.

The Officials, who had been forced into taking a military stance against their better judgement, gained some short-term kudos, and, as they analysed the situation after the event, some members of the Belfast Brigade concluded that they had given the British military machine too much respect. But the real winners in the Falls Curfew were the Provisionals, whose actions had sparked the conflagration in the first place. The Provos, especially the likes of Joe Cahill and Billy McKee, longed for war with the British, but they were not yet in a position to execute one. For the time being they had to be content with training and acquiring weapons. But the Officials had shown them that it was possible to take on the Brits.

Following the 'Battle of the Lower Falls', the Provisionals were anxious to prove they could at least compete with the Officials on the military front. A small group of Provo gunmen had even assisted the Officials during the curfew. It was only a matter of time before the Provisional IRA, which had only been in existence for seven months, went on the offensive.

Sean MacStiofain, the Provo chief-of-staff living in Navan, Co. Meath, had also assumed responsibility for an IRA unit based at Inniskeen, Co. Monaghan. Another member of that unit was Tom 'Slab' Murphy, a millionaire pig farmer, whose property straddled the border at Ballybinaby. Murphy had been born and brought up in a staunchly nationalist region of south Armagh, which for generations had been a place apart from the rest of Ireland.

The area, a region of stunning natural beauty, was steeped in rich folklore, and people paid little attention to the laws of the land, be they Irish or British. The imposition of an international land border running through the area following Partition only served to encourage locals to break the law in pursuit of an extra pound or two. Smuggling became a way of life and customs officers on both sides of the border found it extremely difficult to glean evidence when pursuing known lawbreakers. As far as the British Army was concerned, the place would simply be known as 'bandit country' – and not without good reason.

Tom Murphy had shown some interest in the republican movement, prior to the split. He had attended a meeting addressed by Cathal Goulding in north Louth in the mid-1960s, but when a choice had to be made, he opted for the physical force line of the Provos. In the years to come, Tom 'Slab' Murphy, as he was known, would go on to become a pivotal figure in the IRA, rising to the exalted position of chief-of-staff, and his reputation would be both feared and respected in the local Gaelic Athletic Association (GAA) club as well as the House of Lords.

Members of Murphy's Inniskeen unit listened intently as Sean MacStiofain explained how they should use the southern side of the border to launch attacks on security forces in the North. In 1969, MacStiofain had personally led an attack on Crossmaglen Barracks and he was anxious to repeat his earlier success. Much of MacStiofain's motivation stemmed from his desire to prove his old jail-mate Cathal Goulding wrong.

On 7 August, two IRA volunteers stole a red Ford Cortina car from outside the Ardmore Hotel on the northern approach to Newry. Two days later, after IRA volunteers had placed a 15 lb gelignite bomb in it, the car was left at Lisseraw Road on the outskirts of Crossmaglen. Nothing in this area goes unnoticed for very long and within a day or two it attracted the attention of some local farmers. One man approached the vehicle and tried all four doors without success. Clearly the vehicle had been abandoned.

Eventually, Constables Sam Donaldson and Robert Millar, both based at Crossmaglen RUC Barracks, decided to have a look at the Cortina. The officers hoped to gain access to the vehicle by using a piece of wire hooked around the lock button. Unknown to the police officers, however, the IRA bomb team had placed a triggering device in the car which would go off the second the interior light came on. When the door opened, the bomb detonated, blowing both police officers over a hedge and into a field. The huge explosion caused locals to come running and someone phoned an ambulance. Constable Donaldson, who was just 23 years old at the time, received horrendous facial wounds and was practically unrecognisable. His 26-year-old partner Constable Millar lost a leg, but was still conscious and able to speak. As he lay waiting for medical help, Robert Millar told his sergeant, who had arrived at the scene: 'God save me, I'm going to die. You're a good man and I'll see you in heaven.'

Both officers died in Daisy Hill Hospital in Newry the following morning. They were the first RUC officers to die at the hands of the Provisional IRA and they were also the first people to lose their lives in south Armagh. The beautiful place would soon become a theatre of slaughter where the lives of hundreds of people – police officers, soldiers, UDR men, as well as innocent and not so innocent civilians – would be lost. By the time the 1970s were fading to make way for the 1980s, Tom 'Slab' Murphy's IRA unit had claimed the lives of 68 British soldiers as well as 7 RUC officers. Murphy's unit was, without a doubt, the most successful section of the IRA and it earned grudging respect from professional soldiers of all ranks.

Constables Donaldson and Millar were both Protestant. But despite this, a month after their deaths a special memorial service was held in their honour at St Patrick's Catholic Church in Crossmaglen. Local people in this mostly Catholic village attended in their hundreds and many expressed outrage at the actions of the IRA. People donated money to buy floral wreaths in the policemen's honour.

The death of Constable Sam Donaldson on 12 August 1970 was not to be the last time the south Armagh IRA brought heartache to the Donaldson family home. Shortly after 6.30 p.m. on 28 February 1985, the south Armagh unit, working alongside their Newry counterparts, launched nine homemade mortars at Corry Road RUC Station in the centre of Newry. Eight of the devices, which had been developed and perfected in south Armagh, missed their target, but the last one scored a direct hit on a Portakabin inside the station complex which was being used as a temporary canteen. Nine officers were killed, including Chief Inspector Alex Donaldson – a brother of Constable Sam Donaldson. The Newry attack marked the largest number of RUC officers killed in a single IRA operation throughout the entire Troubles. The Donaldson brothers were cousins of Jeffrey Donaldson, now the Ulster Unionist MP for Lagan Valley at Westminster, and possible future leader of the Ulster Unionist Party.

In November 1970, veteran RUC officer Graham Shillington was appointed Chief Constable of the recently reformed police force. Shillington's appointment was welcomed by unionists, but several Catholic politicians voiced reservations. During his term of office, Shillington, a native of the Protestant citadel of Portadown, oversaw the most violent period of the Troubles when almost 1,000 lost their lives in a three-year period.

Less than 24 hours after being sworn in as Chief Constable, Graham Shillington learned of a double murder carried out by the IRA, which marked the instantaneous demise of one of Belfast's most enduring working-class characters – the so-called 'hardman'.

Like most industrial cities, Belfast's working-class districts had their fair share of street fighters – men who liked nothing more than having a 'fair dig' to assert their manhood and in some cases to secure an elevated position in the pecking order in the deprivation which surrounded them.

Arthur McKenna and Alex McVicker had been mates since primary school. By the time the Troubles erupted in 1969 they were both 34 and well set in their ways. In west Belfast McKenna and McVicker enjoyed reputations as 'hardmen' and they did not entertain fools gladly. They lived life on the edge of the law, getting involved in a range of nefarious activities ranging from illegal gambling and money-lending to fencing stolen goods and the odd robbery. They also feared no one. And, having absolutely no interest in politics whatsoever, McKenna and McVicker carried on much as they had done for years while the fabric of society began to crumble around them. Neither of the men had any liking for the IRA or any other paramilitary group, believing that those involved in such organisations hid behind the balaclava and the gun to exert their authority over the communities in which they lived.

On the west Belfast housing estate of Ballymurphy, the Provisional IRA was steadily growing in strength and the organisation's leaders, who included a young man called Gerry Adams, were steadily preparing for the inevitable confrontation with the ancient enemy – the British Army. The Provos, and the Official IRA for that matter, believed they were on the cusp of a revolution. But there was no room on the blueprint for petty criminals or, worse still, petty criminals who were also 'hardmen'. It was generally perceived that such people at best did not take the IRA seriously, and at worst could actively hinder the organisation. Arthur McKenna and Alex McVicker fitted both these categories perfectly and the decision was taken to execute them. It was also agreed that the 'hit' would have to be done as publicly as possible in order to let the wider community know the IRA meant business and that the era of the 'hardman' – a facet of urban living for over a century – was well and truly over. There was only room for one group of 'hardmen' in nationalist west Belfast and that was the IRA.

Shortly after 3.00 p.m. on 16 November 1970, Alex McVicker left his home in Ballymurphy telling his wife he would not be away very long. She was anxious for him to complete some interior decorating at the family home and Alex insisted he would be back soon to finish it off. Minutes later he and his friend Arthur McKenna were driving along Ballymurphy Road when they spotted Vincie Clarke, a local man known to both of them. They stopped the car and began chatting. Seconds later a gunman struck, firing several shots into both men. They died instantly. The brutality of the killings in the run up to Christmas stunned the entire Catholic community, but the effect the IRA desired was achieved. The day of the freelance 'hardman' who did not pay homage to the IRA was well and truly over.

– CHAPTER SEVEN –

Informers – A 'Dirty War' Case Study

Old Stock, part of who we are,
Of time and race and place,
Beyond ourselves.
That's the story anyway,
A bit of a hard sell,
If you ask me.
I'll choose my own race and place,
And won't thank you for the choice.
I can do without your mystic twist.
From 'The Volk' by Sean O'Callaghan – a Kerryman who, sickened
by IRA violence, chose to operate as a Garda informer inside the
IRA leadership. In 1998 O'Callaghan handed himself in to police
in Tunbridge Wells, Kent, where he confessed, amongst other
terrorist crimes, to the murder of an RUC Special Branch officer.
He received a sentence of 539 years.

In the New Year of 1971, the horror of civilian killing in Northern Ireland
continued to gather pace, and, before the month of January was out, as the
Provos continued to hone their war machine, that old ghost 'the informer'
returned to haunt this stage of death and destruction.

John Kavanagh, a 28-year-old married man with two children, lived in the
Clonard area of west Belfast – the scene of some of the worst violence of the
early Troubles – but originally, Kavanagh, a Catholic, had come from the
Roden Street district off the Grosvenor Road, a distance of less than one
mile. As street violence continued to escalate, 'wee John' as Kavanagh was
known, became deeply immersed in the defence of the small district where he
had been born and brought up. He knew everyone in the area and everyone

knew him and, despite the fact that he had moved away, there was little going on around Roden Street that he didn't know about. Roden Street became a battleground for sectarian combatants and often came under attack from roaming bands of loyalists from the nearby Donegall Road district, which was staunchly Protestant.

Makeshift barricades were hurriedly thrown up around the area for protection, and John Kavanagh, a roof tiler by trade, was often to be seen helping people move their belongings or offering advice on how residents could best secure their home from sectarian attack. Naturally, Kavanagh had an emotional attachment to his home territory, and he was outraged that people who had been his friends and neighbours for most of his life were being forced to face such a serious threat to their very existence. He willingly took his place beside the other men of the area who manned the barricades day and night. It soon became clear to him, however, that words of reason and appeals for calm offered no defence against people who were determined to force others out of house and home or perhaps worse.

Two years previously, however, Kavanagh had been sentenced to six months' imprisonment after he was caught in possession of four shotgun cartridges during the street disturbances. A solicitor for Kavanagh told the court that the accused came to have the ammunition only because another man, who was not named, pushed the cartridges into Kavanagh's hand before running off.

While he was being questioned by police following his arrest, Kavanagh was approached by two Special Branch officers who asked him to keep an eye on the movements of known Provos in his area in return for the policemen asking the authorities for leniency when he appeared in court. As the hours towards his appearance in court ticked away, Kavanagh's thoughts remained firmly fixed on his wife June and the couple's small children aged four and five. John could not bear to be separated from his family for any length of time and he told the policemen he would accept their offer.

The ever-watchful Provos became concerned about Kavanagh following a number of arms finds in the area. They knew he was aware of certain activity, but thought he could be trusted. Following the seizure of arms at a number of homes in the Roden Street district, however, IRA leaders met to discuss the situation. They narrowed down a list of people who may have known about the guns and it wasn't long before the finger of suspicion pointed at John Kavanagh. His movements were monitored and a decision was taken to execute him.

Shortly after 7.00 a.m. on the morning of 27 January 1971, John Kavanagh left his home at Lady Street to go to work. Less than an hour later he was dead.

Unknown to Kavanagh, an IRA gang were lying in wait. They had been given orders to abduct him and shoot him dead at a place known to locals as 'the black patch' – a muddy stretch of river bank near his parents' home.

The black patch section of the Blackstaff River was a natural boundary between the mainly Catholic west Belfast and predominantly Protestant south Belfast, and in the early hours of the morning the area is deserted. It was an ideal spot to dump a body before daybreak.

In the nearby Kelvin Secondary School, the caretaker was getting ready to open the school gates prior to the arrival of the pupils. He decided to wait inside his house a few minutes more so as to catch the eight o'clock news bulletin, which would inevitably be its usual catalogue of death and violence.

Suddenly a shot rang out. The caretaker looked at his watch. It was exactly 7.55 a.m. A short distance away, an IRA assassination squad had frog-marched John Kavanagh from a pathway next to the school down the bank and onto the black patch. He was ordered to get down on his knees. One of the IRA men raised a handgun and shot Kavanagh in the head. He died instantly. Kavanagh was the first of a host of murder victims the IRA accused of being informers.

An immediate police investigation swung into action. As murder squad detectives did their best to track down Kavanagh's killers, they were assisted by two London police officers who were sent over from Scotland Yard. One of them was George Churchill-Coleman, who, at the time of John Kavanagh's murder, held the rank of detective sergeant. Churchill-Coleman went on to head Scotland Yard's anti-terrorist squad and in the years that followed became widely recognised as an expert on IRA tactics and strategy.

Despite the best efforts of the police, no one was held to account for Kavanagh's murder. The execution had the desired effect as far as the IRA leadership was concerned – an informer had been weeded out and the message to the Catholic community was loud and clear.

Since its inception the IRA has been plagued by 'informers' – IRA volunteers who have been persuaded for one reason or another to pass on details of IRA business to members of the security forces. The RUC Special Branch became adept at recruiting 'touts' as they are known in paramilitary as well as police circles. Using fair means or foul, Special Branch officers built up an impressive network of informers and as a result were able to save hundreds of innocent lives. It is now clear that an alarming amount of IRA operations were compromised on the word of informers and that this situation went a long way to forcing the republican terror group to call its military campaign off after a quarter of a century of almost non-stop violence.

One IRA veteran who became embroiled in the murky world of Ulster's so-called 'Dirty War' was Belfast man Martin Meehan, now an extremely active Sinn Fein politician. A docker by trade, Meehan joined the IRA in the early 1960s when it was neither profitable nor fashionable. He was a member of the organisation's 3rd Battalion who operated from Ardoyne in the north of the city to Short Strand in the south. Following the failure of the IRA border campaign in 1962, the new IRA leadership under the control of Dubliner Cathal Goulding found its ranks, particularly in Belfast, seriously depleted. The guns, or what was left of them, were safely in dumps as Goulding's volunteers began to concentrate on political matters. When Martin Meehan joined the organisation, the IRA's 3rd Battalion had only nine members, whose time was largely taken up by housing action groups and tenants' associations. Weapons training was still part of IRA life, but the volunteers of that era saw little need for their use in what looked likely to be a gradual movement towards a socialist republic which would be achieved by peaceful means.

When most other young men of his age were doing the rounds of Belfast's many jazz and blues clubs, Meehan was attending civil rights lectures or going to demonstrations to demand better housing. But in his heart of hearts, Martin Meehan was a 'physical force' republican in the tradition of Dan Breen and Sean South and when the IRA split at the outbreak of the Troubles he went with the Provos.

He quickly developed a reputation as a courageous and fearless fighter, defending the Ardoyne district where he lived. He also became a hate figure for the British tabloid press, which viewed him as nothing more than a ruthless gunman who had masterminded the deaths of British soldiers. Despite having served several terms in jail, Meehan's commitment to the republican cause remained undiminished. Although the IRA leadership did not view him as the most intellectual volunteer in the ranks, he was nevertheless a trusted member of the organisation who had stuck with the IRA through good times and bad.

In the autumn of 1980, Martin Meehan received a letter which gave him the shock of his life. The writer said he was willing to supply the veteran republican with the names and addresses of RUC touts. The letter, which had been sent to a safe house, went on to suggest that the writer and Meehan should meet at a prearranged time in Belfast's waterworks – an area of parkland off the city's Antrim Road which was a short distance from the city centre.

It wasn't so much the content of the letter which stunned Meehan as the fact that it had been sent to him by a serving RUC officer! The policeman, consumed to the point of obsession after being told he would not be considered for Special Branch duties, had embarked on an elaborate plan to teach his RUC bosses a lesson in espionage. His plan involved passing on highly confidential material about informers to the IRA. In return, although he did not mention this to Meehan in the letter, the RUC man hoped to recruit a senior member of the IRA as a police informer. The man he had singled out for this role was none other than Martin Meehan.

Having been a member of the IRA for almost a generation, Martin Meehan was a highly experienced and streetwise republican who viewed the policeman's approach with extreme caution. Nevertheless, he was still intrigued enough to turn up at the suggested time to test the water for himself. Meehan knew first-hand that the IRA's campaign had been severely thwarted by informers and he decided he had nothing to lose by meeting the cop. The meeting was brief and the connection established. But, unknown to both men, they were secretly being filmed by an RUC surveillance team. The undercover RUC men were working on an unrelated matter and couldn't believe their luck when Martin Meehan and the police officer strayed into the view of their camera lens.

Meehan reported details of the meeting to the IRA leadership and, after deciding it had nothing to lose, the IRA directed 33-year-old volunteer Peter Valente, a trusted Belfast Brigade member, to rendezvous with the policeman in future.

Having been alerted to the intriguing situation by accidentally stumbling across the Meehan meeting, the RUC Special Branch kept close tabs on their rogue member and an undercover surveillance team was placed in the waterworks area 24 hours a day. Their interest was rewarded a few days later when Peter Valente was filmed meeting the police officer. Determined to show Valente he meant business, the cop told him that a young Catholic barman called Stephen McWilliams was in the pay of British Military Intelligence. The RUC man added that McWilliams was also working for the RUC Special Branch and he also named a number of others he claimed were police informers.

Valente relayed this information to his IRA superiors. Although a little shocked at the policeman's claims, from the IRA's point of view this was manna from heaven. At last the IRA was confident it could remove the biggest thorn in its side – the RUC Special Branch. It would only be a matter time before all RUC informants would be flushed from its ranks and the organisation could get on with the job of forcing the British out of Ireland.

A few days later Valente was arrested and taken to Castlereagh Holding Centre in east Belfast, after he was positively identified by a Special Branch officer who had viewed film footage of his meeting with the rogue RUC officer. Valente was shown the film and threatened with serious sedition charges which would surely guarantee a lengthy prison sentence. Over the next few hours, teams of Special Branch officers carried out interviews with Valente and gradually broke down his resistance. He agreed to work as a police informer supplying his 'handlers' – officers detailed to look after individual touts – with details of IRA business.

Valente was easily persuaded to work for the police by the lure of regular cash that would boost the low wages he received at that time working as a part-time plumber. On his release back onto the streets, Valente failed to inform his IRA superiors that he had even been arrested, far less that he had agreed to work as a police informer. But Valente was careless and cavalier and it wasn't long before the IRA rumbled him. Valente couldn't resist the temptation to display his new-found wealth and a number of IRA men were detailed to keep a close eye on his movements.

A growing number of military operations which were either compromised or called off completely as a result of police activity was giving the IRA cause for concern, and after an internal investigation it was agreed that all avenues of investigation led straight back to Peter Valente.

On 12 November 1980 Peter Valente disappeared. Two days later he was found shot dead in an alleyway on the Protestant Highfield estate, giving the initial impression that the killing had been carried out by loyalists. As Valente lay dead on the ground, one of the IRA gunmen who murdered him pressed a new twenty-pound note into his hand. The action was a macabre message to the RUC Special Branch that their mole had been uncovered.

Eighteen-year-old Stephen McWilliams, who had been fingered by the renegade cop, worked as a barman in the republican Felons' Club in the New Lodge area of Belfast. Full membership of this establishment is restricted to republicans who have served prison sentences for the cause and as a result the place is a favourite haunt of past and present IRA volunteers and supporters.

McWilliams was abducted from the club by an IRA internal security investigation team. He was questioned for many hours at a time over a four-day period at three different locations. In a house in Oakfield Street in Ardoyne, the young barman admitted to his captors that the security forces had recruited him after he was arrested for shoplifting. During his ordeal, McWilliams was blindfolded and severely beaten. He was quizzed by two groups of IRA interrogation teams – one from Ardoyne and the other from the New Lodge area – who took it in turns to wear him down and eventually break him. He confessed to passing on low-grade intelligence about republicans who frequented the club where he worked and he also pleaded for his life.

When a member of the IRA internal investigation unit – known in republican circles as 'the Nutting Squad' – left the house where McWilliams was being held to receive orders about what to do with their prisoner, his interrogators took a break from the proceeding, leaving him to contemplate his future.

Suddenly an army patrol burst into the house, releasing McWilliams and arresting his captors. During debriefing by police, and probably at the behest of his handlers, McWilliams fingered Martin Meehan and a number of other republicans as the people who abducted and held him during his four-day interrogation.

The following March, Martin Meehan appeared in the dock at Crumlin Road Courthouse charged with kidnapping. He was sent to prison for 12 years following a trial.

At the time a number of people, including Meehan's defence team, raised questions about the strength of the evidence against the IRA man. As he was taken from the dock down a flight of stairs to a tunnel which connected the court to the nearby Belfast Prison, a defiant Meehan told the trial judge: 'I know, McWilliams knows and God knows, I was not involved.'

He later went on hunger strike to protest his innocence, but quit after 66 days. Other republican prisoners who served sentences alongside Meehan suspected he was secretly taking food during his protest. One Belfast republican who was in prison at that time said:

> The hunger strike did nothing for Martin's credibility inside the jail.
> Almost everyone else believed he was accepting food. The episode
> dented his reputation and it took him a long time to gain the trust of
> other republican prisoners who were inside at the same time.

When the disaffected RUC man met Peter Valente in the waterworks, he also told the IRA man about another RUC informant who was a leading member of the IRA. Maurice 'Isaac' Gilvarry from Butler Street, in the Ardoyne district, proved to be a major source of embarrassment to the Belfast Brigade of the IRA. As a teenager Gilvarry had joined the local unit of the IRA and for around four years he had been passing top-quality intelligence information to the RUC Special Branch. His activities practically decimated the IRA in Ardoyne, which had become one of the most staunchly republican areas of Belfast. In the past many men from Ardoyne had served with the British Army, but the Troubles put an end to soldiering as a means of earning a living. For the best part of 12 years, Ardoyne had been a safe haven for IRA members and yet the organisation in the area had not latched on to the fact that Maurice Gilvarry was a rogue element within its ranks.

Gilvarry enjoyed the blessing of Martin Meehan and was given a trusted position in charge of the local so-called punishment squads, which dispensed republican 'justice' to anyone deemed to have been involved in wrongdoing.

During Ireland's War of Independence, kangaroo courts under IRA control were established as an alternative to the British justice system and when the Troubles broke out in the North, the IRA once again set up its own courts in an effort to encourage the Catholic community to have no contact with the RUC.

As police and army patrols moved through Ardoyne, many officers took the opportunity to publicly harangue Gilvarry, unaware that he was and had been working for their own Special Branch for years. The abuse Gilvarry was subjected to at the hands of the security forces went a long way to establishing his street cred and throwing republican 'police' off his informer's scent.

In June 1978, Gilvarry made his handlers aware of a planned IRA operation which was to take place in the Protestant Ballysillan area of the city. The IRA intended to firebomb a Post Office depot and four volunteers, including 28-year-old Denis 'Dinny' Brown, 28-year-old James Mulvenna and 31-year-old Jackie Mailey, were ordered to mount the attack. Mailey was the senior member of the IRA unit. The men, who were all married with children and came from north Belfast, were members of the Ardoyne unit of the IRA and they knew Maurice Gilvarry well.

The IRA men drove to Ballysillan in a hijacked Mazda car and parked near the Post Office depot. Unknown to them, a joint SAS/RUC undercover team was waiting for them. The security forces were working on information supplied by Maurice Gilvarry. Three of the IRA men, Brown, Mulvenna and Mailey, who were all wearing socks on their hands, died in a hail of bullets before they were able to plant their firebombs. A civilian, William Hanna, who was walking nearby, was also killed by the fusillade of shots, but a fourth IRA man somehow managed to escape.

It later emerged that none of the IRA men was armed, sparking speculation that the men were victims of a shoot-to-kill policy. In a bizarre twist following the controversial shooting incident, Maurice Gilvarry, who was single, moved in with the widow of one of the dead IRA men.

In order to maintain his cover, Gilvarry also took part in IRA operations and, following a shooting incident on the Old Park Road, Gilvarry, who was positively identified as being one of the gunmen, was arrested and taken to Castlereagh for interrogation. Within minutes of entering the interrogation block Gilvarry named two other IRA members as the gunmen. He was then released and was free to carry on his double dealing.

Maurice Gilvarry was also the trigger man in an outrageous double murder which still leaves a question mark over the activities and motives of some Special Branch officers. On the evening of 3 February 1979, he and two other IRA gunmen burst into the home of retired prison officer, 60-year-old Patrick Mackin and his 58-year-old wife Violet. The couple lived at 568 Old Park Road and were watching television when Gilvarry shot them. They both died instantly. The bodies of Mr and Mrs Mackin were not discovered until the following morning when their son, an RUC detective, called to visit with his wife and family. Forensic evidence revealed Mr Mackin had been shot three times. He was found slumped in his chair. His wife Violet had apparently tried to save her husband and was shot once as she struggled to get the gun from Maurice Gilvarry.

The IRA hit team escaped back to its Ardoyne base, where the car used in the double killing was later found burnt out. Gilvarry then phoned his RUC handler telling him the names of his accomplices, but also naming a completely innocent man as the person who pulled the trigger. It was only the diligent work of murder squad detectives which prevented this man from going to jail. Exactly how much of this was known by Special Branch remains a mystery and whether an officer was prepared to let an innocent man go to prison to prevent their agent, Maurice Gilvarry, from being exposed will never be known.

Luck was running out for Maurice Gilvarry, however, and eventually the IRA's internal investigation unit decided to put him under the microscope. The IRA leadership in Belfast was desperate to stem the tide of information which was flowing from the ranks and through the front door of the RUC Special Branch HQ at Castlereagh. Members of the IRA's internal investigation unit were ordered to follow Gilvarry any time he left the Ardoyne district. A few days later he was spotted making his way first of all into the city centre and then onto Royal Avenue, which at that time was Belfast's main shopping thoroughfare.

Suddenly Gilvarry entered the Grand Central Hotel, now demolished, which the IRA knew was used by members of the British Military Intelligence service. From this base, undercover members of the army ran a range of covert intelligence-gathering operations ranging from massage parlours to laundry services. It was obvious to the IRA man tailing Gilvarry that he knew his way about and that he had visited the premises before.

So far, however, all the evidence against Maurice 'Isaac' Gilvarry was circumstantial. Damning proof was needed. A short time later Gilvarry was asked to drive a car bomb into Belfast city centre, although he wasn't told the device was in fact a hoax. As usual, he informed his handlers and the vehicle was intercepted. Gilvarry was arrested but soon released without charge as no explosives were found. This action sealed his fate. Maurice Gilvarry was abducted and taken to an IRA interrogation centre in the republican heartland of south Armagh. He made a full confession after enduring hours of horrendous torture and was shot dead. His body was dumped on a border road on 20 January 1981.

A month later Pat Trainor from west Belfast, a 28-year-old married man with three children, was pushed out of a black taxi on the Falls Road. Seconds later he was shot dead by gunmen in a second car which had pulled up behind. The IRA issued a statement claiming he was a police informer. His family strenuously denied the claim. Like Stephen McWilliams and Maurice Gilvarry, Pat Trainor had been fingered by Peter Valente in the list of alleged informers supplied to him by the rogue RUC officer.

Another Ardoyne man named as an informer by the policeman was Anthony Braniff. The policeman claimed Braniff had been ordered by his IRA handlers to conceal a rifle in an arms dump and after doing so informed his handlers, who immediately arranged to have the weapon seized.

On 27 September 1981, Braniff, a married man who came from Etna Drive in the Ardoyne, was found shot dead off the Falls Road. Burn marks found on his neck sparked speculation that he had been tortured prior to execution, although it is more likely that the marks were as a result of gunpowder flash at the moment the fatal bullet entered his head. The IRA issued a statement detailing his alleged betrayal. Again, his family vehemently denied he was a police informer. It is now generally accepted within the republican movement that Anthony Braniff was not a police informer and that the accusations levelled against him were false.

But the singular most shocking piece of information the rogue officer passed to Peter Valente had a devastating effect on the IRA leadership and in particular Martin Meehan. It was potentially so explosive that Valente pained himself as to whether he should keep the information to himself or pass it on to his IRA superiors.

The traitor cop told Valente that Martin Meehan's brother Sean – or Seannie as he was known – was not only an RUC Special Branch agent, but also worked for the British Secret Service agency MI5. Well-placed security sources say the authorities managed to turn Seannie Meehan after convincing him they were in possession of evidence which directly implicated him in a number of terrorist killings, including the murders of three young Scottish soldiers on 9 March 1971, which are detailed in the next chapter.

Following the murder of a young police officer in north Belfast ten months later, Seannie Meehan skipped across the border to Dublin. However, he maintained his links with the British Secret Service. According to the RUC man who met Valente, Seannie Meehan had also worked with the IRA's 'England Dept.', responsible for bombing campaigns on the British mainland. And, again according to the policeman, he had passed on vital information that had led to the arrests of IRA personnel as well as the seizure of massive quantities of explosives. This part of Seannie Meehan's double-dealing life has been confirmed by Sean O'Callaghan.

O'Callaghan held the position as head of the IRA's Southern Command, which had responsibility for IRA operations in England. In his book, *The Informer: The Real Life Story of One Man's War Against Terrorism*, O'Callaghan tells of how he was warned by another member of the IRA not to have anything to do with Meehan regarding IRA bombing missions in Britain as the IRA man considered Meehan 'bad news'.

Despite their suspicions, the IRA leadership continued to use Seannie Meehan until a series of compromised operations once again pointed the finger at him. He was extremely lucky to escape the clutches of the IRA 'Nutting Squad'.

Seannie Meehan, IRA killer several times over, proved to be such a good servant to the British Secret Service that MI5 lost no time in arranging a safe passage to the United States for him and his family as an IRA dragnet closed in.

According to Sean O'Callaghan, Seamus Twomey, a one-time IRA chief-of-staff, believed Meehan had settled in the Fort Worth area of Texas, where he was thought to be running a haulage business. O'Callaghan says Twomey sent an IRA volunteer to the States with specific orders to track Meehan down. The investigation drew a blank, O'Callaghan claimed, and was eventually dropped. However, it is still a major source of embarrassment that a man with close family ties to such a senior and trusted republican as Martin Meehan should end up working for the IRA's sworn enemies.

Privately, a number of IRA volunteers who were interviewed as part of the research for this book have voiced concern that, of all the IRA members named as touts by the traitor cop to Peter Valente, Seannie Meehan was the only one to escape traditional IRA 'justice' – a bullet in the back of the head.

Officially the RUC – now the Police Service of Northern Ireland – refuses to discuss or even accept the existence of the rogue officer who made the approach to Martin Meehan by letter. However, it has emerged that the officer was arrested on 26 October 1980 – months after Martin Meehan was safely off the streets, having been scooped on charges relating to the kidnapping of Stephen McWilliams. Under interrogation, the policeman admitted the IRA had 'turned' him with the lure of large amounts of cash.

After a series of top-level discussions, which went as high as the Attorney General's office, the officer was squeezed out of the police without ever having to face charges. He is now believed to be living in England, where he spends his time reading the Bible and spreading the word of Christ. The case against him was dropped in the interests of national security because at the time it was deemed unwise to highlight aspects of the so-called 'Dirty War' which were previously unknown to the general public.

Although his name was not on the rogue cop's tout list, Paddy Tier was probably the most successful police agent, from the RUC's point of view, to operate inside the Ardoyne section of the IRA.

Before he was 'turned', Tier had been a high-ranking and trusted member of the terror group for ten years. It was Tier – known in republican circles as the 'poison dwarf' – who supplied the Belfast Brigade of the IRA with the information which led to the murder of RUC officer Ernest McCrum.

Sergeant McCrum had been injured when a group of young men from the Ardoyne district broke into his home with the intention of robbing the place. The men spotted Sgt McCrum's police uniform in a wardrobe and, at gunpoint, forced the officer to hand over his warrant card and personal issue firearm before leaving. The McCrum family home had been targeted by the gang because they knew Mrs McCrum was an antique dealer and the armed robbers presumed she would keep cash in her home. Paddy Tier learned of the raid on the McCrum home and told the men responsible that all items taken should be handed over to the IRA immediately, including Sgt McCrum's personal protection weapon.

The men had no alternative and reluctantly agreed to Tier's request. It was from the items taken from the McCrum home that the IRA intelligence team was able to glean enough information about the police officer to plan his murder. Following the attack, 61-year-old Sgt McCrum took time off work to recover and a few weeks later he was well enough to do a few hours' part-time work at his wife's antique shop in Lisburn. An IRA hit squad walked into the shop on 13 April 1991. Earlier it had been a busy Saturday afternoon for shoppers but by now the shop was empty. A gunman shot the police officer at point-bank range before calmly locking the premises and taking the keys with him.

But supplying information which led directly to such murderous efficiency was not typical of Paddy Tier, because he had been in the pay of the RUC Special Branch for years. During his time working as a paid police informer,

Tier had successfully messed up several major IRA operations, which resulted in many lives being saved as well as terrorists being put behind bars.

Tier was personally responsible for the seizure of three tons of explosives, the loss of 17 assorted weapons and the imprisonment of 15 IRA volunteers. A security source with many years' experience of working for the RUC Special Branch said of Tier: 'He was one of the best agents we ever managed to recruit in Belfast.'

Tier even managed to thwart an IRA plan to kill the leader of the Ulster Volunteer Force. The IRA had received information that a leading loyalist – a man who is currently the most senior officer in the UVF – was a short-term patient at the Mater Hospital on Belfast's Crumlin Road, less than a mile from the republican stronghold of Ardoyne. An assassination squad was selected and the IRA planned to execute the man in his hospital bed.

The IRA codename for the murder bid was 'Operation Bunter', and the 'hit', if it was carried out successfully, would have been a major propaganda boost to the IRA, particularly in north Belfast. The UVF leader who was the target of the assassination plot was acutely aware of his personal security, and had arranged for a team of bodyguards to keep a close watch on him during his stay in hospital. It was with this danger in mind that the IRA put three of its most experienced operators on the job. A top-grade getaway driver was also detailed to take the men to and from the operation. But, as the IRA team sat in a house in Ardoyne waiting for weapons to arrive from an arms dump, a team of burly police officers from the RUC's E4A smashed down the door and arrested the four occupants. They were taken to Castlereagh Holding Centre for interrogation but were released without charge after seven days.

Paddy Tier's time in the IRA was drawing to a close. He was asked to produce a man without any previous IRA involvement who would transport a 330 lb bomb into Belfast city centre. He approached two Ardoyne men who refused to do the job before he found a willing 'patsy'. This man was given instructions about where to rendezvous with two IRA men who would then prime the device prior to planting it at its target. As the handover was about to take place, the police pounced and the bomb, which turned out to be a fake device, was made safe. The incident also highlighted the ruthless nature of the IRA leadership, which was prepared to allow a previously unconnected man to be caught while Paddy Tier's loyalty was tested. The spotlight was now well and truly on Tier and his every move was being reported to the head of the IRA's internal security unit.

Around this time, a crooked businessman from north Belfast approached a lorry driver who worked for a tobacco wholesaler's. The man was asked to supply a lorry-load of contraband at a reasonable price. The driver explained that he wasn't in a position to do so because he had already supplied three loads of fags to Paddy Tier, assuming that the cigarettes delivered to Tier were destined to boost the IRA's coffers. When the businessman then appealed directly to a senior member of the IRA with a view to purchasing tobacco, it became obvious that Tier had earlier bought the goods for himself.

A leading IRA man nicknamed 'Il Duce' was tasked with carrying out a second investigation into Tier's activities. The case against Tier was substantial and he was ordered to attend an IRA kangaroo court, convened by the 'Nutting Squad'. But, unknown to the IRA, Tier knew he had been rumbled and was busy making plans to get out. He was assisted by his RUC Special Branch handlers, who conceded his time working as an RUC informer was up. Tier was trying to buy a little time before heading off in order to make arrangements for his wife and family.

A few days later, Tier arrived at the house where the court of inquiry would take place. In an incredibly devious act, Tier carried a toddler in his arms. His interrogators were furious and refused to convene the court until Tier came alone. He was ordered to attend another court a few days later but, before that day dawned, a furniture van appeared outside Tier's home and his property was removed by police officers who later drove Tier, his wife and children to a new life in England.

Paddy Tier, now 45 years old, knows he escaped execution by the skin of his teeth and now lives a quiet life in the greater Manchester area. The details of his past in the murky world of paramilitary espionage are unknown to his neighbours.

– CHAPTER EIGHT –

Filled with Irish Beer and Bullets

It's over the mountains and over the maine,
Doon through Gibraltar tae France and Spain,
Wi' a feather in your bonnet and a kilt aboon yir knee,
Enlist bonny laddy and come awa' wi' me.
'*The Twa Recruitin' Sergeants*', *British Army Recruiting Sergeant*

On 6 February 1971, Gunner Robert Curtis, a 20-year-old member of the Royal Artillery Regiment, secured a unique place in Ulster's bloody history when he became the first serving British soldier to lose his life on Irish soil since the War of Independence 50 years previously.

He was killed by an IRA bullet during an exchange of heavy gunfire in the New Lodge district of north Belfast. Earlier the area had been the scene of serious rioting.

Gunner Curtis, a married man whose wife was expecting the couple's first child, was the first of 503 British soldiers to lose their lives in Ulster. Gunner Curtis had only been in the army for 18 months. He was shot dead by Billy Reid – a member of the Provisional IRA – who was himself shot dead by soldiers during an exchange of gunfire three months later.

In the normal way of things Irish – at least as far as republicanism is concerned – Billy Reid, who had previously led a fairly uneventful life, apart from being known as a keen amateur boxer, became a legend in death. A song, 'The Ballad of Billy Reid', was specially penned to immortalise his memory. However, the doggerel also highlighted the dangers IRA volunteers faced when using old and unreliable weaponry like the Thompson sub-machine gun – the weapon he used to kill Gunner Curtis. One verse from the song says:

> While returning the guns, Billy met British Huns,
> And when the fight had begun,
> His position was dire,
> When his gun wouldn't fire,
> So he died with that old Thompson gun.

The day after Gunner Curtis died, the Unionist Prime Minister, James Chichester-Clarke, made a TV appearance during which he announced: 'Northern Ireland is at war with the Irish Republican Army Provisionals.'

The leadership of the Provisionals were delighted with the respect the Unionist politician had afforded their organisation by referring to the conflict as a war. Nine days later, John Lawrie, a 22-year-old lance bombardier with the Royal Artillery, the same regiment as Gunner Robert Curtis, died in hospital after being shot in the head the previous week during an exchange of fire in Ardoyne.

Then five-year-old Denise Ann Dickson lost her life when she was struck by a car driven by military personnel near her home at Lepper Street, Ardoyne. This part of north Belfast continued to be the crucible of the conflict and on 27 February two policemen, Detective Inspector Cecil Patterson and Constable Robert Buckley, were shot dead at the junction of Alliance Crescent and Alliance Parade. DI Patterson, a native of Belturbet, Co. Cavan in the Irish Republic, had been a serving member of the RUC's Special Branch for many years. He was known to have an encyclopaedic knowledge of the all the major players involved in terrorism in Belfast. The deaths of two police officers marked the end of unarmed police patrols in Northern Ireland. The following day, the RUC Chief Constable Graham Shillington announced service revolvers would once again be issued to police officers on duty.

By far the most shocking incident of this period, however, was the murder of three young Scottish soldiers, two of them teenage brothers, who were lured to their deaths on the pretext of going to a drinks party.

John McCaig, 17, and his 18-year-old brother Joseph, both from the Scottish seaside town of Ayr, were privates in the Royal Highland Fusiliers. On Wednesday, 9 March 1971, they were off duty and went for an afternoon's boozing session in the centre of Belfast, where they met other squaddies, including 23-year-old Dougald McCaughey from Glasgow, who was also a private in the same regiment. It is thought the young men may have attended a cabaret session at Belfast's famous Abercorn Restaurant before going on to Mooney's Bar in nearby Cornmarket for more drinks.

Unknown to the soldiers, the Provisional IRA in the Ardoyne area of the city had devised a plan to attack and kill off-duty members of the British Army. Until this time, violence in Belfast was mainly confined to interface areas largely in the north and west of the city. But that was all about to change, with devastating consequences.

As the soldiers enjoyed their drinks in Mooney's, they were joined by a number of local girls and later by a group of young men who were known to the females. Off-duty soldiers in Belfast at that time were easily spotted. They stood out in a crowd, not just because of their short haircuts or different accents, but also because they dressed differently. Some had a penchant for wearing brightly coloured socks, which became a source of amusement to many local people.

One of the men who was introduced to the soldiers by the girls was 24-year-old Paddy McAdorey, a senior member of the Provisional IRA who lived in Ardoyne. He was accompanied by 20-year-old IRA man Seannie Meehan, brother of the infamous republican Martin Meehan. McAdorey, who was married, was a popular and well-liked person within his own community. Of stocky build, he liked to wear a pork pie hat and often sported a moustache. As a result of his appearance, some of his friends occasionally liked to refer to him as 'Odd Job', after the larger-than-life character in the James Bond film *Goldfinger*.

Someone, possibly Paddy McAdorey himself, suggested moving to another pub on the outskirts of Belfast before going on to a party which, the soldiers were assured, would be 'full of women'. Everyone was in good spirits as the IRA men and their Scottish guests piled into a car to make the journey to Ligoneil, just north of Belfast. They were all in party mood and beer bottles were opened on the way. Irish people are famous for their hospitality and the three young Scots felt they had nothing to fear from their new-found friends. But this was no chance meeting: the IRA men knew exactly what was going to happen next.

At 7.55 p.m., as the spring sun set on a lonely mountain road at Old Squires Hill overlooking the city of Belfast, the car in which the soldiers were travelling stopped. Police say a second car may have also travelled in convoy. The beer intake that afternoon had been substantial and the cheery revellers got out to relieve themselves at the side of the road. As the soldiers stood urinating on the grass, they were so relaxed they did so with beer glasses still in hand. Suddenly and without warning, John McCaig was hit on the back of the head with the butt of a revolver and, as he fell, the gunman who struck him fired two bullets into his skull. Joe McCaig was shot three times through the head and Dougald McCaughey was shot once in the head. The IRA murder gang made their escape, back to the riot-torn streets of north Belfast, which was destined to become the most dangerous killing field in the whole of Ulster.

Children living nearby who had heard the fatal shots found the bodies a short time later. As they looked at the motionless figures lying on the grass at the side of the road, the children noticed that two of the men still had half-filled beer glasses in their hands. Some of the youngsters stood by the dead bodies as others ran for help.

The triple murder sparked a wave of worldwide condemnation and shook civilised society to its foundations. Church leaders, politicians and community leaders stood shoulder to shoulder as they took turns to express outrage at the slaughter. For many with no hard and fast views on how a future Northern Ireland should be governed, it was the betrayal of trust they found so shocking. Back in the soldiers' native Scotland, the gruesome tale was described as having echoes of the famous Massacre of Glencoe, when, at the behest of King William of Orange, the Campbells slaughtered their Highland hosts the MacDonalds as they slept in their beds, after accepting the hospitality of their fellow Gaels for two whole weeks.

Belfast came to a standstill as thousands of workers downed tools and marched in protest to the city centre, carrying wreaths in honour of the young Scottish squaddies. Flags on public buildings were lowered to half-mast as 20,000 people stood in silence outside Belfast's City Hall. Photographs of the soldiers in full battle fatigues and sporting the distinctive headgear of the Highland regiments, the Glengarry, were displayed in shop windows and in bars.

The British Cabinet met hurriedly to discuss the deepening Ulster crisis and army chiefs considered changing the rules so that boy soldiers could no longer be sent to Northern Ireland.

In loyalist areas, youths began wearing tartan scarves to publicly display their affections for and association with the country across the Irish Sea the soldiers called home. The Tartan Gang – a new phenomenon in the pantheon of Ulster's killer gangs – was born. Each gang was distinguished by its own particular tartan, which became a kind of 'uniform'. Tartan gangs became particularly strong in the predominantly Protestant east side of Belfast and clashes with Catholic rivals, as well as the police, became a common feature of life in the city. As time went on, however, the Tartan gangs became a natural recruiting ground for loyalist paramilitary organisations, particularly the Ulster Defence Association.

The Official IRA was quick to issue a statement saying its volunteers were not connected to the murders in any way, while a spokesman for the Provisionals, speaking from the organisation's Dublin HQ, said he would not be commenting on the matter at all.

Some people even went as far as to suggest that a rogue element of the IRA from south of the border had sneaked into the North and carried out the triple killing before disappearing again. But hard-bitten Special Branch officers using their vast wealth of experience and relying on well-placed local sources of information had absolutely no doubt about who was responsible – the Provisional IRA from the Ardoyne district of Belfast.

It was felt that the Provos killed the soldiers – the softest of soft targets – to demonstrate to the world they meant business. They also wanted to shock British public opinion to move from indifference to action. The Provo offensive was clearly aimed at producing a British declaration of intent to withdraw from Ireland. Another element of the murder strategy, as far as the Provos were concerned, was to let their republican rivals the Official IRA know in no uncertain terms that it was they, the Provos, who were the true inheritors of militant Irish republicanism. To a certain extent they succeeded, but not to the degree they desired.

Widespread revulsion in the wake of the soldiers' murders soon turned to anger and led to increased pressure on the Unionist Prime Minister, James Chichester-Clarke, to introduce tougher security measures to quell what many Protestants believed was a Catholic and republican uprising.

Around this time, internment – the detention of civilians without trial – was seriously being mooted as a means of restoring law and order. It had worked in the past, the unionists argued, and there was no good reason to think that it wouldn't work again.

In March 1971, Brian Faulkner, a shirt manufacturer and industrialist, succeeded Chichester-Clarke as Prime Minister and he relentlessly pushed for the introduction of internment. Before the month was out, the Provos killed another soldier in Ardoyne and on 22 May the Official IRA got in on the act when Joe McCann, the organisation's Officer Commanding in the Markets area of Belfast, shot Corporal Robert Bankier of the Royal Green Jackets Regiment. Three days later, the Provisionals threw a suitcase containing 30 lb of explosives into the reception area of Springfield Road police station, which was busy with civilians, including two children. Michael Willets, a 27-year-old soldier in the Parachute Regiment, threw the youngsters aside and shielded them with his body as the bomb went off.

The children survived but the soldier died at the scene. Across the street, the blast blew a baby in a pram through a shop window.

In the run up to the 12 July Orange celebrations, two men, Seamus Cusack and Desmond Beattie, were shot dead by the army in Derry. In the House of Commons, Lord Balneil, the Tory Secretary of State for Defence, said the soldiers' actions were justified. More soldiers lost their lives in Belfast and finally, on 9 August 1971, internment without trial was introduced.

In the early hours of the morning, British troops swamped Catholic areas throughout the North, making hundreds of arrests. They were using RUC intelligence files dating back to the 1950s and many men who were totally unconnected to paramilitaries or violence were scooped from their beds and dragged off to camps at Long Kesh, a few miles from Belfast, and Magilligan, an old military base to the north of Derry. The move, instead of calming things down, only made matters worse as the North descended into bloody reaction.

In Belfast, Father Hugh Mullan, a 40-year-old Catholic priest, was shot dead by soldiers as he went to the aid of a man who had been wounded a few minutes earlier. Father Mullan had seen the man fall and, waving a white rag above his head, he bravely made his way across to him to give him the last rites of the Catholic Church. Ironically, the man he went to assist survived, but Father Mullan was the first of two priests to lose their lives in the Troubles.

Later the same day, members of the Ulster Defence Regiment (UDR), which had been formed the previous year to replace the notorious B Specials, set up a vehicle checkpoint outside Strabane. The soldiers were assisting the regular army in the wake of the internment swoops. An IRA volunteer, using a Thompson sub-machine gun, opened up on the troops. Private Winston Donnell was killed instantly as a hail of gunfire rained down on the soldiers. He was the first member of the UDR to die.

Some observers had seen internment as inevitable, and many IRA members anticipating its introduction took the opportunity of skipping south of the border to the perceived safe haven of the Irish Republic.

As the morning of 9 August wore on, Catholic areas of the North were in uproar. In the Ardoyne, 200 Protestant families were forced to flee their homes, setting fire to them as they left, rather than leave them empty to be occupied by Catholics. In the same area, Paddy McAdorey, the IRA man who had killed the three young Royal Highland Fusiliers the previous March, vowed to resist the aggressive actions of the British Army. Local people say that 24-year-old McAdorey appeared totally oblivious to the fact that his callous killing of the Scots soldiers had contributed greatly to the decision to introduce internment. As far as McAdorey was concerned, the Brits were the enemy and any action taken against their army was justified.

McAdorey went to an IRA arms dump and removed a brand-new rifle. Soldiers from the Green Howard Regiment had flooded the area but, in spite of the obvious dangers, McAdorey positioned himself on the roof of a shop near his home at Brompton Park. The move afforded the IRA man a more commanding view of the district where a serious riot situation had developed. As McAdorey raised his weapon into position, he could see Malcolm Hatton, a 19-year-old squaddie, taking cover at the junction with Crumlin Road. Through the sights on his rifle, McAdorey noticed he still had a clear view of the soldier. He took aim and squeezed the trigger. The crack of the rifle caused the soldiers to duck, but Private Hatton gave a dull sigh before staggering and falling to the ground. He had been shot in the head. One soldier saw where the shot had come from and, after spotting McAdorey's position, quickly loosed off two shots in his direction, but the IRA man, who had an intimate knowledge of the immediate area, made good his escape.

McAdorey continued to pose problems for the soldiers as they struggled to gain control of the area. A few hours later an army marksman noticed the IRA man firing at soldiers once again and he continued to focus on his line of fire until he had an unimpeded view of the gunman. Paddy McAdorey was just about to alter position when a high-velocity round hit him square on the forehead. The man who had befriended Fusiliers John and Joe McCaig and Dougald McCaughey before shooting them through the head had suffered the same fate.

Paddy McAdorey's body lay in state at a local community centre where other members of the IRA's 3rd Battalion formed a guard of honour. A short distance away at Girdwood Park army base, British soldiers cracked open a bottle of Scotch whisky in celebration.

In total, 14 people lost their lives on that fateful day. Internment signalled the start of the most violent period of the Troubles and nearly 1,800 people were to die in the next five years.

As 1971 wore on, the sectarian battlefield of Ulster continued to broaden. There were 131 bomb attacks in Northern Ireland during August, mostly the work of the IRA. The following month this figure rose to 196 and in October there were 117 explosions, which became increasingly reckless with each attack.

Tit-for-tat pub bombings soon became a feature of Ulster life as both communities retreated into bunker-type premises for the dubious pleasure of social drinking. In September, The Bluebell Bar in loyalist Sandy Row, which, during the 1950s and '60s, had been a favourite watering hole of Irish writer and former IRA prisoner Brendan Behan, was bombed. Twenty-five people were injured.

Two people were killed and twenty injured when the IRA blew up The Four Step Inn in the Shankill district. In December of that year, during an eight-day period, a number of murder milestones were passed as events continued to spiral out of control.

The Tramore Bar on Belfast's North Queen Street was better known in that area of the city as McGurk's. The pub was owned and run by Patrick McGurk and his wife Philomena, who lived above the premises with their four children. That area of the city was close to Belfast's rapidly declining industrial base and many residents were still employed in the docks and the nearby Gallacher's tobacco factory. McGurk's was an extremely well-run establishment, although Pat McGurk was seen by some of the rougher elements of the community as being too strict and consequently the pub had an older clientele.

Just after 8.45 p.m. on Saturday, 4 December, a car containing four UVF members pulled up near McGurk's. One man wearing a mask over his face got out of the vehicle holding what looked like a large parcel covered with plastic sheeting. He walked over to the pub entrance and placed the parcel in the hallway. A young boy who was standing nearby looked on as the man produced a box of matches from his pocket and appeared to light what looked like a fuse, before running back down the street to the car, which sped off. Within seconds, a huge explosion ripped through the evening air and the entire pub collapsed, killing 15 people, including Mrs Philomena McGurk and her 14-year-old daughter Maria. Thirteen-year-old James Cromie, who was a friend of Mr McGurk's sons, was also killed. Three of the victims were pensioners, the eldest of whom, Philip Garry, a school crossing attendant, was 73. All of them were Catholics.

Almost immediately, malicious rumours that members of the IRA were using the pub to construct a bomb when it went off prematurely spread across Belfast like wildfire. The speculation was fuelled when army personnel began briefing journalists on the technicalities of bomb-making, as that appeared to back up the claim. Even Mr McGurk himself refused to speculate about who was responsible for fear of sparking further civil unrest. During a radio interview three months after the atrocity, he said: 'It doesn't matter who planted the bomb. What's done cannot be undone. All I can do is mourn my loved ones. The only thing I do regret is that in our society so many people have been jumping the gun and putting their own conclusions to it.'

But the boy who had seen the terrorists plant the bomb also said that the car which helped the bomber escape had a Union Jack draped across the rear window, and seven years later, David McKittrick, a highly respected journalist with intimate knowledge of the Protestant paramilitary organisations, revealed that the UVF was responsible for the attack.

McKittrick discovered that North Queen Street pub had not been the intended target of the bombers, but, unable to reach their destination, the UVF killer gang chose to divert and leave the deadly package at the entrance to McGurk's. Before the Omagh bomb atrocity on 15 August 1998 claimed the lives of 29 innocent people, including the mother of unborn twins, the bombing of McGurk's Bar remained the biggest single loss of life in a terrorist incident in Northern Ireland.

Years after the bombing, Robert Campbell, a Shankill Road man with a known loyalist background, was arrested on a completely unrelated matter. He was interviewed by detectives at Tennent Street police station, who had been instructed to quiz him over a number of criminal matters. After a short period of time, one of the detectives terminated the interview. He realised the man was telling the truth when he said he hadn't a clue what the officer was talking about. The man was placed back in a holding cell while the RUC man went upstairs to consult a senior officer. There he discovered that uniformed police had mistakenly scooped the wrong suspect and that in actual fact it was another man with a similar name that the police really wanted to speak to. The CID man was instructed to leave Campbell in the holding cell for the time being while the uniformed branch scoured the area.

Eventually, when the real suspect was apprehended, the CID officer returned to the custody suite to tell Campbell he was free to go. Nothing could have prepared the police officer for what happened next. As he was about to explain that it had all been a big mistake, Robert Campbell interrupted, saying there was something he wanted to get off his chest.

Hesitantly he said: 'I was part of the UVF team which blew up McGurk's Bar.'

The RUC man asked the prisoner to repeat his claim, before closing the cell door again and reaching for the interview sheets. 'Where do you want to start?' asked the detective, as he pulled up a chair and settled down for one of the lengthiest and most important police interviews of his life.

Years later he told colleagues: 'That was the day I cleared 15 murders . . . by mistake!'

Despite its tough image, the UVF was too embarrassed to claim the McGurk's Bar bomb under its own name and chose the rather nebulous title of 'Empire Loyalists' when staking its responsibility for the blast.

On Saturday, 11 December – one week after the McGurk's Bar atrocity – the Provisional IRA took it upon itself to retaliate. IRA volunteers carried out a no-warning bomb attack at the Balmoral Furniture Store on the Shankill Road. Hugh Bruce, a 50-year-old commissionaire, who was employed to keep an eye on security at the shop, was killed instantly, as was Harold King, a 20-year-old Catholic lad who worked as a salesman.

As the bomb exploded, two-year-old Tracey Munn was in a pram outside the shop. Also in the pram was 17-month-old Colin Nicholl – a baby boy whose adoptive parents were away in England on business. He was being looked after by Tracey's mum. The blast caused a wall to fall on the babies. Tracey lay dead in her pram, but baby Colin's head had been blown off. Dozens of innocent shoppers, including Tracey's mum, were badly injured. The Shankill Road is one of Belfast's best shopping streets and on a Saturday afternoon in the month of Christmas it was packed.

When the funeral of the babies took place a few days later, 1,000 men walked in the cortège, many of them weeping uncontrollably. In a mirror image of the UVF behaviour after the McGurk's Bar blast, the IRA squirmed off to the safety of the Falls Road without claiming responsibility for its actions. Many men who later went on to play major and, in some cases, extremely violent roles in Loyalist paramilitary organisations trace their decision to join up to the no-warning bomb which claimed the lives of the two babies.

One man who traced his decision to become a Protestant paramilitary to this incident was Frankie Curry, who went on to become one of the most notorious loyalist assassins of the entire Troubles. Curry, a nephew of Gusty Spence, the UVF leader jailed for his part in the Malvern Street shootings in 1966, was himself murdered by former colleagues on St Patrick's Day 1999. The spot where he was executed was just yards from where the Malvern Arms stood – the pub visited by the Catholic barmen prior to Peter Ward's murder.

Curry once claimed to journalists that as a schoolboy he had helped dispose of the UVF weapons after Ward was killed. Frankie Curry's mother, Cassie, is a sister of Gusty Spence and it was at her house the Shankill UVF team called following the Malvern Arms shootings.

Cassie Curry, now 77, wears a gold locket with a photograph of her son inside around her neck. Mrs Curry traces her son's involvement in violence to the Balmoral Furniture Store car bomb. 'He was distraught at seeing those babies carried out of that building. He came home – a teenage boy of 16 – and cried. The IRA were killing innocent people.'

Cassie Curry insists that it was then her son joined the notorious loyalist paramilitary group, Red Hand Commando, which has close links to the Ulster Volunteer Force. Ironically, it is believed that Curry was gunned down by people linked to the UVF.

During a terror career spanning nearly three decades, Frankie Curry is believed to have been directly involved in killing between 16 and 19 people. These figures were given to journalists during interviews with Curry following his release from prison and prior to his death.

Many victims of terrorist violence in Northern Ireland have been described as simply being 'in the wrong place at the wrong time'. One such person was Thomas Holmes Curry, a ship's captain who was killed by Frankie Curry on 31 May 1973.

Captain Curry, a native of Preston, Lancashire, was a regular visitor to the coast of Ulster and he was a well-known figure at the seaports of Larne and Belfast. During trips to the North's capital city, the Captain was fond of going for an early morning pint to the famous dockside pub Pat's Bar on Princes Dock Street in the heart of an area known as Sailortown. He would spend a pleasant hour or so chatting to the pub owner Pat Brennan as he prepared his premises for the day's trade.

Pat's Bar was, as it is now, a traditional, welcoming Irish pub with its big coal fire and home cooking served daily. Around lunchtime Captain Curry would send word to his ship inviting the rest of his crew to join him for a meal. An affable man, he enjoyed the camaraderie of his shipmates, but on trips to Belfast he particularly savoured an early drink at Pat's on his own. The publican kept a small dog on the premises and, after opening up and lighting the fire, Pat Brennan allowed the animal out onto the quayside for a bit of fresh air and exercise.

Kerry, the dog, got to know Captain Curry and when his ship tied up alongside it would run over to the craft and bark until crew members threw it a few scraps from the ship's galley. The dog barking was Captain Curry's signal to get dressed in civilian clothes before heading over to the pub for his usual pint of Guinness.

On the morning of 31 May, Pat Brennan awoke suffering from a dreadful toothache and instead of heading to Princes Dock to open the bar he went to the dentist. On board his ship, Captain Curry wondered why his four-legged friend hadn't called over to the quayside to deliver his usual early morning alarm call. After a while, the Captain got dressed and, on seeing Pat's Bar still shut, headed further down the docks area to Muldoon's Bar opposite the magnificent Harbour Commissioner's Building.

The seafarer walked in and ordered himself a pint. A short time later Captain Curry was wondering how he was going to let his crew members know where he was, when he heard a commotion at the pub entrance. Standing there, dressed completely in black with a hood masking his face, was Frankie Curry.

The terrorist levelled a sub-machine gun at the customers and pulled the trigger, spraying the bar with gunfire. As Curry raced from the premises to a waiting getaway car, he threw a homemade pipe bomb back into the bar and seconds later a huge explosion wrecked the place. Captain Curry lay dead on the floor, having been struck by a number of bullets.

Five days later, members of Belfast's seafaring community attended an emotional quayside service before a coffin containing Captain Curry's body was placed on board his own ship prior to its setting sail for Preston. The seaman was one of four people Frankie Curry murdered that same year.

During Frankie Curry's lengthy paramilitary career, he joined almost all of Ulster's deadly divisions of loyalism. At various stages he found himself in the Red Hand Commando, the UVF, the UDA and the shadowy Red Hand Defenders, which is a cover name or a flag of criminal convenience. He also spent lengthy spells in prison during a three-decade period.

But by far the greatest insight into the way Curry's murderous mind worked came into sharp focus when he murdered ex-Red Hand Commando chief Billy Elliott, who was shot in the back of the head on 28 September 1995. Elliott had fallen foul of the organisation following the brutal murder of a young woman in a seedy loyalist band hall in the staunchly Protestant Village area of Belfast.

Margaret Wright, a 31-year-old Protestant, had gone to the club for a late-night drink with a woman she met at a taxi rank a few hours earlier. Once inside, members of the club started quizzing her about her religion. It has since emerged that some of the men questioning her may have wrongly assumed that she had at one time served a prison sentence for the IRA.

Margaret Wright, an attractive blonde, lived with her Scottish-born mum on the Forthriver estate. Her mother worked as a cook in the Rosemary Street HQ of the Masonic Order in Belfast. Margaret had a history of depression and alcoholism, but was believed to be coping well with her problem.

Margaret was taken to a side room where she was savagely beaten with pool cues and a brush shaft. A hood was placed over her head as her attackers refused to listen to her tortured pleas for mercy. Billy Elliott was by far the fiercest of the young woman's attackers, and through a haze of alcohol and Ecstasy tablets he placed a gun next to her temple and shot her four times through the head.

Margaret's body was then thrown into a wheelie bin and pushed to a derelict house where it was unceremoniously dumped. Her attackers then returned to the club where they carried on drinking and drug-taking. Acting on information received, the RUC arrived at the club in the early hours of the morning but were refused entry. The officers were forced to smash a hole in the wall with sledgehammers in order to get inside. It was obvious the club had been the scene of a serious crime and the police arrested everyone who was present. Margaret's battered, bruised and bloodied body was found by police the following day.

During an application for bail by one of those arrested, the court was told that the man admitted seeing Margaret sitting in a room at the band hall with a hood placed over her head. He claimed one of the others told him: 'We have a Taig [a Catholic] in here.' And by way of explanation to the police, he said: 'It's like a Prod going into a Provie club. You wouldn't expect to come out alive.'

Billy Elliott, a 32-year-old married man, was arrested but refused to speak to the police and was released without charge. Embarrassed by the bad publicity which was now being heaped on loyalists, and particularly those associated with the Margaret Wright killing, Billy Elliott bolted to Scotland, where he was looked after by loyalists in the Glasgow area. The UVF killed one of its members, Ian Hamilton, claiming he had assisted in the killing.

After the loyalist ceasefire of October 1994, Billy Elliott presumed, wrongly as it turned out, that it was safe to return to Northern Ireland. Scotland was all very well but he missed the buzz of home. However, Elliott was wise enough not to return to the Village area of Belfast and instead settled in the Cloughy district of the Ards Peninsula with his wife and two children. Elliott knew Frankie Curry well and used to meet him regularly at a house on the Bloomfield estate in the seaside town of Bangor. The pair frequently discussed the state of the burgeoning loyalist drugs business and Curry lured Margaret Wright's killer into a false sense of security.

Curry devised a plan to execute Elliott. He arranged to meet Elliott at a house on Ballyree Drive, on Bangor's Bloomfield estate. Curry also arranged for another man, Tommy 'Muggsy' Maginniss, to wait in a car in a nearby parking bay.

Maginniss was known as 'Muggsy' because he bore a striking resemblance to the tough guy character of the same name in the Jimmy Cagney gangster movie, *Angels With Dirty Faces*. But Maginniss was no angel; he was in fact a hardened criminal capable of extreme violence.

Curry asked Elliott to accompany him across town while he arranged a drugs deal. Elliott, who did not suspect anything, readily agreed. Curry's plan was to lure Elliott out of the estate, shoot him dead and then dump the body somewhere before disappearing for a few days.

As the pair stepped from the house shortly after 8.00 p.m. to walk the short distance to the car park, Curry changed his mind and decided Elliott would die there and then. Curry had a compulsive obsession about clean shoes and he was horrified when Elliott stepped from the footpath onto the wet grass. It had been raining for days and the grass had turned into a quagmire. Curry took a handgun from his waistband and shot Elliott twice through the head. He then calmly stepped over the dead body and ran to the waiting car containing Muggsy Maginniss. He then drove out of the estate and went to visit his girlfriend in the Shankill area.

Two years ago, Maginniss became a cause célèbre when he walked free from Belfast's Crown Court where he had been facing two counts of murder and a host of other terrorist charges. All charges against him were dropped.

The case against Maginniss had been built on the fact that Johnston 'Jonty' Brown, a legendary and highly experienced RUC detective, had managed to get a confession from Maginniss. The confession was secretly recorded on sound and film. Maginniss had spoken to Brown and another officer in the back of a car, but he was unaware that the interview was being recorded. He was later interviewed again and told that this confession had been recorded on audio tape and he was subsequently charged with a series of terrorist offences, including two of murder. However, when his trial opened, the judge ruled that Maginniss would have been unable to offer a proper defence because of the manner in which the confession was obtained and as a result he was dropping all charges against Maginniss. The judge also said he was not directing any criticism towards the RUC investigation team or their superior officers.

A look of astonishment came over Maginniss' face when the judge told him he was free to leave the dock. Maginniss wasn't sure if he had heard the judge correctly and he had to check the situation with a court official before he left the court a free man. He subsequently gave a television interview about his experience.

– CHAPTER NINE –

These Things Don't Happen in the United Kingdom

They taught me how to shoot at wogs,
and treat a black man like a dog,
It's just like pulling legs off frogs,
In the bloody British Army.
Parody of army song by Jim McLean

Contrary to expectations, internment failed to reduce the levels of violence on the streets. But it was not only subversive loyalist and republican groups which were intent on using force and coercion – elements within the British establishment were every bit as keen to make their mark on that front. However, a secret note smuggled out of Belfast Prison forced the British government to call a halt to a programme of torture aimed at smashing the IRA.

An internee who was one of twelve men subjected to round-the-clock torture techniques for a full week arranged for a piece of paper, documenting the horrendous ill-treatment he was forced to endure, to be given to Cardinal Conway, the most senior figure in the Catholic Church in Ireland in 1971.

None of the 12 men who endured Britain's 'Seven Days of Shame', as it was described in newspaper reports of the time, were charged with a single terrorist offence. The techniques used in their torture, however, were reminiscent of those employed in Japanese prisoner of war camps during the Second World War.

Retired headmaster Paddy Joe McClean, speaking 30 years after the events that ended with the British government landing itself in the dock at the European Court of Human Rights, says he is convinced it was the speedy action of the Catholic cleric which prevented another dozen men being singled out for the torture treatment.

It was McClean who persuaded a Presbyterian prison officer in Belfast's Crumlin Road Prison to deliver a document written by him to the Cardinal. Paddy Joe, now a member of the Civic Forum set up under the Good Friday Agreement, said: 'I believe that if I had been unable to get that note to Cardinal Conway the torture would have continued unabated.'

When internment without trial was introduced on 9 August 1971, McClean from Beragh, Co. Tyrone was a 39-year-old schoolteacher and father of eight children. He was rounded up along with 341 others. All were Catholics. Although he was never involved with any paramilitary groups, McClean was the chairman of the Tyrone branch of the Northern Ireland Civil Rights Association (NICRA), and therefore deemed a threat to national security. Within days he was removed from a detention centre at Magilligan Point, Co. Derry, and taken to a secret torture chamber, which he later learned was within the British Army's Shackleton Barracks at Ballykelly, also Co. Derry.

A hood was placed over McClean's head and he was ordered to take off his clothes and put on a blue boiler suit. He was forced to stand with his legs wide apart and his hands against a wall. This room was to be his home for a week, although he didn't know that at the time. McClean was deprived of sleep and subjected to hours of continuous beating. Loud noise was played in his ear throughout.

So confused was his state of mind that at one point he thought he had died and was witnessing his own funeral. Two days later McClean was taken out of the torture chamber for a while. He was rushed by helicopter to another base where he was handed detention papers signed by the Northern Ireland Prime Minister Brian Faulkner. Up until that point, McClean and the other 11 had been detained illegally. The beatings were sometimes interrupted for periods of interrogation, when he was quizzed about IRA activities.

After seven days of almost continuous torture, McClean was flown again by helicopter to Girdwood Army Barracks in Belfast, where the hood was at last removed from his head. He was ordered to walk through a hole in a wall and into Crumlin Road Prison. Prison staff were shocked at McClean's physical condition. He had lost 40 lbs in weight and looked as though he had been through hell.

Despite his physical and mental state, McClean had enough savvy to ask for a warder he had known from the last time he was interned during the IRA's border campaign of the 1950s. At that time, he had been lifted because he was a member of a completely legal republican grouping.

The prison officer, who was a Presbyterian from Co. Antrim, called to see him, asking if there was anything he could do to help. McClean requested a pen and writing paper on which he recorded everything that had happened to him during the past seven days. He listed 24 torture techniques which had been used on him. The warder was then asked to smuggle the document out of prison and on to Cardinal Conway.

After reading McClean's note, the churchman caught the first available flight to London and demanded a meeting with the British Prime Minister Ted Heath. At a late-night meeting with Conway, at 10 Downing Street, Heath was polite as he offered tea, but his demeanour changed when he realised the nature of the churchman's business.

Heath looked shocked as he read about the treatment his army had been meting out to UK citizens, but, as the reality of the situation began to sink in, Heath then switched tack to one of damage limitation. He knew that, any day now, the story of Britain's torture chamber in Ulster would be making headline news all over the world. There and then the Tory Prime Minister ordered senior army personnel to drop future torture plans.

The torture treatment meted out to the internees and documented by Paddy Joe McClean was to form the basis of the Irish government's case against Britain at the European Court of Human Rights in Strasbourg. It became known in the press as 'the Hooded Men Case'.

In court, Britain offered no defence and it is thought that this was to allow the politicians who had ordered the torture to remain anonymous. Their names have never been revealed. During the proceedings it emerged that the techniques employed in the Ballykelly torture chambers were taken from a KGB blueprint used against dissidents in the former Soviet Union. They had been developed by the boot boys of the tyrannical Russian leader Joseph Stalin.

Bricklayer Mickey Donnelly was married with a young family when he was arrested at his home in Derry's city centre. He was taken first to Ebrington Barracks and from there to Magilligan Camp, before being flown by helicopter to the Ballykelly torture chamber.

Like McClean, Donnelly was hooded and, during the flight, a soldier opened the side door of the craft and threatened to drop him into the sea. He felt the wind swirling around him when he was suddenly grabbed from behind and thrown out.

He was convinced he was falling to his death but a split second later he hit the ground with a bump which took his breath away. He had been dropped from a distance of ten feet.

Mickey Donnelly was physically very strong and extremely fit and as a result he was better equipped than most to cope with the torture treatment. At one point, he even managed to get his hood off and look every one of his torturers straight in the eye. He insists he would recognise every one of them today.

At 19, Joe Clarke was the youngest of the group. A gifted mechanic, he was involved in the upper levels of the motor rally industry and by all accounts had a rosy future in front of him. Clarke was arrested at his parent's home in the Falls area of Belfast by members of the Parachute Regiment. He was taken to Crumlin Road Prison, where an RUC Special Branch officer told him he was one of a group of five who were to be given 'special treatment' – he would soon learn this was coded language for torture.

Hoods were placed over their heads and they were frog-marched to a waiting helicopter. When the craft was airborne, the soldiers told Clarke he was going to be thrown out into the Irish Sea. The Paras told them they would receive the same treatment 'as the Yanks gave the Vietnamese'.

Twenty minutes later the helicopter landed at Ballykelly. From the second Clarke entered what he was soon to learn was a torture chamber, a number was written on his right arm and from that moment on he wasn't addressed by his name again for a full week.

Clarke was subjected to the same treatment as Paddy Joe McClean and he was convinced he was going to be killed. Like McClean, he was forced to lean on the torture room wall, legs wide apart, for 72 hours continuously. The food he received was an occasional piece of bread with a glass of water.

After seven days, although he had lost all track of time, his hood was removed and he was given a proper meal. The hood was again put over his head and he was once again placed in a helicopter. A man who identified himself as a police officer told him he was going to Crumlin Road Prison in Belfast. As the helicopter touched down, the cop removed the hood from Clarke's head. He was told not to look back and walk straight in front of him through a hole in a wall. As the policeman pushed Clarke from the aircraft, he whispered in his ear: 'Good luck to you, Joe.'

Although he was unsteady on his feet, Clarke made it through the prison wall and into the main building. A shocked prison officer told him: 'Don't worry, son, nothing is going to happen to you here.' Joe Clarke had lost 18 lb in weight.

Three decades later, no individuals have yet been made amenable or claimed responsibility for the torture treatment. The British government was called to answer allegations of torture in the European Court of Human Rights but Paddy Joe McClean says the people he would like to hear from are ex-Tory Prime Minister Ted Heath and his former Defence Secretary Lord Carrington. 'These are the men who have to answer questions about what happened at Ballykelly.' Despite the deafening silence of Heath and Carrington, it is widely believed that these two senior politicians were kept fully briefed about what happened in the immediate aftermath of internment. When the Irish government raised the matter with the European Commission for Human Rights, the British failed to cooperate fully.

On 3 September 1976, the Commission released its report on the matter. In a unanimous decision, it ruled that the techniques used on the men at Ballykelly amounted to torture and inhumane and degrading treatment. The judges also ruled that Britain had failed to 'accord the Commission full assistance' as required by Article 28 of the European Convention on Human Rights.

In Dublin, the government thought the ruling was incomplete since no individuals were held responsible for the actions of the soldiers and police officers who inflicted the torture. As a result, it took its suit to the European Court of Human Rights, where the Commission's decisions can be appealed.

It was seven years after the events at Ballykelly by the time the Court finally made its ruling. By a vote of thirteen to four, the judges ruled that the techniques used amounted to inhuman and degrading treatment, but not torture. The Irish government, which had wanted the techniques outlawed, was stunned. Amnesty International stepped in and announced that despite the judges' decision, it considered the Ballykelly interrogation techniques to be torture.

The compensation paid to each of the torture victims averaged just fourteen thousand pounds.

Over three decades have passed now and Paddy Joe McClean holds no ill will to the men who brutalised him: 'They were just carrying out orders,' he says. But McClean is not so forgiving about Lord Carrington: 'If Carrington gave the order then it is he who should be held responsible and if he did not, then he should be taken to task for not ferreting out those who are.' McClean says he contents himself in the knowledge that the guilty men still have to live with their consciences.

Now 70 years of age and retired, the father of 12 (he had 8 children in 1971) has managed to put the past behind him and he still makes an enormous contribution to public and political life in Northern Ireland. A serving member of the Civic Forum, he also sat on the Police Authority until that body disappeared with the change from the Royal Ulster Constabulary to the Police Service of Northern Ireland. He is a strong supporter of the police and believes that a responsible police force is the basis of a stable society. McClean is, however, scathing about political parties like Sinn Fein which have so far failed to nominate members for the newly formed policing boards while continuing to sit in government in Northern Ireland.

Paddy Joe McClean and Joe Clarke never saw each other after their release from internment until 2002. They met again in the coffee lounge of Belfast's Europa Hotel after some friends organised a surprise meeting. For a few seconds McClean looked blankly at the well-dressed man who stood over his table smiling at him. Suddenly he said 'My God' and got up to throw his arms around the man he last saw 30 years ago.

Both men's eyes filled up as they embraced each other warmly. Neither of them mentioned anything about how history had thrown them together – one a Tyrone schoolteacher and the other a mechanic from Belfast – they didn't have to, their eyes said it all. After chatting for around ten minutes and catching up on what was happening now, Paddy Joe McClean made his excuses and left to attend another appointment. The men shook hands and vowed to meet again soon.

All the tortured men found different ways to cope with the horrors inflicted on them. Some were able to recover and move on with their lives, while other were dogged by ill health until their deaths.

Sean McKenna from Newry was, at 42, the oldest of the group. He was released from internment in 1973 and required psychiatric treatment. He suffered from anxiety brought on by bitter memories of his experiences at the hands of his torturers and on 5 June 1975 he died of a heart attack. He was just 45.

Pat Shivers from Toomebridge, Co. Antrim, claimed after his release his dead son appeared to him during the interrogation. When he was released back to the prison, his hair had turned white. He died of stomach cancer aged 54.

Mickey Montgomery, a member of the Official IRA from Derry, developed a severe drink problem. His wife recalls that he became irritable and bad tempered when confronted with noise. He served as an Official Sinn Fein member on Derry City Council, but quit after just one term. He died of a heart attack on 1 December 1984. He was 49.

Gerard McKerr was probably the fittest of the men before his arrest, but when he was released from internment after three years he found his stamina was gone. He subsequently developed Hodgkin's disease. One day he emerged from his house to find a booby-trapped bomb under his car. It was defused by the authorities.

Joe Clarke, at 19, was the youngest of the hooded men. On his release from custody, he joined the Provisional IRA, but quit to go back to his first love – motor cars. Today he runs a successful garage business and is deeply involved in providing aid for orphans in Belarus. He has adopted two Russian children who live with him and his family in Belfast.

Brian Turley – like all the others who were forced to undergo the week-long torture treatment – did not have his difficulties to seek when he emerged from custody. A native of Armagh city, on one occasion when he travelled south of the border he mistakenly took the Gardai for the RUC and required medical treatment to calm his nerves. Joe Clarke, who underwent torture alongside Turley, said: 'Big Brian was a lovely man. He had a quiet country manner about him and he was a complete gentleman.'

Kevin Hannaway, a cousin of Sinn Fein chief, Gerry Adams, claimed his republican background prepared him better than most for what happened. He says he didn't expect anything else.

Frank McGuigan was the eldest son of a staunchly republican family from the Ardoyne district of Belfast. After the torture treatment, McGuigan was removed to Long Kesh Internment Camp. He hit the headlines when he walked out of the heavily fortified base dressed as a Catholic priest. He suffered flashbacks for some time, but has largely managed to put his experiences behind him. He now lives in Dublin.

Jim Auld, known to his friends as 'Archie', was one of the younger members of the group. He got involved with the republican movement on his release from prison and for many years he also suffered from blackouts. Today he runs a restorative justice programme in west Belfast.

Mickey Donnelly from Derry is still a deeply committed republican who has no time for Sinn Fein's role in the devolved administration at Stormont. He is convinced that the root cause of Northern Ireland's problems is the British presence. In 1998 he was savagely beaten in his own home by members of the Provisional IRA. He claims his 'crime' was that he had spoken out about Sinn Fein's acceptance of Partition.

Following the attack, in which he suffered a broken leg, Mickey Donnelly said:

> The old Stormont regime attacked and beat me 30 years ago. And two years ago, cohorts of the Sinn Fein Ministers at Stormont attacked and beat me in front of my family. Nothing has changed. In fact I think we were better off under the old regime.

Patrick McNally still has a recurring dream relating to his days at Ballykelly. He has suffered nightmares for years. Today he is involved in fundraising events to aid Romanian children.

As 1971 drew to a close, the Official IRA made history by carrying out what was termed the 'first political murder' since 1922. Senator Jack Barnhill, a 65-year-old businessman, was shot dead at his farmhouse home outside Strabane,

Co. Tyrone. Jack Barnhill's senator status came from his membership of the upper house at Stormont, which was totally under Unionist control.

Barnhill, who was steeped in the loyalist institutions of the Orange Order and Apprentice Boys of Derry, was in his home with his wife when the IRA murder gang came calling. When he answered a knock at the door, he was shot twice. The intruder carried in a gelignite bomb which was placed beside Barnhill's body. Mrs Barnhill was ordered out of the house and, as she raced towards a neighbour's house for help, she was stopped in her tracks by a huge explosion. The bomb had demolished her two-storey home with her husband's body still inside.

In a statement admitting responsibility for the murder, a spokesman for the Official IRA said it had not been their intention to kill Senator Barnhill. Its members only intended to plant a bomb in Jack Barnhill's home, said the spokesman, but they were forced to shoot him because he tackled the intruders.

Following the incident, the IRA men made their way to the nearby River Foyle, where a small craft was waiting to ferry them to the safety of neighbouring Co. Donegal. The gunmen had used a caravan near Lifford as a base to mount the attack and, after dumping their weapons, they went to a pub in the East Donegal village of Porthall to enjoy a celebratory drink.

Jack Barnhill's funeral, which was attended by around 1,000 people, included senior figures from both sides of the political divide. Standing at his graveside, John Hume called the grisly act 'callous cold-blooded murder' and Bernadette Devlin condemned the killing, saying John Barnhill was no threat to the IRA.

As a depressed and violence-ridden Northern Ireland prepared for Christmas, the murder sounded a warning of what lay in store.

– CHAPTER TEN –

Ever Onward into the Abyss

I pray that my coming to Ireland today may prove to be the first step towards an end to strife among her people, whatever their race or creed.

King George V speaking at the opening of the new Stormont Parliament, Belfast, 22 June 1921

Seannie Meehan's eyes lit up when one of his IRA associates told him: 'I know where you can get a cop.' Ten months had passed since he and Paddy McAdorey had put paid to the lives of three young Scottish soldiers. Meehan wanted another 'hit' badly. For him, killing had become a drug – like a junkie needing a fix. He was prepared to go down any road to get it, but if an easy route could be found, then so much the better.

Unwittingly, Raymond Carroll provided that easy route. Raymond Carroll's family home was in Dunmurry on the outskirts of Belfast on the road to Lisburn, but he worked as a policeman in Belfast. Aged 22, he held the rank of constable and had recently qualified from the Royal Ulster Constabulary training school at Enniskillen, Co. Fermanagh, where his father was employed as an instructor. Several of Constable Carroll's relatives also worked as police officers. The Carrolls were what is described in Ulster as a 'police family'.

Raymond Carroll loved his job but it wasn't his first love. The thing which drove him to distraction in the nicest possible way was rally driving. At every opportunity he was either away watching rallies or taking part in them himself. So fanatical was he about cars that his wife used to complain that they couldn't have a normal conversation while walking down the street because Raymond's eyes were always being diverted to the windows of shops which sold car components.

Raymond Carroll was delighted the day he bought his first rally car and he looked after the machine in the same way a mother would a new baby. In his time in Belfast, Constable Carroll had made good contacts in the motor trade and he was delighted when he met a man who said he would allow him the use of his garage workshop to repair and service his rally car.

Maximo de Magollon Guerrero was a Queen's University student who had come to Belfast from his native Peru to study medicine. At first he threw himself into his studies, but after meeting and falling in love with a local girl he dropped out of academic life. Guerrero had previously worked as a car mechanic and, with the help of some cash his family sent him from South America, he was able to rent a small car repair unit at a filling station on Belfast's Old Park Road.

On 28 January 1972, Raymond Carroll was preparing his car for a rally that night. He needed a few parts replaced and decided it would be easier if he took the vehicle to the Old Park Road workshop where he could give it a thorough going over.

It was there that a man associated with the Provisional IRA in the nearby Ardoyne district spotted him. He had recognised Carroll from when he once called at the garage to speak to the owner wearing his RUC inform.

It was obvious he was going to be working on his rally car for some time and so the man rushed back to Ardoyne to pass on the information to the Provos.

Seannie Meehan couldn't believe his luck. He gave orders that a number of named associates were to be called to a meeting immediately. William Bates from nearby Valsheda Park arrived first at the Northwick Drive house after receiving the cryptic message: 'Seannie Meehan wants to see you.' Those words later played a major part in determining the direction Bates' life would take.

Brendan Mailey, now a spokesman for the Ardoyne Residents' Group, involved in the headline-hitting schools dispute, arrived next. At the time, Mailey was a 20-year-old member of the Provisional IRA.

Another local man, 31-year-old Joe Lynch, was also called to the meeting. When the men arrived at the house they found Seannie Meehan sitting on a bed with a rifle beside him. Mailey was given a small handgun and ordered along with Lynch to hijack a car from a passing motorist and return to the Northwick Drive house.

Bates and Mailey were ordered to drive to the garage to take another look at the intended target. When they returned, all were issued with combat jackets and masks. Meehan, armed with an American M1 Carbine high-velocity rifle, walked briskly to the car. The gun was hidden inside his jacket.

Mailey, Bates and Lynch followed. Meehan and Bates got into the back and Mailey got into the front passenger seat. Lynch was the driver. The four drove to the Deerpark Garage on the Old Park Road, where Bates, Meehan and Mailey got out. All three jumped over the garage wall and Bates moved forward to open the door to the service bay.

Inside, Raymond Carroll was busy working on his rally car. The vehicle was on the hydraulic lift and the off-duty policeman was underneath it. The door opening had attracted his attention and he looked out from under the vehicle. As he did so, Bates shouted 'Watch out!' and ran back outside. But it was already too late. Seannie Meehan's finger was already on the trigger and he began firing. The policeman was hit nine times and died instantly. As the assassins sped off in the getaway car, Meehan began laughing and shouted: 'I got the bastard!'

At the time, the Scotland Yard detectives sent to Northern Ireland to investigate Seannie Meehan and Paddy McAdorey's murderous work the previous year, when the three Scottish soldiers were killed, were installed at a property called 'The Oaks' off the Springfield Road in west Belfast. They were now given further instructions to look into the murder of Constable Raymond Carroll.

English detectives taking charge of the murder investigation sparked a wave of resentment among experienced RUC officers – a situation that recurred throughout the Troubles. Local police officers felt the government believed the RUC murder squad wasn't capable of handling the investigation.

The team of Scotland Yard officers were led by Detective Superintendent Etheridge from Leeds. Etheridge loved publicity and regularly did press interviews. Some years later, however, he was to make the headlines for quite different reasons.

The Scotland Yard men became frustrated at their lack of success. Efforts to mount a prosecution on the Fusiliers' killings were fruitless. Etheridge eventually decided that local RUC knowledge was vital to the investigation and that, rather than alienating his RUC colleagues, he would bring them on board.

One important informant for the RUC in Ardoyne was, however, Jimmy 'Nailer' Clarke, known locally as a 'hardman' and the father of IRA volunteer Terence 'Cleeky' Clarke. Cleeky wrote himself into republican mythology in the early days of the Troubles as one of eight volunteers who escaped from Crumlin Road Prison by jumping over the wall.

Unknown to Cleeky, or the rest of the IRA in Ardoyne, Nailer Clarke had been a police informant since long before the Troubles and was ideally placed to pass on information about republican activity in the area. After a while, police inquiries into Constable Carroll's murder began to make headway.

Anticipating that he was going to be arrested, Seannie Meehan went on the run to the Republic. He was later scooped by the Gardai while carrying out a robbery and sent to prison. In Belfast, Bates and Lynch were arrested as the police net closed in. Largely based on statements made by the accused men themselves, they were charged with murder. A number of others, including the woman who owned the house where the murder was planned, were also charged, but after a period of time the charges were dropped.

Around this time Detective Superintendent Etheridge led a police raid on the Etna Drive home of the Whelan family in connection with the Carroll investigation. Three of the Whelan boys, Timmy, Robin and Owen, were asleep in an upstairs bedroom. The boys, all teenagers, shared the room with two of their young nephews and there was uproar in the house as burly English police officers charged upstairs.

One officer was searching a set of drawers which was used for storing underwear, when one of the boys noticed him placing a gun underneath a pile of socks. The youngster shouted downstairs to his mother: 'Ma, they're planting a gun!' Timothy, Robin and Owen Whelan were all arrested and charged with possession of a firearm.

The trial of William Bates and Joseph Lynch opened at the Crown Court in Belfast in June 1972 in front of Lord Justice Maurice Gibson, who was later killed along with his wife when an IRA bomb blew up their car as they were about to cross the Irish border returning from holiday. Lawyers for the men argued that, whilst they admitted involvement in the murder of Constable Carroll, they had done so under the duress of the man who pulled the trigger, named in court as Sean Meehan. By this time, Meehan was serving a sentence in the Republic for armed robbery. During the case the court was told Meehan had been allowed out of jail on short-term parole to get married.

Lord Gibson had a reputation for being a tough judge and, despite the eloquent cases presented by the legal teams representing Bates and Lynch, he refused to allow 'duress' to be used as a defence and the men were both convicted and sentenced to life. Appeals in both cases failed.

In August 1973, Brendan Mailey was arrested and charged with possession of a gun and ammunition in connection with the Carroll killing. When he appeared in court the following year, he was sentenced to 14 years. In true republican style, Mailey refused to recognise the court.

Lawyers for Joseph Lynch, however, were troubled by the life sentence their client received and decided to mount an appeal on the 'duress' issue which went all the way to the House of Lords. Their Lordships ruled that 'duress' was a legitimate defence to murder, quashed the conviction and ordered a retrial. The case, listed simply as 'R v. Lynch,' made legal history and had huge implications for the Northern Ireland justice system. The English Law Lords had rewritten the legal textbooks. The landmark ruling did not do Lynch much good, however, when a judge at his retrial ruled that Lynch was an unconvincing witness. He said he found 'beyond reasonable doubt' that Lynch was a willing participant in the murder and, accordingly, he was convicted and sentenced to life imprisonment.

His co-accused William Bates was much more fortunate three days later, however. The judge said he was not satisfied beyond all reasonable doubt that Bates was guilty of murder and acquitted him.

The trial of the Whelan brothers, Timmy, Robin and Owen, accused of possession of a gun and ammunition during the same investigation, was heard at Crumlin Road in front of Lord Justice Jones. The judge, whose full name was Edward Warburton Jones, was an ex-army officer and a former Unionist MP. He enjoyed a reputation as a hardline Unionist, and was also seen as a legal and religious bigot as well as a snob.

When the three Catholic teenagers appeared before Lord Jones he was in no mood to listen to the legal arguments put to him by the boys' counsel. On principle, he said, each of the boys must have known the gun was in their bedroom and he had no hesitation in sending each of them to jail for six years. The boys' solicitor, Pascal O'Hare, knew the conviction was far from safe. After consulting the Whelans' counsel, Harry McDevitt QC and Liam McCollum QC (now Northern Ireland's senior criminal judge), an appeal was lodged. It was heard in the Appeal Court in front of Lords Robert Lowry and Turlough O'Donnell.

After considering all the evidence, Turlough O'Donnell enunciated what became known in law as 'The Whelan Principle'. This meant that when more than one person is charged with a crime like the possession of a weapon, to ensure conviction the Crown must prove that each of the accused had 'custody, assent and knowledge' of the crime. If any one of these ingredients is missing then the case against them all fails. In layman's terms, the ruling meant 'the State must prove its case'. The Court upheld the appeal and the Whelan brothers were freed.

All legal advances made in these two cases were overturned with the introduction to Northern Ireland of the non-jury Diplock Courts. This controversial legal system, named after the man who devised it, Lord Diplock, was in part an attempt to get over the problem of jury members being intimidated, which was a common occurrence at this time. Thousands of terrorist cases were dealt with under the Diplock Court system.

Detective Superintendent Etheridge returned to England with his tail between his legs, having failed to teach the Paddies a lesson. Years later he found himself on the other side of the law and was convicted in a police corruption case.

A number of years later, during a search of a premises owned by Guerrero at Alliance Avenue, police found a handgun and ammunition. The garage owner Maximo de Magollon Guerrero was arrested and charged with the illegal possession of the arms. It was fairly obvious from the start that the Peruvian mechanic had absolutely no knowledge that the weapon was on his premises. At one point the case descended into farce during an exchange between the accused and the prosecuting counsel. The row centred on a black French-style hat, which is also favoured in Ireland by members of the IRA. The Crown wanted to know if Guerrero was aware that a black beret was discovered on his premises. The accused, who spoke with a thick South American accent, had great difficulty in understanding what the prosecution was talking about. But eventually the problem was solved when the garage owner realised the problem lay with the lawyer's pronunciation of the word 'beret'. (In Belfast, the t is pronounced.)

In a classic piece of courtroom drama, Guerrero leaned forward in the witness box and told the Crown lawyer: 'Ah . . . no is beret.' And to hammer home his point he repeated: 'No is beret . . . is beret!' (Parisian style). The courtroom collapsed in floods of laughter.

There was no case to answer and Maximo de Magollon Guerrero walked from court a free man. Years later, however, terror returned to haunt the Guerrero family. In 1993 loyalist gunmen walked up to the door of his Belfast home and, when his wife Terese answered, shot her dead. To terrorists, 'The Whelan Principle' or anything resembling proof or justice was meaningless.

Two days after Constable Raymond Carroll was murdered, an event in Derry changed the course of Irish history. Members of the 1st Battalion Parachute Regiment shot dead 13 civilians and wounded 17 others. The slaughter began at the end of a massive civil rights rally, which had been attended by around 10,000 people. Stone-throwing enraged the soldiers, who replied with plastic bullets and the use of a water canon. The rioting began to escalate, with more and more young people joining in. Most civil rights supporters were still trying to make their way home when things took a deadly turn for the worse.

Suddenly a shot rang out, probably fired by a member of the Official IRA, which was still strong in the city at that time. This was the catalyst for the troops to engage in a 15-minute gunfire frenzy which changed the city of Derry forever.

Most of the civil rights marchers who died were shot as they ran away and some as they tried to assist the dying.

Before the Troubles, Derry, whilst it was always nationalist in the aspirational sense, was never what could be described as 'republican'. Members of the republican movement were viewed as oddballs, native oddballs, but oddballs none the less. A majority of families had some connection with the British forces, not least because a stint in the services was a way of easing the chronic male unemployment problem which had blighted the city for generations.

Every bullet fired by the Paras on what became known as 'Bloody Sunday' took a little bit of Anglo-Irish good relations with it and, with the death toll mounting, by the end of the day there was nothing left at all. The city was stunned. Fear turned to panic and then anger.

Within hours, Lord Balneil, the British Defence Secretary, exonerated the Paras. They were responding to gunmen and nail-bombers, he said. The waves of anger that swelled in Derry began to flood across the rest of Ireland in a massive tidal movement. Social Democratic and Labour Party (SDLP) spokesman in Derry, John Hume, who did not attend the march that day, but who lived on the hill overlooking the Bogside district where the shootings took place, caught the mood of the moment when he said in a TV interview: 'Many people down there [the Bogside] feel that it's now a united Ireland or nothing.' It was a statement made to reflect the sea change in his city but it followed John Hume for the rest of his career, not least because unionists believed it revealed where Hume's true sentiments lay.

The shootings were headline news everywhere. British soldiers shooting UK civilians dead was the biggest story involving the army since the Nazi surrender of Second World War. Britain stood condemned throughout the civilised world.

In the House of Commons, Bernadette Devlin MP accused the Tory Home Secretary Reginald Maudling of lying to the House. In a bitter exchange, she snarled: 'No one shot at the paratroops, but someone will shortly . . .' The MP, who was present in Derry during the firing, then ran across the chamber and pulled Maudling's hair and slapped his face. In an interview later she said: 'I didn't shoot him in the back, which is what they did to our people.'

The British Embassy in Dublin was burned to the ground and in Britain too people took to the streets to vent their anger. Some British newspapers began demanding a 'Troops Out' initiative. The sight of the row of coffins in front of the altar of St Mary's Catholic Church in the Creggan, where many of the dead came from, brought not just grief, but again anger.

As the dead were buried, many young people vowed revenge and the biggest beneficiary was the Provisional IRA. It seemed that six months after internment without trial, the British had changed tactic and were now shooting civil rights demonstrators. Something had to be done and many of the young men and women who stood in that bleak cemetery in February in 1972 were ready and more than capable of doing it. Within a few short years, many of those young people who joined the Provos in the wake of 'Bloody Sunday' were either dead or languishing in jail having claimed, or attempted to claim, the lives of others.

There were no winners on Bloody Sunday. Everyone, even the soldiers who fired that hail of death, lost. Any remaining trust the nationalist community had in the British was gone. As far as the people of Derry were concerned, this was the Black and Tans in different uniforms. The event left an open wound in Derry that, 30 years later, remains to be healed. The Widgery Tribunal set up by the British shortly after the shootings offered some flicker of hope to the families that the truth of that day might be told. But in the end it came to nothing. Widgery was a whitewash and the people of Derry knew it.

In announcing the current Saville Inquiry into the events of Bloody Sunday, Tony Blair, the British Prime Minister, offered the families of the victims renewed hope. Sinn Fein's Martin McGuinness – a former chief-of-staff of the Provisional IRA, and now Minister for Education in the devolved administration at Stormont – has agreed to give evidence in person. There has been much speculation about McGuinness' movement on that day and some have even gone as far as to say that it was he who fired the first shot. McGuinness has denied this and he has also denied he had planned a nail-bomb attack on troops which was subsequently cancelled.

One irrefutable consequence of Bloody Sunday was the collapse of Stormont and the introduction of direct rule from London. In one fell swoop, 50 years of continuous Unionist rule was swept away. On 24 March, the Conservative Prime Minister Edward Heath announced the suspension of Stormont for one year, after the Unionists refused to accept that powers of law and order should be transferred to London.

It would be over a quarter of a century before Stormont would be reinstated and this time, following the signing of the Belfast Agreement (the Good Friday Agreement), the Unionists would share power with sworn enemies – the representatives of Irish nationalism and republicanism, including those of the IRA. Bloody Sunday had changed everything.

Republican terrorist organisations competed to avenge Bloody Sunday. The Provos were still struggling to develop as an organisation. There were

Mick Ryan at Sean South's funeral.

LIEUT. CONNIE GREEN
WHO DIED FOR IRELAND

A rare picture of Connie Green, Second World War hero and Saor Uladh volunteer.

Manus Canning, John Stephenson
(later Sean MacStiofain) and Cathal Goulding after
they were arrested for the arms raid on Felstead
Barracks in 1953.

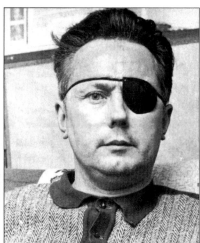

Cathal Goulding, 1970.   Sean MacStiofain, 1970.

The Rev. Ian Paisley demonstrating against the liberal Unionist
prime minister, Captain Terence O'Neill.

Gusty Spence after his
arrest for the Malvern
Street shootings.

Free Derry Corner.

Gerry Adams
(front row, centre)
on a barmen's
outing to the
Guinness Brewery.
Private Collection.

ABOVE (*left*): Nine-year-old Patrick Rooney, the first child to become a victim of the Troubles.

ABOVE (*right*): RUC Constable Victor Arbuckle, the first policeman to be killed in the Troubles.

RIGHT: Gunner Robert Curtis, the first serving British soldier to lose his life on Irish soil since the War of Independence 50 years previously.

Paddy Joe McClean, one of the 'Hooded Men' tortured by the British Army.

Colm Carey, first victim of an IRA 'punishment' shooting.

The devastation wreaked by an IRA pub bomb.

Willie Carlin at the house in Limavady
where he used to meet his MI5 handler.
Picture by Alwyn James, courtesy of the
Sunday World.

Mickey Mooney, the first big-time drugs
dealer to be executed by the IRA.

Noel 'Nogi' Shaw, who became a Shankill Butchers' victim as a result of an attempt by the UVF leadership to clean up the image of the organisation.

Gerald McLaverty, the only known person to have entered the Butchers' torture chamber and lived to tell the tale. Picture by Alwyn James, courtesy of the *Sunday World*.

A modern-day UVF hit squad from the Mount Vernon area of Belfast.

Johnny Adair –
Director of Terrorism.

Martin O'Hagan, the first
journalist killed by terrorists
in Northern Ireland.
Picture by Alwyn James, courtesy
of the *Sunday World*.

hundreds of young people willing to join up, but without proper military training they were more likely to be a danger to themselves. In the aftermath of Bloody Sunday dozens of young Provo recruits lost their lives in premature explosions – testimony to their lack of arms and explosives training.

The Officials, on the other hand, had a network of members and supporters throughout Great Britain. Seamus Costello, the Officials' director of operations, wanted the British government to know in no uncertain terms that his wing of the Irish Republican Army had no intention of allowing the British Army to mow down Irish civilians without reply. The Officials hadn't wanted a war – and they viewed the impending removal of Stormont as a retrograde step – but, they claimed, some sort of stance had to be taken and the Paras, as the elite force of the British Army, were a good target.

As Costello based in Dublin plotted a 'spectacular' attack on the Paras, local units in the North seized every opportunity to exact revenge. On 6 February, the body of David Seaman, a former psychiatric patient who had had the briefest of flirtations with the Parachute Regiment, was found shot dead in south Armagh near the Louth–Monaghan border. He had been shot five times in the back of the head and his eyes had been taped. He had the crest of the Paratroop Regiment tattooed on one of his arms.

Six months before, using the name Hans Kruger, Seaman had appeared at a press conference organised by the Official IRA. He claimed he was a British soldier who was involved in 'dirty tricks' aimed at discrediting the IRA. In reality, Seaman was a fantasist. He had been born in Manchester to a family called Barber, but had changed his name. In 1957 Seaman joined the Paras, but was booted out after a month.

Exactly a week later, the gun which killed David Seaman claimed the life of Thomas McCann, a Dublin-born soldier serving with the Royal Army Ordnance Corps. The body of 19-year-old McCann was found hooded and gagged at Newtownbutler, Co. Fermanagh. The soldier had asked to be transferred to Northern Ireland so he could visit his mum in Dublin on a regular basis. The army had agreed to his request on compassionate grounds.

On 16 February, the Provos underlined a warning given to the Catholic community two months earlier. Shortly before Christmas, republicans had shot dead Sean Russell in his home at Ballymurphy, Belfast, in front of his wife and family. He was the first Catholic member of the UDR to be executed. The killing was a stark reminder to Catholics of the dangers of having anything to do with the British system of government and the Provos were determined to let everyone know Sean Russell's murder wasn't a mistake.

The Ulster Defence Regiment had been set up in the wake of the Hunt Report to replace the Protestant militia, the notorious B Specials, and

Thomas Callaghan, a 47-year-old married man from Limavady, had joined up. Mr Callaghan, a Catholic who worked as a bus driver for a living, was one of a number of his co-religionists who felt the time was right for Catholics to embrace the changes by making some sort of contribution. But the Provos had other ideas. As he drove his one-man-operated bus through the Creggan district of Derry, Thomas Callaghan was dragged from his cab and, as screaming passengers looked on, was bundled into a car. Three hours later his hooded and gagged body was found near the River Foyle.

Less than a week later, a member of the Official IRA, in Parachute Regiment uniform, drove a Mark 1 Cortina car into the headquarters of the 16th Parachute Brigade at Aldershot, Hampshire, and parked it next to the officers' mess. The driver, who was himself a former Para, got out and walked away. Minutes later a massive explosion ripped through the three-storey building, bringing most of it to the ground. All that was left was the frame of the property.

Five women, Jill Mansfield, Margaret Grant, Thelma Bosely, Cherie Munton and Joan Lunn, all members of the domestic staff who were preparing meals, lost their lives. John Haslar, a 58-year-old gardener, was also killed, as was Father Gerry Weston, a 38-year-old army chaplain with the rank of captain. Father Weston had served in the Ballymurphy area of Belfast and a week before the bomb had been awarded the MBE for his work in that trouble-torn part of Ulster. Seventeen others, including serving soldiers, were injured.

Very quickly the Official IRA issued a statement claiming responsibility and adding that the attack was in direct retaliation for the deaths of Irish civilians in Derry on Bloody Sunday. Clearly the Officials, and Seamus Costello in particular, were delighted with their handiwork. But at the time the first statement was issued, details of the casualties were unknown.

The Aldershot blast was the first of many murderous operations mounted by Irish republicans at military bases on the British mainland. The day of the car bomb had arrived and its significance was not lost on the Provos, some of whom were jealous that it was their former comrades-in-arms and not them who had delivered the headline-grabbing retaliation for Bloody Sunday.

Within hours, however, it emerged that the IRA hadn't killed any soldiers. With five women kitchen workers, a gardener and a priest murdered, the Aldershot attack did not seem such a great blow for freedom after all. Unlike the Provos, the Officials prided themselves on being a revolutionary militia out to defend the rights of poorly paid workers. Now they were murdering them in the name of people of Ireland.

In a bungled effort at damage limitation, the Officials issued a second statement claiming their own intelligence reports revealed that at least 12 high-ranking officers had been killed. The Brits were lying through their teeth, they said. According to them, the British had somehow managed to smuggle out mangled bodies of officers as part of a black propaganda exercise.

The Officials were wrong. There were no dead Paras, officers or men. The only dead in Aldershot were the five female domestic staff, the elderly gardener and the Catholic padre. It was hardly a blow for the revolution.

The catalyst for the Aldershot attack had been Seamus Costello, the Official IRA's director of operations. Costello, from Bray, Co. Wicklow, was a veteran of the '50s campaign. He achieved hero status among republicans in south Derry when he burned down Magherafelt Court House (now refurbished, it is a tourist attraction). A one-time used-car salesman, Costello commanded widespread respect among the 'physical force' elements still in the Officials and following the introduction of internment he had been keen to pull off a spectacular on mainland Britain. He was determined not to allow the Provos the stage to themselves.

The Officials tapped into their network of members throughout the UK and shortly before Christmas the push was on to produce a major military operation. An Offical IRA unit based in Bristol stole a massive amount of gelignite from a quarry in the West Country. But, unknown to the IRA, one member of the unit – a man known in IRA circles as 'Flasher' – had been turned by Bristol Special Branch and the cops were kept aware of most developments.

The Bloody Sunday shootings sent Costello into a frenzy and he demanded an immediate response. The explosives were moved into position, as were detonators stolen from a quarry in Scotland. Anthony Doran, the Official IRA's Operations Officer in Belfast, was despatched to Engand to oversee the operation. Another man with bomb-making skills was also sent to England. The outcome of Doran's trip was the bombing of the officers' mess at Aldershot.

Anthony Doran returned safely to Ireland, but massive police swoops right across Britain put the Officials' UK network under severe pressure. Noel Jenkinson, a native of Co. Meath and a member of Clann na hEireann, a support group for the Officials, was arrested as a result of information supplied by Flasher, and when the police discovered another bomb in a garden shed at Jenkinson's house there was always only going to be one outcome. Whether Jenkinson played a significant role in the Aldershot bombing is open to debate, but he is the man who was prosecuted and he was handed a 30-year sentence when he appeared at the Old Bailey charged with mass murder.

Roy Johnston, the Marxist guru who had thought he could help transform the IRA into a revolutionary machine, left the organisation after this atrocity. Revolutionary theory was one thing but bombing poorly paid workers and priests was another. This belonged to the Fenian Movement of the last century, he thought. In the end, Johnston did not have the stomach for it and he realised not all IRA volunteers had the same outlook as his friend Cathal Goulding.

Two years after the Aldershot atrocity, Seamus Costello was dismissed from the Officials following a court martial. He was found guilty and he immediately formed the Irish National Liberation Army (INLA). One of Costello's first recruits was Anthony Doran. A substantial section of the Official's membership in Belfast and Derry also left to join the new terror group.

The army held a small remembrance service for the Aldershot victims on the 30th anniversary of the bombing – but only decided to do so after being contacted by *Daily Telegraph* journalist David Sharrock. Unlike republicans', establishment memories are short.

Three days after the Aldershot bombing, the Officials went on the offensive again. This time John Taylor, the Stormont Minister of State for Home Affairs, was the target. As Taylor emerged from his office at The Mall in the centre of Armagh, he was ambushed by four Official IRA gunmen, including Joe McCann. As he stepped into his car, Taylor was shot. Five bullets hit him in the head, shattering his jaw, and another ten missed him by inches. Miraculously, Taylor survived and today a wooden replica of his jaw is used in the training of paramedic staff employed by the ambulance service.

Back in Derry, however, rank and file Officials didn't care if the Aldershot attack had been bungled. It was the thought that counted. The 'Stickies', as the Officials were known locally, set about the task of building on their recent 'success' as they saw it. The new influx of volunteers who joined the Officials after Bloody Sunday were delighted to find out that they were 'revolutionaries' as well. They hadn't realised they were part of a worldwide communist conspiracy. But, of course, as guns were now flooding into the North like never before, the Stickies had competition in the form of the Provos. Many an argument broke out on the streets of Derry about which group was the true inheritor of the mantle of republicanism. There had never been great support there for physical force republicanism, and so the tension between the two groups tended to manifest itself in rows about not having enough respect to stop at each other's vehicle checkpoints. Most recruits wanted action, and if that meant facing down a rival republican faction, then so be it. However, the vicious and murderous feuding which consumed republican areas of Belfast when the Officials and the Provisionals disagreed was largely absent in Derry.

Writer Eamonn McCann, who has been active in left-wing politics in Derry for most of his life, believes the all-embracing power Derry mothers exert over their families, and sons in particular, went a long way to preventing that kind of bloodshed. It is a matter of historical record that the protesting action of women contributed greatly to the demise of the Official IRA in Derry.

On the morning of 4 March the body of Marcus McCausland was found on wasteground near the rear entrance to the Termonbacca Boys Home, close to the Creggan district. He had been shot three times. Forensic evidence revealed he had been tortured before his body was dumped on a mound of snow. One bullet had removed part of his thumb, whilst another had entered his neck. The third bullet was fired into his temple at close range. Thirty-nine-year-old McCausland was a member of a wealthy land-owning family which had been in Ireland since the time of the Elizabethan Plantation in the seventeenth century. The family estate at Drinagh, near Limavady, Co. Derry, was sometimes a venue for National Trust open days where members of the public were encouraged to view the delightful gardens. Marcus McCausland, who was 6 ft 5 in. tall, had been educated at Eton and had served in the Irish Guards Regiment, as had his father, Lt. Colonel Connolly McCausland. His mother, Lady Margaret McCausland, was the vice-president of the Alliance Party. Marcus McCausland and his Argentinian-born wife June had two sons and a daughter. At the time he was killed, he was a captain serving with the Ulster Defence Regiment.

Given their background, steeped in the landed gentry and the military, the McCauslands were a most unusual family in that they were followers of the Roman Catholic faith and regularly worshipped at the local Catholic church in Limavady.

Lt. Colonel Connolly McCausland had renounced his Protestant faith after coming into contact with some Jesuit priests prior to the Second World War. Converting to the Church of Rome had not been an easy experience for Connolly McCausland because some trustees of the Drinagh estate – the McCausland family seat – attempted to prevent the estate being passed on to Marcus McCausland in the event of his father's death. One of the trustees pushing for this action was Sir Norman Stronge, a veteran Unionist politician and landowner who was shot dead by the IRA along with his son James, when masked men broke into their home at Tynan Abbey.

Sir Norman was 86 years old at the time and was one of the oldest civilians to be killed in the Troubles. His efforts at altering the McCausland family inheritance proved unsuccessful, however, because Marcus McCausland was at that time still a Protestant. It was sometime later before he followed his father into the Catholic Church.

On the night Marcus McCausland was abducted and killed, he was visiting friends on Inch Island, a popular beauty spot near Buncrana, Co. Donegal, around ten miles from Derry. He enjoyed a drink and the social intercourse which went with it. McCausland particularly liked lively political debate because he cared passionately about the country which had been home to his family for over 300 years.

Marcus told his friends that he was considering resigning from the UDR because he could not reconcile his membership of the regiment with the government policy of interment without trial. It was against the way of natural justice, he argued. He maintained that republicans were good people at heart and they were only adopting their current position because unionism had failed them. McCausland's friends accused him of being naïve and, in a reckless act of bravado, he decided to prove them wrong. He jumped into his car at 4.00 a.m. and drove straight to Derry's Bogside, which was at that time a no-go area for troops and police. He was never seen alive again. Marcus McCausland was the third Catholic member of the UDR to be murdered by republicans.

Captain McCausland was killed by the Official IRA. The organisation claimed McCausland was in the process of building up an intelligence network for the British. The allegation was nonsense and anyone who knew Marcus McCausland knew it.

In April of the same year, Joe McCann, the Belfast IRA officer who had become a thorn in the side of the British Army, was shot dead by Paratroopers as he tried to evade them in the Markets area of the city. He was unarmed and could easily have been arrested instead of killed. A known gunman who was a member of the organisation which had bombed Aldershot, there was no way the Paras were going to allow him to escape. Without doubt, McCann was directly responsible for the deaths of several British soldiers, but, by any standards, Joe McCann, too, was murdered. He was the first victim of an unadmitted shoot-to-kill policy by the security forces.

By now, members of the Official IRA working out of its GHQ in Dublin were becoming increasingly alarmed at the direction the organisation was taking. Where were all the noble sentiments of peace, work and class politics? Was the execution of Marcus McCausland what class warfare really meant? There were precious few answers coming out of Derry, that's for sure, and the political gap between Dublin and Derry was growing. But the gun-toting faction of Officials weren't finished yet.

The leadership of the Official republican movement wanted a coalition of left-wing interests to stand firmly together in opposition to the tit-for-tat sectarian slaughter which was emerging in the North. It believed the people of both religious camps would support such a move. And, although the Dublin-based Officials always kept one jaundiced eye on growing support for the Provos, they were convinced they would win out in the end. However, they had one major problem – a substantial minority of the membership of the Official republican movement still believed political power could be achieved through the barrel of a gun – particularly in Derry.

Shortly before 7 a.m. on 21 May 1972, a male nurse found the dead body of 19-year-old William Best lying on waste ground near Quinn's Lane off William Street at the entrance to the Bogside. He had been shot and marks on his body indicated he had been punched and kicked. William Best, from Rathkeele Way in the Creggan estate, was a soldier serving with the Royal Irish Rangers Regiment of the British Army. He had been home on leave and had spoken to friends about deserting.

The evening before his body was found, William Best left his parents' home to make a phone call, but never returned. He had been abducted by members of the Official IRA. The teenager was questioned at the Officials' Derry HQ and then beaten before being sentenced to death and executed. One of those involved in the soldier's interrogation later drank himself to death.

No one in the Officials in Derry could have anticipated the fall-out from Ranger Best's execution. This wasn't one of the Paras who had gunned down civil rights protesters on Bloody Sunday. William Best was a local boy who had joined the army to find a job. He had family in the Creggan and he was one of their own. Soon the power of the 'Derry mother' Eamonn McCann had spoken about came into full view and it was a fearsome sight. Two hundred women, including Mary Nelis, now a Sinn Fein MLA (a Member of the Legislative Assembly at Stormont), but then an SDLP supporter, marched on the Official IRA's premises demanding they get out of town. The hapless Stickie volunteers cowered inside wondering what to do. One unarmed soldier they could easily handle, but 200 angry women were something else.

The officials had issued a statement locally, saying Ranger Best had been 'apprehended in suspicious circumstances, tried by an IRA court and sentenced to death'. Then, in an astonishing display of arrogance typical of dictatorial paramilitary organisations, the statement added: 'The ruthlessness shown by the British Forces against the people of Free Derry could only be answered in similar terms.'

It was, however, the final words of the press release which spurred the women into action and finished the Officials as a paramilitary force in Derry. It read: 'Regardless of calls for peace from slobbering moderates, while British gunmen remain on the streets in the Six Counties, the IRA [Official] will take action against them.'

The Officials had committed political suicide as far as Derry was concerned and on 28 May, 6,000 people attended a peace rally in Shantallow, a sprawling housing estate on the other side of town. The following day, 29 May, the Official IRA called 'an immediate cessation of all hostilities'. The organisation said it was doing so in accordance with the wishes of the vast majority of the people in the North. The Officials did, however, reserve the right to self-defence in the face of attack by sectarian elements or the British Army.

The statement, which was issued from the Officials' HQ at Gardiner Place in Dublin, was a strong indication that those in the leadership who favoured political activity over the gun had won the internal debate. Although there were others who would later leave to form the deadly divisions of the Irish National Liberation Army, for the Officials, the war against the British at least was over.

Following Ranger William Best's murder, Frank Cahill, a brother of Provo boss Joe Cahill, approached a leading member of the Officials, demanding a meeting with Billy McMillen, the Official's Belfast leader, as quickly as possible. The reason for calling the meeting, he said, was because 'Yous are killin' too many Catholics', and he cited the deaths of Father Gerry Weston at Aldershot and Marcus McCausland and Ranger Best in Derry as examples.

Less than five years later, however, the Provisionals had clearly got over their qualms about killing Catholics who were in some way linked to the military. John Lee, a 35-year-old married father of three, was shot six times in the back of the head. The IRA killed him by rifle fire as he emerged with his wife from the Crumlin Star Social Club.

John Lee lived at Mountainview Gardens, and had been born and raised in Ardoyne. He was just 18 when he joined the Parachute Regiment. The Lee family were all very hard-working and John's decision to join the army was based purely on economics. When he left the army, he came back to Belfast, but, as he was concerned about bringing his family up during the Troubles, he and his wife took their children back to England, where once again he joined the Paras. Lee managed to get an agreement that he would not have to serve in Northern Ireland and he was given a job in the army stores.

Lee, who was known to his friends as 'Jackie', quit the army for the second time in 1975. He and his family moved back to Northern Ireland, where they set up home in a loyalist estate in Bangor, Co. Down. However, the former soldier became concerned that his young family were being subjected to sectarian abuse and decided that they would be better off living in the place where he was born – the Ardoyne district of Belfast. John and his wife Mary were delighted when they managed to get a house in Chatham Street, where they were welcomed by their neighbours.

John Lee felt safe in Ardoyne. He believed the IRA would never bother him because his father, Thomas 'Tansy' Lee, had helped keep the flame of republicanism alight in the area during the barren years of the 1930s and '40s. During the War of Independence in 1921, Tansy Lee's uncle had been taken from his Ardoyne home by the Black and Tans (a notoriously vicious section of the British Army) and tied to a tree before being shot dead.

In the year 2002 only one death notice in the local newspaper, the *Irish News*, recalled John Lee's memory. It was from his wife and made no reference to the appalling circumstances of his death.

By the end of its brief foray onto the stage of paramilitary murder, the Official IRA had claimed the lives of 54 people. Its republican rival, however, the Provisional IRA, was responsible for the deaths of 1,778 or 48.7 per cent of the total deaths.

The terrible year of 1972 was without a doubt the worst in three decades of unremitting slaughter. Nearly 500 people lost their lives – the vast majority unarmed civilians. In July of that year the Provos gave an indication of what was to come when on 21 July, on what became known as 'Bloody Friday', the IRA detonated 22 bombs in Belfast in the space of one hour. Nine people were killed and 130 were injured. Police believe Seamus Twomey – a former bookmaker's clerk who was the Officer Commanding the IRA in Belfast at that time – gave the go-ahead for the attack. Twomey's second-in-command was Gerry Adams. Thirty years after this dreadul event the IRA issued a statement of apology for killing what it called 'non-combatants' and, days after the apology was issued, Gerry Adams denied any involvement in the Bloody Friday atrocities. He also denied ever being a member of the IRA – a statement which both shocked and amused some of his republican comrades.

-CHAPTER ELEVEN -

Bernard Moane, Patsy Gillespie and James McAvoy – Family Men Doing a Day's Work

> Daddy, sing the 'Forty Shades of Green'.
> *A request from Benny Moane's children to entertain them during*
> *long car journeys back to Fermanagh*

The vast majority of those killed in the Troubles were not paramilitaries, police or army personnel. Many of those who died were just ordinary people going about their own business or doing a day's work. Drinks salesman Bernard 'Benny' Moane, cook Patsy Gillespie and filling station owner James McAvoy were all victims who fell into that category.

The Moanes originated in a place called Moanes' Cross, which, as the name suggests, is a crossroads in the townland of Cooneen, near Roslea, Co. Fermanagh. But as work was hard to find in that beautiful part of Ulster, known as the lakelands, some members of the family left and settled in Belfast, where they found employment.

Benny Moane was 46 years old when he was killed. He lived with his wife Dorothea and two sons, Bernard (15), who was called after his father, and Michael (10), who would later follow in his father's footsteps by carving out a successful career in the drinks industry. Bernard and Dorothea also had four daughters, Dorothea (14), named for her mother, Ann (12), Lorraine (9) and the youngest member of the family was Patricia, who was six. Bernard and Dorothea lived for their family and the Moane children were encouraged to respect others regardless of their religion or political conviction. The Moanes lived in a comfortable semi-detached house on Ailesbury Avenue, off Belfast's Ormeau Road – a mixed area which prided itself in a degree of tolerance sadly missing in other parts of the city.

Benny's pride and joy was his eldest son Bernard. A keen footballer, Bernard had been a trialist goalkeeper with Glentoran, the east Belfast side which, under the guidance of ex-Celtic star John Colrain, had taken the legendary Benfica (Eusebio included) to the wire in the European Cup in the mid-'60s.

Benny Moane had a reputation for being a hard worker in his job as a traveller with the local drinks company Irish Bonding. But he also had a great sense of humour and enjoyed a joke.

Young Bernard, through his father's connections, managed to get a part-time job working as a glass collector in the Parador Hotel which was just a short walk from the Moane family home and once, for a laugh, Benny Moane knocked on the pub door after time and when his son answered asked if it was all right if he and his friends came in for a late drink. 'I'm sorry, Daddy, we're closed now,' said Bernard before the publican, who was a personal friend of Benny's, intervened to bring the men inside.

Benny Moane was popular with a wide circle of friends and he was known the length and breadth of the Falls and Shankill Roads, where he plied his trade as a drinks salesman. Nothing was ever too much bother for him as far as his customers were concerned. After all, it was the publicans of Belfast who kept him in a job and therefore helped provide the money he needed to bring up his family in the best possible manner. Benny Moane understood the drinks business, he knew what publicans needed and he was only too willing to provide a service for them.

As a man who enjoyed the camaraderie of the pub himself, Benny Moane was never found wanting when it came to buying his round. He also often bought a pint or two for customers when he called into pubs during working hours.

As he sat eating breakfast in his home on 17 May 1972, Benny Moane contemplated the busy day in front of him. It was his day to cover the Shankill Road area of Belfast, a district packed with pubs. It was Benny's job to ensure they were kept well supplied.

It was a fine Tuesday morning, the sun was shining that day and business was brisk. So Benny decided to carry on working through the lunch hour to ensure all his calls were covered. After leaving the Rex Bar, he made his way to the Woodvale Arms at the corner of the Shankill Road and Ainsworth Avenue. The publican there had a problem with his previous delivery and Benny was anxious to sort it out.

As he walked through the door of the Woodvale, Benny noticed three men, who were all regulars and lived locally, sitting at a table in the corner of the pub. Being a good sales representative, he also noticed the men's glasses were almost empty, so he instructed the barman to replenish them. The men, 19-year-old Joe McAllister, 24-year-old James Welshman and 38-year-old Sam 'Saucie' Swain, were all unemployed and so a free pint from an unexpected source was more than welcome. When the pints arrived on the table the men, all members of the local branch of the UDA, raised their glasses in acknowledgement of the kind act. The UDA had been formed the year before out of vigilante groups which had sprung up in Protestant areas as a means of defence against possible IRA attack.

The UDA men were within earshot of the bar and could hear Benny discussing business with the man behind the bar. The bartender explained that in his last delivery he had received whiskey in bottles which were too small for the volume of business the pub was doing and he wondered if Benny could replace them. After that, the conversation drifted on to family matters and it must have been obvious to the UDA men that the affable salesman who bought them a drink was a Catholic.

In Belfast, even simple things like names can be a guide to a person's religious background. Certainly the Christian name 'Benny' is much more prevalent in men of Roman Catholic faith and it could have been this which alerted the UDA members to the fact that the kind stranger in their midst wasn't 'one of our own'.

Benny Moane was so busy chatting to his customer he almost forgot the reason why he had called to the Woodvale Arms in the first place. But a glance at the small whiskey bottles on the gantry reminded him and he went out to his Austin Maxi car, which was parked outside, and brought two large bottles into the bar and accepted a smaller one as a return. As he made his goodbyes, Benny Moane waved over to the young men in the corner before heading for the exit.

Suddenly, as he opened the pub door, he felt a blunt object being pressed into his back and turned to see Joe McAllister pointing a gun at him. 'UDA, move outside,' McAllister said sternly and as he walked out the door. James Welshman and 'Saucie' Swain followed. It was 1.45 p.m.

All four men got into Benny Moane's car, but what happened immediately after this is unclear. What is known, however, is that around 15 minutes later the car containing its four occupants arrived at the County Antrim War Memorial, known locally as the Knockagh Monument – a well-known beauty spot high above the outlying district of Greenisland on the northern shore of Belfast Lough. The monument, which is 1,000 feet above sea level, commemorates the fallen heroes from County Antrim – both Catholic and Protestant – who lost their lives in the First World War.

McAllister, who appeared to be the leader, ordered Benny Moane out of the car and they all walked over to the edge of the cliff, which has commanding views over Belfast Lough as well as large parts of Co. Antrim and Co. Down. On a clear day the Ayrshire coast in Scotland can be seen easily and, as a result, it is a popular place for hillwalkers, as well as for family picnics.

Benny Moane knew the Knockagh Monument well. In fact, when he was doing his rounds along the towns and villages of that part of Co. Antrim, he would often call up there for an hour at lunchtime to relax and enjoy the sandwiches and flask of tea Dorothea had packed for him.

For a moment or two, Benny wondered if the men would be foolish enough to try to push him over, but then he relaxed somewhat when McAllister ordered him back to the base of the monument, which is some distance back from the cliff edge. McAllister then told 'Saucie' Swain, who was the eldest of the UDA men, to check the boot of the car to see if there were bottles of alcohol in it. Swain came back with a bottle of whiskey and some small bottles of Guinness, which he opened by banging the tin tops on a cornerstone. For a while a degree of normality descended on the situation, as the UDA gang started to relax over a few drinks. Saucie Swain was asked to take another trip to the car to retrieve more Guinness and McAllister displayed an element of compassion by offering Benny Moane a bottle, which he accepted. Police believe Benny Moane thought he may have been able to persuade the men, who were all several years his junior, to let him go.

A short time later a car arrived at the monument car park and when the occupant, who was intending going for a walk, got out, he was approached by Sam Welshman who asked him if he was a 'Mick or a Prod'. The man, who had a mystified look on his face, told Welshman he was a Presbyterian. The UDA man then said: 'You've walked into something here, we're going to fill this guy in. He's an IRA man.'

Welshman then told the man that the reason he and his friends were going to murder the man in their custody was that he had been involved in the killing of a UDR man in Co. Tyrone. The claim was, of course, nonsense, as Benny Moane had never been involved in politics or paramilitarism of any kind.

Within minutes, two other cars arrived and Welshman, who was by now acting as look-out, ordered the first driver to let the tyres down on the other two vehicles. There was an argument and Welshman told them to 'F★★k off!' He then turned to one of the men, who was with his wife and child, and said: 'There's something bad going to happen here and enough bad things have happened in this country without that child seeing any more.' At that, the couple hurried off, but rang the police at their first opportunity.

One of the men, who spoke to Benny Moane briefly, was held at the scene and he was still there when Joe McAllister walked up to Benny Moane and raised an automatic pistol to his forehead. Mr Moane was heard to say 'Ah, no, boys' before three shots were fired in quick succession into his head. McAllister shot Benny Moane between the eyes. He died instantly. The gunmen then ran to Mr Moane's car and forced the man who witnessed the brutal shooting to come with them.

Without a word passing between them, the UDA murder gang drove the man to a nearby road junction before stopping and ordering him out. The killers then travelled at speed back to the Shankill district, where Mr Moane's car was abandoned in Battenberg Street. It is believed that at this point the gang were assisted by a 70 year old, who lived in the street. All three men removed any remaining bottles of alcohol from the vehicle, which they sold for the princely sum of two pounds.

Right-thinking members of the public were outraged as details of the savagery of the murder began to emerge. Two days later Mr Moane's funeral took place at the Holy Rosary Church on the Ormeau Road. Around one thousand people attended the Requiem Mass and the Irish Bonding company closed its Belfast depot as a mark of respect for their esteemed colleague. Five hundred men followed the funeral cortège before the coffin was placed in the hearse and driven to Milltown cemetery. Grown men wept openly as the Moane children climbed into the funeral car to accompany their father on his final journey.

Newspaper reports at the time reflected how popular Benny Moane was with friends and work colleagues. One man said: 'Benny was a terribly decent man who lived for his family. He enjoyed a drink and was popular with everyone.'

An RUC murder investigation swung into action and very quickly arrests were made. McAllister, Welshman and Swain were among the first to be brought in, but of course they denied any involvement in the crime. They also denied ever having been at the Knockagh Monument and one of them even claimed he didn't know where it was, although it can be seen from most of north and west Belfast. But, unknown to the killers, the police had recovered Mr Moane's gold-coloured Maxi car within hours of the murder. The fingerprints of all three were found on the vehicle, as well as on bottles recovered from the murder scene.

When they went on trial at Antrim Assizes, all three UDA men denied the charges against them, but they didn't convince the jury, which was made up of eleven men and one woman. The jury brought a majority verdict of guilty against McAllister and two unanimous verdicts against Welshman and Swain.

Mr Justice Gibson, who, along with his wife, was later murdered by the IRA, told the jury he 'wholeheartedly agreed' with the verdicts before discharging them from jury duty for life.

On 26 June 1973, at Crumlin Road Court House, UDA killers Joe McAllister, Sam Welshman and Sam 'Saucie' Swain, were all sent to prison for life. As they were taken down to the tunnel which links the court to Belfast Prison, the men each gave clenched fist salutes and shouted 'No surrender!' Friends and supporters repeated the loyalist slogan as staff struggled to clear the court.

A year after her husband's murder, Dorothea Moane gave a press interview where she spoke about coping without her husband and trying to plan for the future of her six children. She told the newspaper: 'I still feel numb. The most important thing in my life was my husband. My life has been completely shattered. I tried to cut myself off from the Troubles and I am really trying to get back to normal.' Mrs Moane explained how she had considered moving away from Belfast, but had decided the best thing to do was to stay, as it offered the best opportunities for her children. She said: 'The children are all at school, which means I stay in the home during the day. What else can you do? Life has to go on.' Mrs Moane then said that her children helped her to cope with the tragic loss of her husband: 'I live for my children now. I often wonder what would happen to me if they were not there,' she said.

Following his father's murder, Bernard Moane junior at 14 years of age donned the mantle of his father and assumed responsibility for his younger brother and sisters. The Moanes remain close and occasionally hold simple family gatherings in honour of their father.

Bernard Jnr is a senior civil servant with the Environment and Heritage Service, which is an Executive Department within the Department of the Environment. Ironically, his office has some responsibility for the Knockagh Monument – the beautiful Co. Antrim beauty spot where his father was murdered. Some years ago, he plucked up the courage to visit the monument and when he returned he told friends of the 'chilling feeling' which came over him as he gazed at the spot where his father and namesake lost his life.

Speaking 30 years after the incident, Bernard Moane says he bears no ill will to anyone over his father's death, although he insists the brutal killing was totally unnecessary, as his father was no threat to anyone and wished no harm to any human being. He said:

> Obviously we are still heartbroken about what happened. My mother never got over it, but we all look out for her as well as each other. The people of this country will have to rise above bigotry if we are to

move forward. Some people should learn to temper their language
when they talk about people of a different religion. We still talk about
our father and we have great memories of him singing 'The Forty
Shades of Green' in the car on the way to Fermanagh.

As his eyes filled, Bernard Moane added: 'At least we can be proud of him and
that's all he would have wanted.'

The murder gang which took the life of Benny Moane in such tragic
circumstances admitted in court to being members of the Ulster Defence
Association – by far the largest of the loyalist paramilitary groups. It was
founded in September 1971 as an umbrella organisation for several loyalist
vigilante groups which sprung up around the start of the Troubles. From
almost the beginning, the UDA has been beset with accusations of
involvement in racketeering and murder. Hundreds of its members have been
jailed for the most heinous crimes and yet, remarkably, it took the
government until 10 August 1992 to get round to proscribing the
organisation.

The terrorist attacks at New York's World Trade Center and in Washington
in the autumn of 2001, which claimed the lives of thousands of innocent
people, brought the suicide bombers of Osama Bin Laden into world focus.
The following year, when it became apparent that more Palestinians were
prepared to blow themselves up as well as others, experts on global terrorism
believed a new low had been reached. But in Ulster, the tactics of the Al-
Qaeda and PLO terrorists served to remind people that in this part of the
world the IRA once launched a wave of human bomb attacks across Northern
Ireland.

Derryman Patsy Gillespie and Newry pensioner James McAvoy were
chosen by the Provos to drive their so-called 'proxy bombs' to army
checkpoints near their homes. Those attacks claimed the lives of seven people
and injured dozens of others. On the same night, another man was to drive a
vehicle packed with explosives to the Lisanelly army base at Omagh. That
bomb failed to explode.

The difference, however, between the men who drove those vehicles and
the terrorists who flew the planes into Manhattan's World Trade Center was
that the Ulster men didn't have a choice. The men were strapped into vehicles
and forced to carry deadly cargoes to their destinations. The IRA's 'human
bomb' campaign was eventually called off, not least because of the outrage
expressed by all sections of the population.

It was probably a note smuggled out of Belfast Prison in early 1990 which was the catalyst for the IRA's 'human bomb' tactic. The tiny piece of paper, known in IRA parlance as a 'comm.', revealed for the first time how the men and women who had waged the war of attrition on behalf of the Provos and were now languishing in jail were beginning to weary of the prolonged violence. The closing lines of the note, which was sent to a leading member of the IRA on the outside, read:

> Hoping that this talk of bringing the armed struggle to a conclusion that McGuinness and Co. are talking about bears fruit, as I've thrown the hands up on at least two occasions. But I've an awful feeling that this war is set for at least another decade. Whether we have the ability to break out of the containment the Brits are imposing on the war or not, I think is crucial to the ultimate success or failure of the conflict . . .
>
> At present, I'm not optimistic about our ability to do so. You would not believe the change in attitude and resolve of the northern nationalist community regarding their commitment to the war.

These words demonstrated that the IRA – at least those members behind bars – were aware that the security forces, spearheaded by the RUC Special Branch, had at least managed to contain the IRA campaign and was on the verge of closing it down completely. The prisoners believed the IRA badly needed a new strategy which would once again bring the Northern Ireland conflict to international prominence, as the 'Long War' strategy, advocated by the Adams–McGuinness axis, clearly hadn't worked.

In 1990, Sinn Fein spokesman Martin McGuinness – a former IRA chief-of-staff – was a member of the organisation's Army Council and head of its Northern Command. He oversaw the new plan to kickstart the IRA's faltering campaign as the Army Council decided the human or proxy bomb was the answer to its problems.

Patsy Gillespie, a 42-year-old father of three from Lenamore Gardens in Derry's Galliagh district, worked as a cook in the British Army canteen at its Fort George base on the banks of the Foyle. His occupation was enough to single him out for attention. In October 1990 an IRA gang called at the Gillespie home and, holding his family hostage, the IRA ordered Patsy to drive a van bomb to the Coshquin border crossing on the outskirts of the city, a distance of about three miles.

IRA engineers had devised a detonation technique linked to the vehicle's courtesy light which came on when the van door opened and, as a safeguard, the bomb makers also employed a timing device which would ensure the bomb would go off at precisely the right moment.

The IRA men who took over the Gillespie home assured the family he would return safely and, before he left, Patsy Gillespie put his arms around his wife and daughter and said: 'Everything will be all right, don't worry.'

The security forces claim that Patsy Gillespie was then strapped into the bomb van by a man who is a well-known republican figure in Derry, but republican sources say this is not true. What is known is that, on a number of previous occasions, Patsy Gillespie had been warned to quit his job at the army base or run the risk of reprisal. Once before the terrorists had forced him to drive a proxy bomb inside the Fort George base, but on that occasion the device had failed to go off and he had managed to escape from the vehicle without any difficulty.

When Gillespie pulled up at Coshquin, he tried to get out of the van and at the same time he attempted to alert the young soldiers manning the checkpoint to the danger. But the huge bomb detonated while he was still strapped to the driving seat. Patsy Gillespie's body was blown to bits in an instant. His torso was found in a nearby field in a follow-up search the following day.

Five English soldiers, all members of the King's Regiment, also died: 23-year-old Paul Worral; 21-year-old Vincent Scott; 20-year-old Stephen Beacham, who had two children; 19-year-old David Sweeney; and 30-year-old Lance Corporal Stephen Burrows, who was married with one child.

A short time after the explosion, a group of Derrymen, including Martin McGuinness' brother Willie, were arrested by Gardai on the southern side of the border near the scene of the atrocity. The sound of the explosion echoed across Derry and a member of the IRA gang holding the Gillespie family hostage in their home turned to them and said: 'He'll be home soon.'

In February 1991, Patsy Gillespie's family joined relatives of the soldiers for a small memorial service at Coshquin border crossing, the scene of the atrocity. They were joined by several hundred, mainly Protestant, local people whose homes had been damaged in the blast. Speaking at the ceremony, Patsy Gillespie's widow, Kathleen, said her grief differed from that felt by the relatives of the dead soldiers. She said: 'I don't think it is the same grief. My circumstances are bad, because I have lost my husband. But I feel too, that it must be a terrible thing for parents to bury a child.'

Kathleen Gillespie still keeps in touch with the families of soldiers who lost their lives along with her husband. They are united only by grief and the fact that they were the victims of a terrible new terror strategy aimed at kickstarting a flagging campaign: the 'human bomb'.

The South Down Command of the IRA was ordered by a representative of the IRA Army Council to single out a local man to be used as cannon fodder in a terrorist attack in Newry, which would take place at exactly the same time as the Coshquin blast. A young IRA man from the Armagh Road area of Newry, but who was now in charge of a unit in the Mayobridge/Rathfriland district, offered 68-year-old James McAvoy as the sacrificial lamb.

Mr McAvoy's so-called crime, as far as the IRA man was concerned, was that he owned a filling station where policemen sometimes called to purchase ice cream and soft drinks. At least ten IRA volunteers were involved in the 'human bomb' operation in Newry.

The first thing James McAvoy knew of the attack was when an IRA gang called at his home on the Rathfriland Road, on the edge of Newry town. They forced their way into the house, which is adjacent to McAvoy's family-run filling station. Around the same time, a second IRA team held another family hostage in their home at Mayobridge a few miles away. A blue Toyota Hi-ace van parked outside their house was commandeered by the IRA men. The vehicle was then driven to the McAvoy home, where the family had been herded into a back room. The McAvoy family, minus their father, were then taken in the van back to Mayobridge, where an armed IRA gang held them hostage. This was because, in the words of a former IRA man who was involved in the operation: 'It was easier to hold two families hostage in the one house.'

The Toyota was then driven back to Newry, where James McAvoy was forced into the back of the vehicle at gunpoint with a blindfold around his eyes. The garage owner, who was extremely ill, remained calm as the van was driven to the Flagstaff beauty spot overlooking Carlingford Lough and much of the border region.

There, an IRA team from south Armagh loaded a ton of explosives packed into black plastic wheelie bins into the rear of the van. James McAvoy was then ordered to drive the vehicle to the Cloughogue army checkpoint, via Clontigory Road and the main Dundalk–Newry Road which straddles the border. He was told to transport the bomb to the accommodation block at the permanent army checkpoint on the outskirts of Newry.

Until this point everything was going well from the IRA's point of view, but suddenly a major stumbling block presented itself. James McAvoy had a heart complaint and he hadn't driven for many years. Worse still, the Toyota had a column gear stick and the pensioner had never even seen one before. He explained to his captors he hadn't a clue how to drive the vehicle, but even so he was still strapped to the driving seat and a member of the gang forced the van into second gear. As the Toyota began to move off, a senior IRA man appeared to have a pang of conscience over the pathetic sight in front of him. He lent over and quietly whispered in James McAvoy's ear: 'Don't open the door, get out through the window.'

The deadly cargo was driven at a snail's pace with the van engine roaring along country roads as an IRA team followed in a second car. The lights of both vehicles were switched off. Shortly before the checkpoint, the car containing the IRA men turned off the road and Mr McAvoy continued to drive his deadly load to its final destination as ordered.

The noise of the engine attracted the attention of Cyril John Smith, a 21-year-old soldier in the Royal Irish Rangers Regiment, who was on duty at the checkpoint. James McAvoy remembered the advice the IRA man had given him and, despite his age, managed to get himself out of the window. But as he did so, the soldier was screaming at him to move the van immediately.

Mr McAvoy had successfully managed to avoid opening the door, but he was unaware that the IRA had also inserted a timing device to ensure the bomb would detonate in any event. As the two men faced each other feet from the van, the one-ton bomb exploded. Ranger Smith, who was from Carrickfergus, died instantly and 13 of his colleagues who were standing nearby were badly injured in the blast. Miraculously, James McAvoy survived, although he did suffer a broken leg and ankle in the atrocity.

Mr McAvoy managed to give evidence at the inquest into Ranger Smith's death the following April but he died two months later and friends say he never got over the shock of being used as a bomb courier by the IRA. The man who fingered Mr McAvoy is now a leading member of Sinn Fein and the IRA man who told him to escape through the door went to America, where he escaped the attentions of the FBI until recently.

A third 'human bomb' operation the same night was unsuccessful because a faulty detonator failed to explode a 1,500 lb bomb near an army base at Omagh.

The IRA's 'human bomb' tactic had not come as a bolt from the blue, as far as the RUC Special Branch was concerned. The Branch had some knowledge of what was about to happen because one of its agents, who was also a member of the IRA's Derry Brigade, had passed on information.

Ten days before the Coshquin bomb, 27-year-old Martin Hogan, a trusted member of the IRA's Derry Brigade, and three other IRA men burst into the home of a local family who lived at Elaghmore Park and announced they were taking the place over. Other IRA members removed a van from the garage and then returned it with a huge bomb in the back.

A major terrorist attack had been planned, but shortly after 4.00 a.m. the local parish priest called the house to tell the IRA men the police were aware of their presence. The priest was in bed asleep when the police phoned him asking for his help. Within minutes, Hogan and his gang escaped out the rear of the house and by a strange 'coincidence' managed to evade the considerable police presence in the area.

The Derry Brigade of the IRA thought it had got rid of its informer problem when earlier that year it executed Paddy Flood as a tout, after holding him for six weeks. As it turned out, Flood was not an informer, but Martin Hogan was. Hogan realised his number was up when a senior IRA man told him he wanted him to travel south to carry out an operation. He contacted his police handlers, who were able to tell him that the IRA intended to execute him. Hogan, together with his wife and family, left Derry the same day and now lives under a new identity at a secret address in England. In an amazing act of bravado before he left, Hogan, whose family were steeped in the republican movement, told a senior IRA member, 'I'm a tout.'

In developing the human bomb, the IRA achieved a new low in the murky world of Irish terrorism. Several other human bombs were planned, but it is thought the IRA dropped the idea because of the outrage expressed by leading figures in the Catholic community.

– CHAPTER TWELVE –

Ulster's Answer to the Taliban

Beat him to within an inch of his life.
The order given to an IRA punishment squad before an attack

In his younger days, Colm Carey was an ideal IRA volunteer. Born in Derry in 1954, he was a teenager when the Troubles broke out and regularly attended the many civil rights marches which took place in the city. He particularly looked forward to stoning the police and army at the end of these events and developed a reputation as a being a crack shot with a stone. It wasn't a big step, therefore, to becoming a crack shot with a weapon of another description and when the approach was made he willingly signed up to join the Provos. It was the thing to do at the time and it also gave Carey the feeling of having some standing in the impoverished community he came from in the Waterside district of Derry.

Very quickly Colm Carey came to the attention of the police who regularly stopped him in the street and quizzed him about his movements. Undeterred by the police interest, he continued with his IRA activities and developed a skill for bomb making. But it wasn't too long before he became careless and the police were able to pin a charge on him.

Carey was convicted and sent to prison for a series of IRA bomb attacks in Derry and, in true republican style, he refused to recognise the court. In jail Carey mixed with other IRA prisoners and appeared committed to continuing his terrorist career on his release.

However, the odds were stacked against him from the start, because Carey, who came from Strabane Old Road in the Gobnascale area of Derry, came from a dysfunctional family where alcohol abuse was commonplace. On his release from prison Carey went into a downward spiral, which ended with him floundering in a sea of booze.

People who knew Carey say he was essentially a quiet person who seemed to lose his way. When he wasn't drunk he would be friendly and polite, but increasingly alcohol took over his life and he gradually became a street drinker. Every day, from the minute he opened his eyes, was a constant battle where the most important thing was to get a drink – and the sooner the better.

Carey got into a habit of falling in with other alcoholics who regularly met up at a small inner-city park between Derry's seventeenth-century city walls and the Guildhall Chambers, home to Derry City Council. 'On-street' drinking has been a problem in the city for many years and the park at Foyle Street, which is no longer there, became a magnet for winos. Summertime living may not have been easy for Colm Carey and his drinking pals in the park, but at least it was a lot easier than battling against the elements when the wind and snow swept up the Foyle valley during the winter months.

If wine was available, it was often shared in a communal kind of way and if it wasn't, then the park was a good place to lie in the sun and watch the world go by, and, of course, there was always the chance of begging a few shillings from passers-by, which could be quickly converted into a bottle of fortified wine.

On 16 July 1982, Kevin Barry Johnston woke early in his house in the Bogside. He hadn't been drinking the night before so he didn't have a hangover, but as he had cash in his pocket he was determined to go out and enjoy himself. But drinking for Kevin Johnston, who was known locally as 'Biggsy', wasn't confined to the odd half pint of lager. Alcohol for Johnston was there to be consumed in as large quantities as possible. Biggsy was Bogside born and reared and was very streetwise. He had been arrested by the army when he was just six and kept under armed guard in the rear of a military Land-Rover while the soldiers struggled to contain rioters. He has a picture to prove it. Biggsy had spent time in the Termonbacca Boys' Home, where street rioting was a way of life and a diversion from the strict routine of the home. But, like Colm Carey, he too was a booze victim and a regular visitor to the park on Foyle Street. Two things, however, made Biggsy stand out from the rest of the wine drinkers: one was that, despite his diminutive stature (he was only 5 ft 4 in. tall), he could handle himself in the physical sense; and secondly, he was never short of money because he was capable of living on his wits.

Biggsy drank two cans of beer in his house before heading out to see what was happening on the streets. The sun was warm that July morning and shortly before 9 a.m. he paused on the quay near the Guildhall to look at his reflection in the water, which was shining like glass. As he headed along

Foyle Street towards the park, Biggsy thought to himself: 'It's great to be alive.'

A few moments later he saw the solitary figure of Colm Carey sitting on a bench staring at the ground. Although they lived on different sides of the River Foyle, which divides the city of Derry, the two men knew each other well and enjoyed each other's company.

'Well, Colm,' said Biggsy, 'Where are we going to get a drink?'

'I've no money, Biggsy,' came the reply.

'I didn't ask you that, I asked you where are we going to get a drink?' said Biggsy.

Carey looked up at his friend and a second later his face lit up in a smile. Without a word passing between them, Carey knew his prospects for that day were about to improve dramatically. The smile on Biggsy's face said it all. He was flush with cash and wine would soon be purchased.

Carey stood up and both men hurried off to a nearby pub to buy two bottles of wine and several tins of beer. Colm Carey and Kevin Johnston were like many other drink victims in the city at that time (Johnston now lives away from Derry and quit alcohol soon after leaving the city) they were not allowed to drink in pubs, but some publicans agreed to sell them alcohol on an off-sales basis.

Within minutes, both were back in the park and over the next two hours they proceeded to get drunk on the cheap booze they had just purchased. Colm Carey spoke about his outlook on life since getting out of jail and how he wished he could shake off his addiction to drink. He also said he regretted getting caught up the IRA's bombing campaign. Biggsy agreed alcohol was a curse. But for the moment they were enjoying themselves, he said, and sure they were doing no one any harm, except themselves of course.

After a while, Carey, who had been drinking heavily the night before, felt the worse for wear and Biggsy suggested he should get a taxi home. 'Sure, I've no money,' said Carey. But without another word, Biggsy Johnston arranged and paid for a cab for his friend, and, as he helped him into the rear seat of the vehicle, he put two cans of beer in Carey's pockets and shoved eight pounds into his hand. That was the last time Biggsy Johnston saw Colm Carey alive.

Carey went back to his home in Gobnascale and slept off the effects of the morning's drink. When he awoke later that evening, he drank the beer Biggsy had given him before going out to buy more booze with the money which he 'mysteriously' discovered in his trouser pocket.

A few hours later, when he had no drink and no money left, Colm Carey embarked on a drunken escapade which would end up costing him his life. He ran into an off-sales and stole a bottle of whiskey before running out again.

The shop was busy with customers at the time and, as Carey made no attempt to disguise his appearance, he was easily recognised.

Unknown to the unfortunate Carey, a member of the Provisional IRA was waiting in the off-sales queue and had witnessed the entire episode. Carey returned to his home at Strabane Old Road and took refuge in the stolen alcohol on which he was so dependent. Suddenly an IRA punishment squad burst into the house and a short scuffle took place. Carey, who was incapable of defending himself, was oblivious to the danger of the situation he was in. The IRA men dragged their former comrade-in-arms out into the garden and, using a high-powered rifle, shot him in both legs before skulking off to dump their weapons. At least two of the men involved came from the immediate vicinity and were well aware of Colm Carey's chronic alcohol problems.

Carey's father, who was in the house at the time, was unaware of what was going on because of his own intoxicated state. An eerie silence fell over the Gobnascale area and it was a full hour before an ambulance was called to the scene. But by that time, it was too late. Colm Carey, former IRA prisoner, Catholic civilian and now hopeless alcoholic, died in the street outside his home. One of his legs had been completely blown off and the other was left hanging by a thread.

He was the first, but certainly not the last, person to die in Northern Ireland as a result of a so-called punishment shooting. The irony of the situation clearly wasn't lost on the IRA, which promised a 'full inquiry'. As far as is known, no members of the public, or the police for that matter, were ever made aware of the outcome of that investigation. But it is believed that because one member of the murder gang is connected through marriage to a senior member of the IRA in Derry no action was ever taken against those responsible for Colm Carey's shameful death.

William Joseph Carlin is an unusual and intriguing Irishman. A native of Derry and former British soldier, he managed to operate as an MI5 agent undetected inside the republican movement for nearly 12 years. Now 53, he lives in hiding under an assumed name.

In the mid-1960s Willie Carlin, as he is known, left his home town to join the Royal Irish Hussars and after a nine-year stint in the army Carlin wanted to return home to Derry. He was, however, advised against it by senior officers, because by that time the Ulster Troubles were at their peak. Somehow, secret service personnel who made contact with Carlin managed to persuade him to work for them as an undercover agent.

Carlin was told not to attempt to join the IRA, but instead to concentrate on finding out as much as possible about Sinn Fein, the organisation's political wing. After a couple of years back home, where he existed quietly on the margins, Carlin made his move and was accepted into the republican party. Gradually he gained promotion and was given a job running a community group in the Gobnascale area near where he lived. The former soldier's natural talent for organisation and figures meant he was ideally suited to Sinn Fein's fledgling attempts at building a credible political machine. On that front, Carlin became an aide to Sinn Fein chief Martin McGuinness, now the Minister for Education in the power-sharing executive at Stormont.

Throughout this time, Carlin kept in contact with a series of MI5 handlers, whom he met on a regular basis. He met them in a number of locations near Derry, including Ness Woods and a lonely mountain beauty spot above Benone strand. But he also met them at a large house named 'Old Forge – Cross-na-hEana-Ghonel'. The property, which has only recently been demolished, lies on the northern side of Limavady. This was exactly the same location where, it later emerged, Sinn Fein's Martin McGuinness was meeting Michael Oatley, the MI6 officer codenamed the 'Mountain Climber'.

One of Carlin's handlers during this time was an MI5 man called Michael Bettaney. In 1984, he was hauled before the Old Bailey in London and was convicted of treason after being found guilty of trying to sell secrets to the Soviet KGB. Bettaney almost cost Willie Carlin his life.

Consumed with bitterness at receiving a long sentence, while in prison Michael Bettaney, who was also a chronic alcoholic, approached Pat 'Chancer' Magee, jailed for his part in the bombing of the Grand Hotel in Brighton during the 1984 Tory Party Conference. Bettaney knew all about Magee's IRA activities, dating back to the mid-1970s when Magee was part of an IRA Active Service unit in London. In a bombing spree codenamed by the Provos 'Operation OXO', Magee was directly implicated in IRA attacks at the Greenwich Gasometer and Canvey Island.

Bettaney introduced himself to Magee while both men were attending Sunday mass, and, to gain Magee's confidence, he suggested to the IRA man he should let Martin McGuinness know that Willie Carlin – his plausible Sinn Fein aide back in Derry – was in actual fact an MI5 agent who had been in place for over 11 years!

Very quickly the net closed in around Carlin and he was lucky to escape with his life. Carlin was about to be exposed as an MI5 mole when Margaret Thatcher, the Conservative Prime Minister who had been the target of the Brighton bomb, personally intervened in the affair on 3 March 1985.

Carlin was contacted by an MI5 operative and within an hour the father of three was smuggled out of Derry with his wife and young family. They were spirited away in Maggie Thatcher's private jet, which she personally made available.

Undercover agent 3007 – codenamed 'The Fox' on account of his red hair – had survived, but only just. The British government valued Willie Carlin's role as an agent inside so highly it continues to pay him a pension.

To this day, Willie Carlin is haunted by one of the most atrocious terrorist crimes of the Troubles. On 7 April 1981, Joanne Mary Mathers, a 29-year-old married woman and mother of a young baby boy, was shot dead by an IRA assassin as she collected census forms on a Derry housing estate. She was standing at a doorway in Anderson Crescent in the republican Gobnascale area when the gunman struck. At that time Sinn Fein was opposed to people participating in the census, accusing the government of using it as a covert way of spying on republicans.

Minutes before she died, Joanne Mathers, who lived on a farm at Tamnabrine, near Strabane, had called at Willie Carlin's mother's house in a state of blind panic. She had been threatened in the street and was afraid for her life. But Carlin, then a prominent member of Sinn Fein, assured the census collector she would be safe.

Twenty years after this horrific event, Willie Carlin sneaked into Ulster and paid a private visit to Joanne Mathers' grave at Mountfield Cemetery in rural Co. Tyrone. Later he explained the build-up to the terrorist attack which has troubled him ever since. He said:

> I will never forget it because it was in the middle of the IRA hunger strikes and two days before Bobby Sands was elected as an MP. I was visiting my mother when a young woman arrived in a dreadful state. She explained that she was a census collector and said she had been threatened with being shot.
>
> The girl told me her name was Joanne and said she hadn't realised she was in a dangerous area or she wouldn't have come. She knew the IRA had threatened to shoot census workers and she just wanted to get out of the area safely.
>
> I told her I was a member of Sinn Fein and I personally would guarantee her safety. I looked at her list of addresses and told her which houses to visit. I believed in my heart she would be safe and after giving her a glass of water I walked her out to the door and told her I would keep watch until she got to the end of the street.
>
> Joanne clasped my arm and said 'God bless you'. As she made her way down the street she appeared to get her confidence back, because she looked up and gave me a wave – I smiled and waved back as she

approached the door I had sent her to. But just as the door was
opening, a masked man brandishing a gun ran round the corner and
grabbed her clipboard. And as she struggled to hold on to it, he shot
her in the head.

Still conscious and despite her injuries, Joanne Mathers tried to escape the
gunman's attentions by fleeing inside the house. The occupier bravely tried to
prevent the gunman from entering the property by attempting to slam the
door behind the young woman, but the gunman brushed him aside and
pursued his quarry. Within seconds, Joanne Mathers, census collector, was
dead.

Carlin continued:

I heard more shots and ran back to my mother's, ordering her to
phone an ambulance immediately. I then ran down to where Joanne
was. The gunman had escaped, but people were yelling at me and
calling me a murdering bastard. I will never forget her happy smile
and that wave she gave me seconds before she died.

He then added: 'All these years later I hope God has forgiven me, but I haven't
forgiven myself.'

Following the murder, the IRA moved quickly to distance itself from the
attack, claiming the killing had been carried out by people intent on
discrediting the election campaign of IRA hunger striker Bobby Sands. But
no one took the IRA's story seriously. Within hours, RUC forensic experts
were able to prove that the gun used in the attack had been used previously
in a number of IRA killings.

Joanne Mathers was married to a farmer. She had quit her career as a town
planner to look after her baby son, but had taken a short-term job as a five-
pounds-per-day census collector.

Twenty years after her murder, Mitchel McLaughlin, Sinn Fein's National
Chairman, urged republican supporters to cooperate with the 2001 census.
McLaughlin's announcement came within days of the anniversary.

Murder-squad detectives say the IRA gunman who executed Joanne
Mathers was a member of the IRA punishment gang who, just over a year
later, shot dead Colm Carey in the same district of Derry for stealing a bottle
of whiskey. He was never convicted of either crime and still lives in the area.
Police believe a leading IRA man who is now a prominent member of Sinn
Fein personally gave the order to execute Joanne Mathers. She was the only
census collector to lose her life in the Troubles.

– CHAPTER THIRTEEN –

Customs Men, Cops, Prison Officers – They're All the Same

A sort of lewd people called Smuckellors, who make their trade to steal and defraud His Majesty and His Customs.
Parliamentary Proclamation, 9 August 1661

The Northern Ireland Land Boundary was established in law in 1923 and, until it ceased to exist in the formal sense in 1992, 'the border', as it became known, was a source of contention, security, fun and extreme danger all at the same time. For many in poor rural areas it was also a lucrative source of income. Many men who started off smuggling a few dozen eggs and couple of slabs of bacon became millionaires, as shortages and subsidies played into the hands of people from both traditions who refused to recognise the existence of the border.

Intricate cat and mouse games were played out in the middle of the night and in broad daylight, as cross-border smugglers did their damnedest to evade the 'excise men'.

Today, smuggling tends to be dominated by shadowy paramilitary figures who are either members of the Irish Republican Army or who are happy to pay a levy to that organisation in return for operating without molestation. It wasn't so long ago, however, that a good-humoured and healthy respect existed between customs officers and smugglers. In those days, if a smuggler was caught red-handed he tended to accept whatever penalty was imposed on him without question.

One such man was Patsy Bradley – a legendary smuggler from the Donegal–Derry border area. Patsy was connected throughout the country and he was also well known in Scotland and in the Glasgow area in particular. One Belfast customs officer made it his life's work to shadow Patsy Bradley as he dreamt up all sorts of schemes to avoid paying excise duty and, before he retired, the officer was presented with an award from the Queen for his unceasing efforts on behalf of the State.

Generally Patsy Bradley accepted whatever was coming to him, as far as smuggling was concerned, and customs men will tell you he always did so with good humour and grace. On one occasion, Patsy was stopped around 3 a.m. while driving a lorryload of pigs on a border road. In a demonstration of genius, he denied the 'outrageous' allegation of the officer that he was smuggling and replied: 'What? Smuggling? Me? Not at all. You see, my wife can't get a wink of sleep because these pigs have been squealing all night. I'm just driving them around to make them tired in the hope that they'll nod off!'

However, there was also another and much more serious side to life on the Northern Ireland Land Boundary. On a snowy December night in 1954, a Customs and Excise Border Patrol was about to knock off work around 11 p.m. when they heard the sound of a van heading at speed towards the Irish Republic in Co. Armagh. They turned to investigate and as they did so they were rammed. As the personnel of both vehicles spilled out onto the streets, fighting broke out. Suddenly a shot rang out. John Turner, a young customs officer, fell to the ground badly injured with a gunshot wound to the stomach. The strangers left their van and headed for the southern side of the border on foot.

An examination of the vehicle revealed it contained a cache of arms and ammunition, including a Thompson sub-machine gun and a .303 rifle, which had been stolen from Gough Barracks in June of that year.

John Turner was rushed to hospital, where emergency surgery saved his life. He was the first customs officer to be shot in Ireland in 200 years.

Eight customs officers were murdered during the Troubles. Ian Hankin and James O'Neill died after being caught in the crossfire during a gun battle between soldiers and the IRA near the Killeen Border Crossing on 27 November 1971. Ian Hankin, a Protestant, originally from Durham, came to Northern Ireland with his wife to follow his chosen career as a customs officer. His colleague James O'Neill, a Catholic, worked as a cleaner for the customs service. Forensic evidence showed the men died after being hit by IRA bullets. The men were the first customs officers to die.

On 16 January 1981, two men walked into the Customs Station at Warrenpoint Docks, in Co. Down, and shot dead Ivan Toombs. A Higher Executive Officer in HM Customs and Excise, Toombs was also a member of the UDR. It later emerged that he had been set up by a colleague, Eamonn Collins, who was a member of the IRA.

When he was arrested, Collins broke down during interrogation and, after admitting his role in the murder, named other IRA personnel.

In the 1990s, Eamon Collins wrote *Killing Rage*, a bestselling and revealing account of life inside the IRA. He also gave evidence at the High Court in Dublin against Thomas 'Slab' Murphy – a millionaire pig farmer and leading member of the IRA – who sued the *Sunday Times* newspaper for libel. The jury found that Murphy was a disreputable man deeply involved in IRA activities, including murder, and Murphy's legal bid failed.

On 27 January 1999, Eamon Collins was found dead on a country road near his home at Barcroft Park, Newry. An iron bar had been rammed through his skull. No one claimed responsibility for the murder, but police believe republicans carried out the killing.

It wasn't just customs officers who were on the receiving end of IRA bullets, as the story of the life and death of 34-year-old building contractor Adrian McGovern reveals.

The father of four was gunned down by the IRA outside his home at Stoneyford, near Lisburn, on 16 September 1993. On the face of it, it seemed just another sectarian killing and a tragedy for the family concerned. But a closer examination of the facts revealed a web of intrigue stretching from the homes of Irish gangsters living in London to MI5 agents tasked with stopping IRA bombs getting into the English capital.

It started with a major police investigation into a massive theft racket of plant and machinery which was being stolen in England and then sold on the black market in Northern Ireland and the Irish Republic.

The focus of the police inquiries was a group of Irish nationals living in the Home Counties area, and the leader of the gang was an Irishman called Cyril McGuinness, who was originally from the fishing village of Skerries, in north Co. Dublin. McGuinness was a huge man of around 6 ft 6 in. tall, with the bulk to go with it. He was well known among the Irish community on the Isle of Dogs, where he was called 'Jimmy'.

McGuinness had a lengthy criminal record, including a conviction for attempted murder – when he drove a lorry over a man's Mercedes while the driver was still in it – and he was also jailed for burning down the house of a man he claimed owed him money.

McGuinness was constantly under the scrutiny of the police because they knew he was involved in illegal dumping, known in the building trade as 'fly-tipping'. But increasingly they began to receive intelligence that he was the 'Mr Big' masterminding the theft of plant and machinery and then shipping it back to Ireland.

In the spring of 1993, an RUC section which specialised in stolen vehicles discovered a strange-looking lorry outside a hauliers at Portadown. The vehicle turned out to be stolen and it was seized by police. Further inquiries revealed that the lorry had been left at the hauliers by a southern Irish-based lorry dealer called John Mullins. But a person arrested at the Portadown depot where the lorry was found refused to say who left it when questioned by the police under caution.

Jimmy McGuinness was well known to police on both sides of the Irish Sea and detectives suspected, correctly as it turned out, that he had a hand in this matter. The police knew McGuinness was associated with a haulage dealer from the Forkhill area of south Armagh, who was also well-connected with the Provos. A joint RUC/Scotland Yard intelligence-gathering operation also revealed that McGuinness was behind huge volumes of building-site theft in London, which resulted in stolen vehicles being sold on in both parts of Ireland. A decision was taken to place him under heavy surveillance.

Shortly after this, in May 1993, police in London tailed a stolen vehicle transporter with a JCB hoist and a digger known as a 'Load-All' on the platform. The lorry was followed as it made its way out of London along the M4, onto the M5 and then later onto the M6. The driver finally ended up at the Scottish port of Stranraer, where he made arrangements to make the crossing to Larne. The RUC were contacted and a surveillance team scrambled.

When he came off the ferry, the suspect was followed to Belfast. He then crossed the city using the west link and onto the M1. As expected, he signalled to come off at the Newry turn-off, but, instead of heading south, he doubled back towards Lisburn. The lorry driver carried on through the market town before heading out towards Aldergrove Airport and then driving back on the road to Belfast. The police surveillance team were baffled.

Suddenly the lorry stopped at a site where two houses were under construction and removed the 'Load-All' from the platform. RUC officers were detailed to keep an eye on the delivered vehicle, while the surveillance team kept tabs on the driver, who was now heading back towards the border. Detectives running the operation were then told that a second suspect vehicle was believed to be in the area and that there could possibly be a connection between the two.

The police decided to stop the first lorry and, after a vehicle checkpoint was hurriedly put in place, the transporter was stopped on the A1 outside Hillsborough. The driver turned out to be none other than Cyril 'Jimmy' McGuinness. The vehicles were all identified as stolen and McGuinness was arrested and taken to Bannbridge RUC station.

Meanwhile, back at the other site, police watched as the 'Load-All' vehicle McGuinness had just delivered was driven to a new bungalow at Stoneyford

Road – the home of haulage contractor Adrian McGovern. The police regrouped and then stopped the second suspicious vehicle, which was being driven by a close friend of Jimmy McGuinness, and it too had stolen vehicles on board.

The police then seized the 'Load-All' at the Stoneyford Road bungalow and Adrian McGovern was arrested. Detectives discovered that McGovern worked for the security forces and he was in possession of false number plates that had been supplied to him by British MI5 agents running covert security operations.

In England, McGuinness' house at Enfield in North London was taken apart. Anti-terrorist police even removed the drainpipes from the property as they carried out an in-depth search operation. His common-law wife packed her bags immediately and headed back to her mother's house in Ireland.

McGuinness and his friend were released without charge, but the vehicles, which all turned out to be stolen, were seized by police. Within weeks, more stolen plant and machinery was arriving in Ireland. Much of it was seized by the RUC, but McGuinness still demanded payment for the goods. Detectives at SO16 Branch at Scotland Yard then arrested McGuinness and he was taken to London for questioning. He was never charged in connection with any of the plant or machinery seized in Ireland.

On 16 September, Adrian McGovern was shot dead. Three high-velocity bullets hit him in the head, upper body and leg. He died instantly. The IRA claimed he was executed because he supplied building materials to the security forces. But RUC detectives believe the real reason is that the IRA knew he was a link in a chain forged by MI5 blacksmiths. McGovern was clearly the weak link.

On 8 April 1976, Patrick Dillon – a 36-year-old married man with five children – was shot dead outside his home at Mountfield, near Omagh. Mr Dillon, a Catholic, was the first serving prison officer to die in the Northern Ireland terror war. He was murdered by the IRA.

Prison officers became 'legitimate targets', as far republicans were concerned, because they were seen to be implementing British policy which denied IRA prisoners serving sentences in the Maze Prison and Armagh Women's Prison 'special category' status, which would allow them to wear their own clothes and exempt them from prison work. The dispute lingered on and culminated in the IRA hunger strikes, when ten republicans serving sentences for terrorism died after refusing food.

The first man to lose his life on hunger strike was Belfast man Bobby Sands. Sands died on 5 May 1981, after 66 days without food. While in prison, he was elected as Member of Parliament for Fermanagh-South Tyrone. The publicity surrounding his death and those of other IRA prisoners is seen as a major turning point in IRA strategy. After the hunger strike, republican candidates began making headway in democratic elections, although it was another 15 years before the organisation called off its terror campaign.

Even after the hunger strike ended, the IRA continued to target prison officers and staff. On 6 March 1984, William McConnell was shot dead outside his east Belfast home in front of his wife and three-year-old daughter.

Mr McConnell, who worked as the assistant governor at the Maze Prison, was killed as he checked under his car for an explosive device. At first it seemed just another savage action by the IRA, with little prospect of the perpetrator being caught. However, a scored-out entry in a diary turned out to be the key that unlocked the secret surrounding William McConnell's murder.

Mr McConnell, a 35-year-old Protestant, was also in charge of security at the prison where he worked. He lived with his wife Beryl and their little girl at Hawthornden Drive, off the Belmont Road. Shortly before he died, Mr McConnell wrote to his superiors outlining concerns he had over his personal safety.

The night before he was shot, an IRA unit, which included a woman, had taken over the house of Owen Connolly, who lived nearby. A 64-year-old pensioner and Second World War hero, Connolly had taken early retirement from his job at Stormont, where he had worked in various government departments.

He gave the Provo hit team full use of his house at Campbell Park Avenue. After the murder, the gun gang returned to Connolly's house, where they were fed and sheltered before the old man helped them escape the clutches of the RUC's follow-up operation.

Connolly walked the killers to the bus stop and a few minutes later they were en route to Belfast city centre and freedom. The IRA gang was so sure of Owen Connolly's support it even left him in possession of the weapons and disguises used. When the coast was clear, two days later, Connolly packed the guns and false beards into a bag and delivered them to one of his IRA contacts in the Markets area of Belfast.

On the face of it, it looked as though Owen Connolly, who had been working for the IRA for eight years, had got away scot-free. But a tenacious RUC detective followed a trail which led straight to his door.

Sixteen hours after the McConnell murder, a UDR patrol positioned on the Albert Bridge, near Belfast city centre, stopped a car containing three men. They told the soldiers they were heading back to their homes on the other side of town. Two of the men, who gave false names, were taken in for questioning and the other – a well-known republican called Eugene Gilmartin – was arrested the following day, after being allowed to continue on his journey.

In the interview suit at Castlereagh Holding Centre, the detained men refused to answer questions put to them by detectives. But a 1984 diary found in one of the men's pockets intrigued one of the policemen. It was completely blank except for a few entries in the days running up to the McConnell murder. However, the writing had been obscured by heavy scoring by a black ballpoint pen. The detective sent the diary for testing and when he drew a blank in England he then sent it to the RUC's own forensic lab, where he got the breakthrough he was looking for.

An odd insertion in the diary entry for 2 March read: '9.00 ETS – Camels – 5 – Dene 20 CPA'. Detectives thought '9.00 ETS' might have been coded language for 9 a.m. Estimated Time of Shooting; and that '5 Dene' could also have been a misspelt code for the McConnell address at 5 Hawthornden Drive, where the murder took place.

The officers were at a loss to come up with a suggestion as to what CPA could have meant, when a young policeman who grew up in east Belfast, piped up: 'I think it is for Campbell Park Avenue, which is nearby.' A quick look at the electoral register reveal that 20 Campbell Park Avenue was occupied by Owen and Margaret Connolly and their daughter Carmel. Suddenly things were looking up.

The police swooped on Connolly's home and quizzed him about suspicious activity in the area the previous week. Connolly was furious at this intrusion by the police and angrily told the officers: 'I am a retired civil servant with an impeccable war record and I object to being questioned like this.' But the old man's indignant tone only served to convince Alan Simpson – a detective superintendent in charge of the RUC investigation team – that he was on the right track. Simpson arrested Connolly, his wife and the couple's 24-year-old daughter Carmel on suspicion of being involved in paramilitary activity.

In Castlereagh, Carmel Connolly at first denied any knowledge of the McConnell killing. But within minutes she changed her story and admitted the gun gang had used her family home as a base to mount the attack, and she admitted wigs were worn by the killers to destroy forensic evidence. The game was now up and during interrogation Connolly made a full confession as to the degree of his involvement in the murder as well as other crimes. It took the police two days to write down Connolly's statement.

In March 1985, a full year after William McConnell died, Owen Connolly appeared in court charged with taking part in the murder. The court heard how Connolly, who came from south Armagh, got involved with the IRA after he became embittered with his bosses at work. Connolly believed that he had been passed over for promotion because he was a Catholic. He had even taken his grievances to the Ombudsman. But when his complaint was dismissed, in disgust he turned to the Provos in the hope of getting even. The IRA couldn't believe their luck when Connolly made contact and an IRA man from the Markets area, who is now a Sinn Fein politician, was detailed to keep close contact with him.

Passing sentence, the trial judge told the pathetic-looking silver-haired pensioner standing in the dock:

> How a man of your intelligence, education, background and age, could descend into the pit of such murderous intrigue and violence to join men capable of gunning down a fellow countryman in front of his wife and three-year-old daughter is almost beyond comprehension.

Owen Connolly was jailed for life, while his wife and daughter received suspended sentences.

In October of the following year, Owen Connolly appeared as the chief prosecution witness at the trial of the three men accused of murdering William McConnell. One of the men in the dock was Eugene Gilmartin, who had been stopped by the UDR patrol 16 hours after the McConnell shooting.

The prosecution was able to prove that a distinctive footprint found at the rear of Connolly's home was that of Eugene Gilmartin (his foot was slightly deformed). Gilmartin was sentenced to life imprisonment.

After seven years, Owen Connolly was allowed out of prison on compassionate grounds after suffering a heart attack. The decision to release Connolly was in stark contrast to the lack of mercy he showed his victim, Assistant Governor William McConnell.

Patrick Dillon and William McConnell were just two of twenty-nine prison officers to lose their lives. Of those officers, the IRA killed twenty-eight and loyalist paramilitaries killed one.

– CHAPTER FOURTEEN –

Mickey Mooney – Getting Away with Murder

Here comes the Dapper Don.

A greeting from a criminal associate of Mickey Mooney

Mickey Mooney was the first big-time drugs dealer to be executed by the IRA using its cover name 'Direct Action Against Drugs' as a flag of convenience, although a small-time dealer Francis 'Rico' Rice had been killed the year before. He was shot dead in a Belfast city-centre pub as he was taking a telephone call from one of his killers. Mooney's murder was also the first time the IRA breached its 'cessation of violence' announced in August 1994. Mooney's death was the first of five IRA assassinations between April and Christmas that year of people it accused of being involved in the illegal drugs trade, although it appears one of these men, Martin McCrory from Turf Lodge, was shot only because the IRA was unable to track down his brother 'Ula'.

In recent years, more murders, including those of Brendan 'Speedy' Fegan and Paul 'Bull' Downey in Newry, Edmund 'Big Edd' McCoy in Belfast and Christopher 'Cricky' O'Kane, followed as the IRA realised it was now possible to get away with murder without political sanction being taken against its Sinn Fein colleagues. Paul Daly, shot dead in May 2001, is the most recent big-time dealer to be executed by the Provos.

The IRA campaign against drug dealers was savage, but the writing had been on the wall for drug dealers for a full six years before Mickey Mooney lost his life. In 1988, as James 'Doc' Halliday sat sipping tea and chatting to a local man called Paddy Seredge in a cafe at the Buttercrane Shopping Centre in Newry, he was shot and seriously wounded by IRA gunmen who escaped on a motorbike. He was hit in the chest, stomach, back and bottom and eyewitnesses say it was a definite murder attempt. Within hours, the IRA issued a statement admitting the shooting and naming Halliday as the boss of a cross-border drugs cartel. Halliday, a former motor mechanic, turned rock band soundman, was well known in the area as a major cannabis dealer. He was on good terms with the notorious loyalist killer Billy Wright, who was gunned down by the INLA while in prison in 1997, and, to afford himself some sort of protection against republican paramilitaries, Halliday bought a house situated inside the security barrier at a British Army base in the Co. Armagh village of Bessbrook.

When he was well enough, Halliday appeared on television to tell the Provos he had no intention of packing in. Doc Halliday told the BBC's *Spotlight* investigative reporter, Jeremy Adams, that he was shot because he refused to pay the Provos ten thousand pounds and when asked by the reporter how long he thought he would get away with dealing in drugs, Halliday answered: 'How long runs the fox?'

As far as the authorities are concerned, James 'Doc' Halliday is an unemployed car mechanic who lives on his own, apart from his pit bull terriers, at Mountcharles Square, in the Quaker-built model village of Bessbrook, near Newry. Of course, the reality is very different. Halliday has served prison sentences for drugs importation offences and he used his time behind bars to build up criminal contacts in the drugs business. His home is a virtual fortress, with top-quality surveillance equipment installed throughout the house, and, with the British Army protecting him 24 hours a day, it is virtually impossible for any would-be assassins to mount an attack on him without risking immediate arrest or worse.

Mickey Mooney agreed with 'Doc' Halliday's stance on not paying the Provos a penny. 'Why should I?' he often said. 'I make my money, they make theirs.' But Mooney lived in Belfast and he did not have the luxury of British Army marksmen to keep guard on his house while he slept.

Mickey Mooney was born into a respectable Catholic family in Belfast during the late 1950s, and when the Mooneys took over the tenancy of a house on the newly built Turf Lodge estate in west Belfast things were looking up. Life for a youngster in Turf Lodge before the Troubles was magical. The Black Mountain, with its panoramic views of Belfast and the Lagan Valley, was on the doorstep and every day was a new adventure.

With the onset of civil unrest, however, Mickey Mooney, like many young men in west Belfast, had to make a decision about whether or not he should join a paramilitary organisation. The choice was fairly simple: either sign up with the Provos, the Officials or the INLA, or go your own way. Mickey, who was making a name for himself on the amateur boxing circuit, decided there was no future in private armies. There was more to be gained from looking after yourself and that is just what Mickey intended to do. But, of course, crime has its problems and it wasn't long before Mooney came a cropper.

While still a teenager, he was jailed for seven years for drugs offences. People who knew him behind bars say that even then Mooney stood out from the crowd because he set himself high standards which he doggedly maintained. A keen and talented boxer, he was constantly in the gym working out and encouraging others to do the same.

Henry Robinson, a founder member of the human rights group Families Against Intimidation and Terror, served time with Mooney in Crumlin Road Prison. Robinson had joined the Official IRA as a teenager and was jailed for shooting a member of the Provisionals. In jail Robinson got on well with Mooney and says the crime boss saved his bacon on more than one occasion.

> I had been the target of a number of attacks from Provos and I had sustained a broken hand. One guy tried to take advantage, by offering to fight me. I was in no position to defend myself. Others were closing in around me. But without asking, Mickey stepped in and the thing was forgotten.

In prison, using his undoubted charm, Mickey Mooney built up a network of contacts including some paramilitary people. He was particularly friendly with 'Sparkie' Barclay – a prisoner who was a member of the terror group, the Irish National Liberation Army. Through him Mooney got to know another INLA man called 'Bobby T', who gave him the authority to carry out robberies in republican areas provided he paid a levy to the INLA. This gave Mooney the protection he needed from other paramilitary groups.

When Mooney was released from jail he needed money badly. One day he spotted Gerard Steenson, the notorious INLA assassin, entering the Falls Road branch of the Northern Bank. The bank (now closed) was situated in the Beechmount area, a few hundred yards from the offices of the INLA's political wing, the Irish Republican Socialist Party. From a distance, Mooney looked on as Steenson lodged around twenty thousand pounds and then left the bank holding his receipt.

Minutes later, Mooney returned to the bank with two of his friends. They were masked and brandishing replica guns, although the terrified bank staff did not know that at the time. The raiders left with a substantial amount of money – including the cash deposited by Steenson!

The INLA, embarrassed by Mooney's cheek, ordered his execution. The group doggedly searched Belfast bars he was known to frequent, but Mooney had been tipped off and made himself scarce. Shortly after this, Mooney bought his first weapon – a Walther PPK handgun. Using his wits, Mooney offered the weapon to the INLA in return for lifting the death threat. The ploy worked and, with the assassination scare out of the way, Mooney was free to build a criminal gang around him. He hand-picked his men and prided himself on their professionalism.

Mooney's team were essentially bank robbers. He did, however, maintain loose links with his INLA contacts and it was this connection which unwittingly got Mooney caught up in the murder of an Official IRA man in Belfast.

An INLA man called Martin 'Rook' O'Prey (later shot dead in an internecine republican feud) asked Mooney to use his contacts to borrow two handguns. Mooney was told the weapons were to be used in robberies and duly obliged. But unknown to Mooney, O'Prey was planning the murder of Eamon 'Hatchet' Kerr – an Official IRA man from the Lower Falls district. O'Prey claimed Kerr was harassing a relative of his. A few days later, Kerr was shot dead as he lay in bed. As he handed the guns back to their owner two days later, Mooney apologised profusely because he had no idea they were to be used in a murder – and especially not the murder of an Official IRA man.

Around this time Mooney married his childhood sweetheart Anne and the couple settled in the Short Strand district, where Mickey had family connections. One night, as the couple were on their way to a party, a leading Provo challenged Mooney to a fight. Mooney declined the offer and walked on. But after thinking he might have looked afraid of the IRA man, he turned back and with one punch knocked him out. Days later, three Provos tried to smash their way into Mooney's home. Their efforts were thwarted by a recently installed and very expensive security system. It now appears the attack on Mooney's home was actually a murder bid, although this was unknown at the time.

Mickey Mooney's reputation as a crime boss continued to grow – as did his bank balance – and as the drugs scene in Northern Ireland began to take off around 1990, Mooney was in a position to buy in at a high level. But he also began to attract the attention of the RUC Drugs Squad.

One day, with the cops on his tail, Mooney was observed throwing a package into the River Lagan as he crossed the Albert Bridge in a car. He was arrested and when the package was recovered it was found to contain a substantial drugs stash. Mooney went to jail for the second time. In prison he stood out, mostly because he was so physically fit and also because of his professional approach to the whole thing – doing his time without a word of complaint. He even earned the respect of some republicans when he single-handedly battered five members of the notorious Shankill Butchers gang in front of their eyes.

Back out on the streets, Mickey Mooney cultivated the image which earned him the title of Ulster's answer to John Gotti – 'The Dapper Don'. He was proud of his dark-brown hair, with flowing permed locks. Dressed in a black leather waistcoat with an expensive raincoat over his arm, he cut an impressive figure. Life was good for Mickey Mooney. He had made it. Having survived the physically dangerous bank-robbing times, he was now a businessman, providing employment for others. It didn't matter that the business was drug dealing and that his workers were Ecstasy pushers. He had done well for a wee lad from Turf Lodge, he thought, and he hadn't had to join the Stickies or the Provies to do so.

But he signed his own death warrant when he threatened the life of an IRA man whose son owed him money. Some people had decided 'The Dapper Don' was getting too big for his boots.

By 1992, Mickey 'Moneybags' Mooney, as he was also known, had firmly established himself as Belfast's number one crime boss. He was highly respected among the criminal fraternity, and, although republicans would be loathed to admit it, he was also liked – in Belfast at least – by the Provo rank and file, who admired his disciplined approach to crime. Mooney wisely knew his days as a bank robber were over. The risks were enormous and it was only a matter of time before a member of his gang was shot dead. The future was drugs, and in the drugs underworld no one cared about stupid things like religion – that was yesterday's business and it was time to move on.

Nightlife in Belfast at that time was dull to say the least, but with the advent of dance music, and the drugs culture which went with it, Northern Ireland began to open up. Drugs began to take over from alcohol and Mooney was determined not just to be a bit player in the Ecstasy business. He quickly worked out where the big money was to be made.

Using his contacts, Mickey Mooney was introduced to a former INLA man called Tommy Savage, who was living in Amsterdam. Savage was earning a fortune as a drugs wholesaler. Mooney flew out to meet him and, through an Asian intermediary called 'Ramadam', arranged for a consignment of drugs to be smuggled back to Ulster.

Suddenly Mooney was a big-time dealer. Using a convicted armed robber called Dominic Thompson as his right-hand man, Mooney built up a lucrative drugs empire. But of course it wasn't long before he once again came to the attention of Customs and Excise and the RUC Drugs Squad, which had been expanded to cope with the growing drug trade.

The Dapper Don was under constant surveillance – and he knew it. Despite this, he successfully controlled a network of local dealers who sold the Ecstasy tabs he had smuggled from Amsterdam. Using a variety of routes,

Mooney regularly went on shopping sprees to the Dutch capital, claiming to inquiring customs officials he was a used-car buyer.

Inevitably, Mooney's narcotics empire began to attract the attentions of the IRA. A small-time crook and serial house burglar, whose father was at that time finance officer for the Provos, starting working for Mooney. At first things were fine, but then the relationship soured when the crook wouldn't pay his drugs debts. His father was embarrassed and angered when other republicans began making comments about his son working for a drugs baron. In an effort to get his boy out of the drugs business, the IRA man bought his son a car. He wanted the youngster to start working as a self-employed taxi driver. But Mickey Mooney somewhat recklessly seized the car in part payment of the outstanding debt. When the IRA man telephoned Mickey Mooney to challenge him on the matter, Mooney adopted an aggressive approach and at one point even threatened the IRA man. Mooney had now overstepped the mark, as far as the IRA was concerned.

An IRA meeting was hurriedly arranged in a former mill property off the Falls Road. It was decided that, despite the IRA ceasefire – which was then only eight months old – Mickey Mooney would be executed and the hit would be claimed by a nebulous organisation calling itself Direct Action Against Drugs. The group would have no premises, spokesmen or press officers. It would only execute uppity drug dealers and then claim the killings. The new breed of drug dealers had to be taught a lesson and Mickey Mooney topped the list.

An IRA man who was at that time operations officer for Belfast was told to carry out an investigation into Mooney's drugs empire. A total of 43 people were pulled in and forced to make tape-recorded statements. They all alleged Mooney was a major dealer. They were forced to supply details of Mooney's regular movements and one man told his interrogators that Mooney called into a Belfast bar called The 18 Steps in the centre of Belfast every Friday night. The tape recordings were to be used to prove Mooney's drug-dealing activities in the event of a backlash against the IRA, which was supposed to be on ceasefire.

Two very experienced killers were specially chosen for the job. They knew Mickey personally because they all lived within a short walk of each other. The IRA men had both previously been involved in the close-quarter killing of a man called Sammy Ward – shot dead in the Sean Martin's Gaelic Athletic Club in Beechfield Street. The men were tasked with killing Mooney during his visit to The 18 Steps Bar the following Friday. All necessary arrangements were made.

On Friday evening a team of IRA 'spotters' were sent into the city centre looking for Mooney. Finally, one man reported seeing the 'Dapper Don' walking into the first-floor lounge of The 18 Steps Bar.

Within minutes, the unmasked IRA hit men were approaching the bar entrance. One of the gunmen used a mobile phone to call the bar and asked for Mooney by name. (Bar staff claimed Mooney took at least 20 calls that night, both on the public phone and his mobile.) By now the gunmen were at the bar entrance and the second they heard Mooney's voice they raced up the stairs. Mooney was standing straight in front of them, still holding the telephone receiver.

As horrified customers looked on, the assassins fired at least six heavy-calibre bullets into his body and he slumped to the ground. The gunmen ran off to a waiting car. The promise made to the IRA Finance Officer had been kept. Mooney was executed in a 'mafia-style' favour – more would follow.

– CHAPTER FIFTEEN –

Lenny Murphy – Local Hero, Shankill Road Style

Here lies a soldier.

Inscription on the headstone of UVF killer Lenny Murphy, at Carnmoney Cemetery, on the outskirts of Belfast.

To this day, even the mention of the notorious loyalist murder gang 'The Shankill Butchers' strikes fear into the hearts of many Catholics. Their apprehension is not without foundation because these were the people who, more than any other collection of killers thrown up by the Troubles, demonstrated the subhuman depths some people were prepared to plumb in pursuit of political and religious domination. The driving force behind this terrifying murder machine was one Hugh Leonard Thompson Murphy.

Known as Lenny, it was Murphy who developed the cut-throat killing technique which became the Butchers' trademark. In many ways, the modus operandi of Murphy's gang was simple. Attacks were usually preceded by a substantial boozing session and in many instances the victims were entirely innocent.

After pub closing, Murphy's men would trawl the practically deserted streets of inner-city Belfast in a black London-style taxi, seeking out victims. Northern Ireland's capital city is unique in that it is quite possible to guess a person's religion based on nothing more than the side of street on which they choose to walk. This is particularly true of interface areas during the hours of darkness.

The Butchers' victims were generally selected at random and were subjected to horrendous and lengthy periods of torture before being granted the small mercy of death. Murphy's men, all members of the Ulster Volunteer Force, were expert at carrying out the usual paramilitary tasks of beatings, bombings and shootings. But without a doubt, the speciality which singled out their leader as psychopathic was his penchant for close-quarter cut-throat killing. Removing teeth by using pliers while the victims were still alive was another of Murphy's trademark techniques.

Police believe Lenny Murphy personally carried out no fewer than 18 murders, although he probably had a hand in another 30. Murphy's marathon murder mission began in 1972 when, aged just 20, he shot dead Eddie Pavis, a 32-year-old illegal arms dealer, in his own home. Murphy believed Pavis had sold weapons stolen from a loyalist arms dump to members of the Official IRA. His accomplice was Mervyn Connor, a 20-year-old UVF member. Both men were arrested and charged with murder. While in jail awaiting trial, Connor made a full statement to the police naming Murphy as the gunman. Days later, Connor died of cyanide poisoning. The deadly liquid was personally dispensed by Lenny Murphy.

The fact that Murphy was able to pull off such a thing while on remand for murder is an example of the kind of power he wielded in and out of jail. Murphy beat the murder rap when he appeared in court the following year and it was many years later before the police realised Lenny Murphy was the man who poisoned Mervyn Connor.

Following his release from prison, Murphy and his Shankill Butchers gang embarked on a five-year killing spree which shocked the public at large and at the same time baffled hardened RUC detectives.

Catholics were routinely and systematically butchered and tortured as Lenny Murphy's bloodlust increased with every killing. But Protestants also fell prey to Murphy and his men, usually because they were mistaken for Catholics or were caught up in a loyalist paramilitary feud. Despite the outrage expressed by many, the detectives faced 'a wall of silence'. This became a recurring problem as the investigation continued. No one was willing to give evidence against the Butcher Gang, under any circumstances. The fear of reprisal was well founded, as Murphy's public execution of a fellow loyalist killer clearly demonstrated.

Noel 'Nogi' Shaw was badly beaten and tied to a chair after Murphy ordered his UVF unit to abduct Shaw and take him to the Lawnbrooke Social Club – a notorious Shankill Road drinking den frequented by loyalist paramilitaries.

Murphy told everyone in the cabaret lounge of the club to gather round as he took the stage. He approached 18-year-old Shaw and accused him of being the triggerman involved in the murder of Archie Waller – another killer and personal friend of Lenny Murphy. The Butchers' boss levelled a gun at Shaw's head and shot him six times. With blood spurting everywhere, Murphy put the gun in his pocket and calmly walked back to the bar to finish his drink.

When the sound of the gunfire died away an eerie silence fell across the room. After taking a sip from his glass, Murphy turned to the 20 UVF men who witnessed the execution and barked: 'Clean up that mess!'

Shaw's body was unceremoniously dumped in a linen basket and removed from the club in a stolen taxi. One of Murphy's most trusted lieutenants hit on a plan to burn the taxi with Shaw's body still in it. But a heavy presence of troops in the Shankill area that day forced the men tasked with disposing of the body to abandon it instead and it was soon discovered.

Writer Martin Dillon, whose book *The Shankill Butchers* is the authorative account of one of the worst chapters in Belfast's bloody history, says the public execution of Noel Shaw was Murphy's way of stamping his supreme authority on the UVF: 'To understand the mind of someone like Lenny Murphy, you have to examine every aspect of the Shaw killing. This was Murphy letting not only his section of the UVF but the entire organisation know that he was in charge.'

Ironically, 'Nogi' Shaw became a Shankill Butchers' victim as a result of an attempt by the UVF leadership to clean up the image of the organisation. Around that time, in 1975, a new UVF leadership was tasked with stamping out the gangsterism which was rife in the organisation at that time and, amazingly, Lenny Murphy was personally asked to oversee the makeover by coming down hard on rogue elements.

An old lady who lived at 161 Shankill Road had been robbed and tied up by a UVF gang which broke into her home. She was left for 12 hours before she was rescued by neighbours. The crime outraged the entire Shankill community and the UVF Brigade Staff asked Murphy to track down the culprits and punish them by kneecapping – shooting through the knee joint.

Murphy suspected three UVF men who frequented the nearby Windsor Bar. He had a word with their boss and arranged for them to be 'arrested' and taken to a room above the Brown Bear pub which Murphy used as his own HQ. The men were systematically beaten until they confessed to robbing the old lady. They were then taken to a derelict garage where placards bearing the words 'Shot For Crimes Against The Loyalist People' were placed around their necks prior to them being kneecapped. But, as he was about to be shot, one of the men, Stewartie Robinson, made a run for it and was shot dead by Murphy's trusted friend Archie Waller.

Lenny Murphy was particularly fond of Waller because he had willingly taken part in the recent cut-throat killing of Catholic man Francis Crossan, whose head was practically severed from his body. Murphy ordered the other kneecappings to go ahead and warned the victims that if they spilled the beans on Robinson's murder they would be killed. The UVF leadership then quizzed Murphy about Robinson's death, but he denied any knowledge of it. However, within days the truth emerged and the leader of the Windsor Bar team ordered Waller's death in revenge.

On 29 November 1975, Waller – a married man with two children – was shot dead as he sat in his car outside a loyalist club in Downing Street. Murphy was furious at this challenge to his authority and ordered his men to abduct Waller's killers. When Murphy's team burst into the Windsor Bar, they found Nogi Shaw drinking on his own. He was dragged out and taken to the Lawnbrooke Social Club, where his ordeal culminated in his public execution at the hands of Lenny Murphy.

A police investigation into the killing drew a blank initially, as right across the Shankill shutters were pulled tightly down. After the furore surrounding Shaw's murder died away, Murphy's Butcher Gang got back to doing the thing they did best – the torture and killing of innocent Catholics.

The RUC was now ploughing extensive resources into tracking down the Butcher gang but were constantly hampered by the fact that many in the close-knit Shankill community were unable or unwilling to come forward. In some cases, their silence came about through fear of reprisals, but in other cases it was because they quietly supported Lenny Murphy's strategy of terrorising the Catholic community, which they saw as providing the necessary succour the IRA needed in order to exist.

A special squad of detectives, headed by Detective Superintendent Jimmy Nesbitt, were brought together with a single purpose – to snare the Shankill Butchers.

Despite the anguish over a growing list of unsolved murders, Jimmy Nesbitt was convinced he was on the verge of a breakthrough and his hunch proved correct. At 4.30 a.m. on 11 May 1977, Jimmy Nesbitt was wakened from his sleep by the ringing of the telephone. It was a police officer from Tennent Street RUC Station, which covers the Shankill, ringing to tell Nesbitt that a man who had survived a serious assault in the area had been taken to hospital for treatment. The victim was 22-year-old Catholic Gerald McLaverty. He is the only known person to have entered the Butchers' torture chamber and lived to tell the tale. At first, Nesbitt did not link McLaverty to the Butcher gang because of the very fact that he was still living.

Once McLaverty had been interviewed, however, Nesbitt knew he was onto something. McLaverty told the police how he had been abducted by four men posing as police detectives and driven to a former doctor's surgery in the Shankill district. There, after offering the victim tea, the men proceeded to assault and torture him. One of the men, using a bootlace, choked McLaverty and he was eventually dumped and left for dead in a back alleyway.

At this time, Ulster was gripped in its second General Strike. The action was provoked by loyalist anger at government policy and, as many people were unable to travel to work due to paramilitary intimidation, the Shankill Road was packed with people hanging around in groups catching up on the latest strike gossip. Jimmy Nesbitt was suddenly struck by a brainwave which was to prove to be the key in solving the case of the Shankill Butchers. He instructed two of his men to disguise McLaverty and drive him around the Shankill. As the RUC car made its way along the busy shopping street, McLaverty pointed out two of the men who had tortured him. A few days later, a massive RUC search and arrest operation swung into action. More arrests followed, including that of Robert 'Basher' Bates, one of Murphy's trusted officers who had witnessed the execution of Nogi Shaw.

Bates was interviewed by Detective Sergeant Philip Boyd (now deceased). 'Bogie' Boyd, as he was known to friends and colleagues, was a tough rugby-playing police officer from Coleraine, Co. Derry. He had worked in the Belfast region for many years and was well up to speed on how to handle so-called Belfast 'hards'.

'Bogie's interviewing technique was brutal, but effective,' recalls his friend, now retired Detective Superintendent Kevin Sheehy. But on the day he was detailed to interview 'Basher' Bates, Boyd decided to employ a new and uncharacteristic tactic: he decided to be nice. With Bates sitting in front of him, Philip Boyd pulled out his trademark Petersen twisted briar pipe and, after taking what seemed like an eternity to light it, said: 'You're fucked this time, Basher!' In an instant, Boyd knew his suspect was about to confess and remained silent. He continued staring at Bates for three minutes before Bates finally decided to speak: 'Bogie,' said Bates in a whisper, 'Go and tell my wife where I am and when you come back I will tell you everything.'

It was nearly teatime and the last thing Philip Boyd wanted to do was to drive across Belfast to the Shankill. But, sensing he was onto a winner, he agreed to Bates' request. When he returned to the custody suite, he took down the confession of Robert 'Basher' Bates, who admitted his part in a five-year campaign of ritual slaughter.

At a subsequent trial, Bates was one of 11 members of the Shankill Butchers gang who were convicted of 19 murders as well as countless attempted murders, kidnappings and bombings. The gang received a total of 42 life sentences as well as prison sentences amounting to almost 2,000 years. Basher Bates was handed ten life sentences and the judge recommended he spend the rest of his life in prison. He was, however, released in 1996, only to be shot dead in a revenge attack the following year. It is believed the man who murdered him was related to one of Bates' loyalist victims.

Jimmy Nesbitt's team was delighted. But the detectives' celebration party was tinged with reservation because three senior members of the Butchers Gang had evaded prosecution, including Lenny Murphy himself. Throughout the trial, Murphy was referred to only as Mr X and his two closest cohorts were named as Mr A and Mr B.

Jimmy Nesbitt, now living quietly in retirement, seldom discusses what was one of the biggest murder investigations ever undertaken by the RUC. But people who know him well say he still feels cheated that he was unable to put Murphy, Mr A and Mr B before the courts.

Martin Dillon insists that the Mr A and Mr B were inextricably linked to Lenny Murphy in a way which would ensure the Butchers leader was never caught. In a bid to throw police off Murphy's scent, they made sure the murder campaign continued while Lenny Murphy was in prison awaiting trial.

The IRA felt duty bound to exact revenge for the shattering effect the Shankill Butchers' campaign had on the Catholic community and, on 16 November 1982, it moved to take out the man who was arguably the most feared loyalist paramilitary figure of all time.

For years IRA leaders had discussed ways of executing Lenny Murphy but always came up against the same problem – little or no information was known about his movements. But once the Provos had enlisted the help of top loyalist racketeer and UDA member Jimmy Craig, Murphy's days were numbered.

Craig operated a massive protection racket based mainly in the building industry, which was booming in Belfast in the 1980s as the government moved to replace large swathes of slum housing. He was doing deals with republicans in order to escape the prying eyes of other UDA people who viewed Craig as a money-grabbing gangster out to line his own pockets. Jimmy Craig built up a dossier on Murphy's movements and was able to tell his IRA contact that the Butchers boss was in the habit of calling at his girlfriend's house at Forthriver Park in the Glencairn district.

The IRA man tasked with taking out Murphy was just 25 when he agreed to put his life on the line by stepping into the Butchers' backyard. In the closed and secret world of the IRA he was known as 'Spik' – because of his resemblance to a glam-rock star popular at that time by the name of 'Spik Spangle'. Murphy's murder was planned down to the very last detail. The hit squad had a van specially converted with spy holes to allow its occupants all-round vision. It was placed near Murphy's usual parking spot outside his girlfriend's home and when Murphy pulled up in his yellow Rover car, Spik stepped from the back of the van and opened fire on Murphy, hitting him 22 times. Seven of the bullets hit his head, while the others ripped through his heart, lungs and chest. The IRA hit team escaped unhurt.

It became apparent that Murphy had been set up by someone within the loyalist community and it wasn't long before the finger of suspicion began to point at Jimmy Craig. Despite his double-dealing, Jimmy Craig managed to survive for another six years, until he was cut down in a hail of bullets fired at him by a member of his own paramilitary group, the UDA.

Lenny Murphy was given a full UVF paramilitary funeral. Men in black uniforms formed a colour party around the cortège and a volley of shots were fired over the coffin. The Shankill district of Belfast came to a standstill as thousands of loyalists turned out to pay their respects. Following the funeral, Murphy's mates Mr A and Mr B – who had both played prominent roles as mourners – settled back down to family life on the Shankill Road.

Friday, 10 August 1998 was a pleasant evening in Belfast and so Lower Falls man Tommy Nelson decided to make the short walk along the Grosvenor Road into the city centre for a drink with one of his pals. The two friends, both Catholics and dedicated followers of Glasgow Celtic Football Club, enjoyed a couple of pints in The Crown Bar and The Beaten Docket before heading home.

On the way, Nelson remarked how things appeared to be improving and that the bad old days of sectarian murder were now a thing of the past. As the two friends waited for the pedestrian crossing light to change at Westlink roundabout, a red Volkswagen Scirocco car collided with another vehicle in front of them. The collision was serious and the two men raced over to the scene of the crash to give assistance. His friend rushed to the nearby Grosvenor Road police station to summon help, while Tommy Nelson delivered what first aid he could to the badly injured man in the Scirocco. Holding his hand, Nelson comforted the man, who had suffered appalling injuries, while he waited for an ambulance to arrive. After giving their names and addresses to a police officer, the two Falls Road men carried on their way. That night before going to bed, Tommy Nelson said a prayer for the 'poor soul' who had been in the car crash a few hours before.

The following day, the police called at Tommy Nelson's house to take a statement from him regarding the car crash he had witnessed the previous evening. An RUC officer explained that the matter was now a fatal accident inquiry as the man Nelson had helped had died on his way to the nearby Royal Victoria Hospital.

What the policeman did not tell Nelson, however, was that the dead man – John Alexander Thompson Murphy – was the 46-year-old brother of Shankill Butchers leader Lenny Murphy, or that John Murphy was in fact the mysterious Mr B referred to at the Butchers Gang murder trial. It was an ironic twist of fate that, as he lay dying and waiting for an ambulance, John Murphy – mastermind of the Shankill Butchers' cut-throat killing crusade – was attended by two Catholic men who were also keen Celtic fans. John Murphy was one of the deadly duo Jimmy Nesbitt was so keen to see behind bars.

Although things had calmed down considerably since Lenny Murphy's murder, another member of the Murphy family seemed destined to follow in the footsteps of the men who had dominated the Shankill Butchers gang. William Murphy was keen to prove he was every bit as tough as his cut-throat killing uncles Lenny and John and so, in January 1997, he battered a 78-year-old man senseless and then left him to choke in a pool of his own blood. William Murphy Jnr was jailed for life for the murder of Second World War hero Andy Spence in his Battenberg Street home in the heart of the Shankill area. During a police raid on Murphy's home nearby, 56 rounds of ammunition were found. His father William Murphy Snr pleaded guilty to possession of the bullets and was given a two-year jail sentence suspended for two years.

Murphy Jnr was only three years old when Lenny Murphy was cut down in a hail of IRA bullets. But by bludgeoning Andy Spence to death, he proved he was every bit the killer his uncles Lenny and John were.

Martin Dillon maintains the triumvirate relationship of Lenny and John Murphy and the shadowy Mr A is the key to understanding the Shankill Butchers case. He says:

> For anyone trying to understand who Mr A was, one would have to look at those who were closest to Lenny Murphy and who would never have been able to betray him. These two guys, John Murphy and Mr A, were the protective cover which allowed Lenny Murphy to operate with impunity for so long. Even when Lenny was in jail, no one was going to go against him, because John Murphy and Mr A were still on the loose and ensuring the killings continued. They were the two people Jimmy Nesbitt and the other cops working on the case could

never bring to justice. But they were also the people who were closest to Lenny in every sense and, therefore, they were able to protect him.

Dillon, who now lives in New York, is considered an expert in terrorist movements throughout the world, although for most of his working life he has concentrated on the paramilitary organisations operating in Northern Ireland. He is convinced that one day, the missing link in the murderous trinity which controlled the Shankill Butchers will be revealed. 'When people discover the real relationship between Lenny and John Murphy and Mr A, then it will make the story of the Shankill Butchers even more frightening.'

– CHAPTER SIXTEEN –

Johnny 'Mad Dog' Adair – Director of Terrorism

We'll march up and down,
On the road to Portadown,
The drums they will rattle like the thunder.
And as the day draws near,
We'll fill the Papish hearts with fear,
We're the bold Orange heroes of Comber.
A traditional loyalist song

These days, Johnny Adair projects an image similar to a number of other Ulstermen who have formerly been involved in terrorism. Aping Sinn Fein politicians, he has even begun wearing expensive Hugo Boss suits with Giorgio Armani ties, and recently he has granted interviews to such respectable publications as *The Sunday Times*. Observers say it appears Adair is desperately trying to clean up his own act and at the same time improve the tarnished image of the Ulster Freedom Fighters (UFF) – the loyalist paramilitary group to which he belongs. Adair, who was once jailed for 16 years for directing terrorism, insists he is now committed to using exclusively peaceful methods of settling political differences – very few believe him.

John James Adair first came to prominence in the wake of a paramilitary power struggle which took place inside the Ulster Defence Association at the end of the 1980s. The leadership, headed by Andy Tyrie, was seen by the young turks coming to the fore as corrupt and completely infiltrated by the RUC Special Branch.

Prior to this upheaval, Johnny Adair was known to the police in the Shankill district as a small-time hood who passed his time sniffing glue and occasionally attending National Front demonstrations, which were promoted in Belfast by the UDA. For a time, Adair was the frontman in a punk-rock band whose song lyrics spewed out racist and sectarian rhetoric in time to a muffled three-chord trick. The aptly named 'Offensive Weapon', which included Adair's mates Skelly McCrorie and Donald Hodgen, had a big following in England and attracted huge crowds when they performed at National Front functions.

But as time moved on and the old guard quit the organisation or were forced out, Adair rose quickly up the paramilitary ladder and was very soon appointed Brigadier in charge of 'C' Company based in the lower Shankill estate. He built up a team of trusty lieutenants around him.

On 23 October 1993, the Provos attempted to wipe out the entire UFF leadership by planting a bomb in Frizzell's Fish Shop on the Shankill Road. Senior loyalists, including Johnny Adair, were in the habit of using the upstairs premises for meetings, but when IRA volunteer Thomas Begley placed the bomb on the shop counter it exploded, killing himself and nine innocent Protestant shoppers, including children. Sean Kelly, another IRA volunteer who was with Begley, was badly injured, but survived.

A week later, on 30 October, two UFF gunmen walked into the Rising Sun Bar in the Co. Derry village of Greysteel during Halloween celebrations. After shouting 'Trick or treat?' the men opened fire, killing seven people. For a while it looked as though Northern Ireland might descend into civil war, but successful RUC investigations into both atrocities helped ease tension.

Johnny Adair's rise to power in the UFF coincided with the mushrooming of the illegal drugs industry in Ulster. This provided a lucrative source of income for the revamped UFF. Adair was on the way up, but he badly needed something to assert his authority over the men below him and, before long, Noel Alexander Cardwell presented him with that opportunity.

Cardwell was a 26-year-old Protestant from the Shankill district. He suffered from a nervous complaint which saw him in and out of hospital and doctors say he had a mental age of an 11 or 12 year old. Noel Cardwell was single and lived with one of his sisters. He worked as a part-time glass collector in one of the local bars and his main interest in life was having a game of snooker. Occasionally, when playing snooker Cardwell would drink two pints of beer, but his friends insist he would have no more than that, because he knew it could affect the medication he was required to take on a daily basis.

One night, shortly before Christmas in 1993, Cardwell, who was also known as 'Big Noel' on account of being 6 ft 4 in., felt like getting into the festive spirit and so he went for a pint to a local bar. He sat down at a table where two UDA men, who were known to him, were already sitting. For a laugh, one of the men spiked Cardwell's drink with an unknown substance (probably an Ecstasy tablet), which some time later caused him to feel unwell. Cardwell was rushed to hospital, where he received treatment for an aggravated ulcer. But he was also questioned by the police, who wanted to know who Cardwell had been drinking with prior to him feeling sick.

Being the trusting type, and not for a second believing he was doing anything disloyal to his friends, Noel Cardwell named the two UDA men. The men were arrested and quizzed about what happened when they met Cardwell in the bar. They were then released without charge.

Around this time, the police had seized a number of weapons from a UFF arms dump and Johnny Adair decided Cardwell, who was known to many UDA members in the Shankill area, must have had something to do with it. He ordered his men to 'arrest' Noel Cardwell as soon as he was released from hospital.

On 12 December 1993, Cardwell's sister collected him from the Royal Victoria Hospital on the Falls Road, where he had been kept in overnight. He was feeling much better and after tea he went to the 'Buffs' club for a game of snooker. He was careful not to take any alcohol that night and sometime later told his friends he was heading home. He never made it.

Cardwell was abducted by two of Johnny Adair's cohorts and taken to a flat at Boundary Way in the lower Shankill district. A hood was placed over his head and he was beaten about the head and body. Big Noel was then kicked and punched as his interrogators tried to 'persuade' him to admit to being a police informer. Cardwell persistently denied the allegations.

Johnny Adair, who was 29 years old at the time, arrived on the scene demanding to know how the interrogation was going: 'He's denying it, Johnny,' said one of Adair's close paramilitary associates.

Adair disappeared and returned a short time later wearing the paramilitary uniform of black jacket and trousers and black shoes. This time he was carrying a Magnum 10 pistol with a silencer attached. The weapon was pointing to the ground.

Adair handed a bag to Gary McMaster, another trusted UDA man, and said: 'When I come out, take this away.' Johnny Adair walked into the dingy flat and yelled to the UFF men present: 'Get him on his knees!' The men did as they were bid. Adair then pointed the gun at Noel Cardwell's hooded head and pulled the trigger. There was a dull thud. A single 45mm round which had been fired from close range smashed its way through Cardwell's skull and exited at the other side. Before Cardwell's body slumped to the floor, Johnny Adair was already walking back outside, where he placed the Magnum in a grip bag and said to the waiting McMaster: 'Move!' Gary McMaster did his boss's bidding and moved the gun out of the area to a safe UFF arms dump in the nearby Silverstream area.

Several hours later the police received a phone call from a man claiming to represent the UFF. He said the 'Special Assassination Section' of the UFF had executed Noel Cardwell in a flat at Boundary Walk because he was a Special Branch informer responsible for a number of arms finds in the Shankill area. The police raced to the scene where they found Noel Cardwell lying in a large pool of blood. Amazingly, he was still alive. The temperature had dropped during the night, preventing the blood from flowing at a normal rate. Noel Cardwell was rushed to hospital, but died there at 10.20 a.m.

As Noel Cardwell's distraught sisters made their way to the morgue to identify him, it was pretty much business as usual for Johnny Adair and the men of 'C' Company.

Adair was impressed by the performance of Gary McMaster when he safely disposed of the weapon after the Cardwell murder. The New Year brought new ideas and Adair decided it was time to go back to the old tried and tested loyalist tactic of 'terrorising the terrorists' – only this time he vowed to take the fight to Sinn Fein's front door and Gary McMaster agreed to be a willing participant in Adair's plans.

Gary Whitty McMaster, a Protestant, was originally from east Belfast. But at 29 years of age, he was married and living on the staunchly loyalist Shankill Road, with no fewer than nine children to provide for. Having joined the UFF 14 months before the Cardwell killing, he was a trusted member of the new breed of loyalist terrorists. McMaster was loyal to Johnny Adair and he was given the job of running a 'shebeen' on the lower Shankill, where drink was sold illegally and drugs, particularly Ecstasy tabs, were freely available.

Adair told McMaster that, although he saw a future for him as a senior officer in the UFF, he would first have to prove he was up to the mark. McMaster was tempted by the promise of 'a few bob' in the event of a successful operation and finally agreed to fill in the detail on Adair's new terror blueprint.

On 7 February 1994, Gary McMaster planted a booby-trap device at Sinn Fein's Connolly House headquarters on the Andersonstown Road. He secreted a grenade in the front garden which was linked to a command wire on the gate. The bomb should have exploded when the gate was opened. But it was spotted by Councillor Alex Maskey, who was at the time Sinn Fein's leader on Belfast City Council.

Maskey, who was elected Belfast's first republican Mayor in 2002, had to endure the indignity of phoning the RUC to have the device made safe by the

British Army bomb disposal squad. The incident attracted widespread news coverage and so Adair paid McMaster one hundred pounds in cash.

The following day, Gary McMaster was back in action. He tried to murder a Catholic man, Joseph Kirby, near the Hatfield Bar on the Ormeau Road. Again he received a one-hundred-pound cash payment from Johnny Adair. Four days after that, McMaster fired an RPG7 shoulder-held rocket at the Sinn Fein centre and again was paid one hundred pounds cash by his UFF Brigadier. The rocket attack caused considerable damage and was headline news for several days.

Then, on 18 February, as a team of workers were busy repairing damage at the Sinn Fein HQ, McMaster opened fire on them without warning. Three tradesmen were hit. Johnny Adair organised a party in McMaster's honour that night and once again gave him one hundred pounds in cash. Under Adair, the UFF were back in business and the IRA was worried. Adair was true to his word: he was bringing the war to the doorstep of the republican movement.

Following the onslaught on Sinn Fein's premises, Adair rested on his laurels for a while and Gary McMaster enjoyed the notoriety of being Johnny's main man. The following month, McMaster was messing around with a .22 pistol when it went off. The bullet blew a piece of his finger off and he required hospital treatment. He received a number of visitors from the UFF, who were worried that their new triggerman on the block was seriously injured. The terrorists were relieved to learn McMaster was well on the way to making a full recovery.

McMaster, however, also received a visit from two people he didn't know. The strangers enquiring after his health were officers from the RUC Special Branch. The men, both experienced detectives, made McMaster an offer he couldn't refuse and he was duly signed up as a paid police agent working inside the UFF.

McMaster's main motivation was money, which is why in May of that year he agreed to take part in a UFF armed robbery at Boardmills Post Office, near Lisburn. The robbery was expected to produce big money and Adair promised McMaster between five hundred and one thousand pounds.

Unknown to the UFF, or the RUC Special Branch for that matter, the anti-racketeering branch of the RUC had the place staked out and when UFF men made their move they were all arrested. McMaster's career as a Special Branch agent was short-lived. It was time for him to hold his hands up and he did so willingly.

McMaster made extensive statements to the RUC detectives who interviewed him and spilled the beans on the Sinn Fein HQ attacks as well as the execution of Noel Alexander Cardwell. In total, McMaster made statements concerning 33 serious terrorist offences, but when he appeared in Belfast Crown Court at the end of June 1995, he decided to contest two of the litany of charges before him. He denied murdering Noel Cardwell and he named Johnny Adair as the guilty party. McMaster also denied possession of the Magnum 10 pistol which was the murder weapon used in the Cardwell killing and once again he named Johnny Adair as the culprit.

After a four-day trial, McMaster was found guilty on all counts and sent to prison for life. RUC detectives planned to mount a case against Adair concerning the Cardwell killing, but decided against it after taking legal advice.

The Cardwell case was, however, a turning point for Adair as well as the RUC. It was while working on the Cardwell murder investigation that Detective Sergeant Johnston Brown first realised Adair was a cold-blooded killer and he pledged himself to putting Adair behind bars. He succeeded.

On 6 September 1995, Johnny 'Mad Dog' Adair, as he was known, pleaded guilty to directing the activities of the Ulster Freedom Fighters. He received a 16-year prison sentence when he appeared at the Crown Court in Belfast.

Adair was the first member of the UFF and only the second person in Northern Ireland to face charges of directing terrorism. The offence had been included in the Northern Ireland Emergency Provisions Act since 1991. The court heard that Adair was trapped when police targeted him and secretly taped conversations with him. As he was led from the dock, Johnny Adair appeared unmoved by the severe sentence and, as he gave a clenched fist salute, he shouted to journalists in the press gallery: 'I applaud the dedication of all the young men of the 2nd Battalion.'

Pat Lynch, prosecuting, had described Adair as a sinister and manipulative terror chief. He said Adair was 'dedicated to his cause which was nakedly sectarian in its hatred of those it regarded as militant republicans – among whom he lumped almost the entire Catholic population'. Mr Lynch said Adair held sway over his foot soldiers with 'a combination of force of personality and the ability to inspire fear'.

In a tape-recorded conversation with a police officer, Adair explained the secret of his success: 'The threat of one [a bullet] behind the ear keeps them in line,' said the UFF boss.

Detective Sergeant Brown wound Johnny Adair in as a fisherman does a salmon. He made a point of getting to know Adair, who believed he was a rogue officer, and, at great risk to himself, he methodically set about getting the evidence on which to build a criminal case against the top UFF man. Brown would sit in Adair's house drinking tea and chatting to his UFF pals.

On one occasion, when Johnny and his mates were all talking at cross purposes, Brown intervened, pointing to the lampshade on the ceiling light and saying: 'Don't all be talking at once, because the bug in that light won't pick it all up.'

Adair and his mates laughed loudly. Johnston Brown was great craic, they thought. As far as they were concerned, it was a pity all cops weren't like Johnston Brown. Later that day, when Brown returned to his police station to knock off duty, a member of the RUC Special Branch asked to have a word with him: 'Johnston, I wish you hadn't said that about the bug in the light in Adair's house. We do have a bug there, but its not in the light!'

Johnston Brown was a detective of exceptional ability and bravery. Only his determination, patience and courage could have snared someone as cunning as Adair. This doggedness and professional skill were enough to scare Adair into pleading guilty in court. He knew too well what type of man Brown was and he didn't want to debate with him in the witness box.

After the Adair trial, the UDA/UFF decided to hit back at Detective Sergeant Brown for what it saw as the humiliation of its beloved leader and UFF men left a bomb outside the policeman's front door. Fortunately, the bomber placed the device too close to the door and when it detonated the blast did not have the desired impact. Detective Sergeant Brown and his family were forced to move home as a result of the UFF attack.

Johnny Adair was released from prison early under the terms of the Good Friday Agreement, which saw some of the biggest terrorist criminals back on the streets. But following a murderous feud between the UFF and its arch-rivals the UVF, Adair was rearrested and put back in prison on the instructions of the then Secretary of State for Northern Ireland, Peter Mandelson, who ruled that Adair had breached the terms of his release licence.

Adair was furious at being incarcerated again and he fought Mandelson and his successor Dr John Reid every inch of the way as he tried to have the ruling overturned in the courts. But in an exhaustive written explanation of its decision, the Sentence Review Commission told Adair he was back in jail because he was involved in a 'paramilitary show of strength in Portadown' and the 'organisation of a colour party of armed men' at a UDA/UFF parade on the Shankill Road on 19 August 2000 – two men were killed that day.

The Commission also accused Adair of 'making from the proceeds of your drug-dealing payments to proscribed organisations'. The 'Mad Dog' was caged and he wasn't getting out until John Reid was satisfied he had changed his tune. So Adair settled down to become a model prisoner. He even took a job as a wing orderly in charge of keeping the kitchen clean.

He was freed again in 2002 and Johnny Adair now says the future, as far as he is concerned, is about politics. He insists he's solely interested in getting the best for the people he represents.

A former police officer who has watched Adair's transformation from punk-rock singer to sharp-suited politician says he remains to be convinced of the UFF leader's long-term intentions. And, as he cast his mind back to that cold night in December 1993, when Noel Cardwell, with a mental age of 12, walked into a dirty dingy flat at Boundary Walk never to come out again, the officer said: 'Johnny Adair has been given a chance to improve his life. It's a pity he never gave the same chance to Noel Cardwell.'

– CHAPTER SEVENTEEN –

Marty O'Hagan – Shot in the Back

Henry, the first time it was tragedy, the second time it was
farce.
Marty O'Hagan's view of the IRA ceasefire

George Chambers was a popular man. In his job as a police officer in the RUC
he was known as a 'solid citizen', but he was also known to have a good sense
of humour and compassion in abundance. At 44, George Chambers still held
the rank of constable, but personal ambition had not been his motivation for
joining the police in the first place. The outbreak of civil unrest on the
streets of Northern Ireland horrified Chambers, because as a father of six
children he worried about what the future held for them. He sincerely hoped
the politicians would be able to work out their differences in a way which
would once again bring peace and stability.

When the Queen Mother visited the RUC training depot at Enniskillen in
1962, Constable Chambers had been chosen to be a member of the guard of
honour. A photograph had been taken to record this event and it was given
pride of place in the Chambers family home at Bannbridge. Many people,
George Chambers included, believed that if a programme of reform had been
properly implemented at that time then the Troubles could have been
avoided.

Being a small-town police officer, George Chambers made it his business to
get to know as many people in the community he served as possible. He was
on good terms with almost everyone and he felt it was his duty to treat people
in a fair and civilised manner.

In 1972, as the Troubles were reaching a peak, Chambers was transferred to
Lurgan, the largest predominantly Catholic town in North Armagh. It was
inevitable that when the Troubles broke out Lurgan polarised, with many folk

retreating into the comparative comfort and safety of their own tribe. Catholics used Catholic-owned shops and pubs, and Protestants used Protestant-owned shops and pubs. There were, of course, a few notable exceptions.

North Armagh, of which Lurgan and its neighbouring town of Portadown were the main population areas, was still steeped in the rhetoric of yesteryear and neighbours being described by neighbours as 'the other sort' was commonplace.

These days Lurgan's Kilwilkie estate is exclusively Roman Catholic, but in 1972 the district had a fair smattering of Protestant residents. Earlier that year in Kilwilkie, eight-year-old Linda Hughes had been caught up in a road accident involving a police Land-Rover. The little girl was badly injured and required emergency hospital treatment after losing a kidney. As Christmas approached, George Chambers thought it would be a good idea if he persuaded his colleagues to contribute towards a present for Linda, who was on the road to recovery. The policeman managed to collect enough money from his fellow officers to buy a watch, a jigsaw puzzle and a box of snakes and ladders. There was also a few pounds in cash left over.

The following day, on 15 December, Constable Chambers suggested to his colleagues they should drive to Kilwilkie to deliver the presents to young Linda. That day was George Chamber's 22nd wedding anniversary and he was anxious to knock off work early as he and his wife intended going out that night to celebrate. Three officers, including a sergeant, agreed to go with the constable, although George Chambers waited in a police Land-Rover while his sergeant was welcomed into the Hughes' home by Linda's mum Elizabeth.

Unknown to the police officers, though, members of the Official IRA were planning to pull off a wages snatch at a local factory around the same time and were using a safe house in Kilwilkie as a base.

Linda Hughes was in the front living room of her parents' house along with her brother and sister when her mum ushered the RUC sergeant inside. The little girl's face lit up with a mixture of delight and embarrassment as the police officer handed her the presents which had been wrapped in brightly coloured Christmas paper. A broad smile appeared on Linda's face as she opened the box containing the watch. She had never owned a watch before and had only recently learned to tell the time. The police officer knew how to handle children. He took the watch from Linda, wound it up and then placed it around her wrist before fastening the strap. He then wished Linda a happy Christmas and after a few words with her mum left to go back to his colleagues waiting outside.

While the sergeant had been in the Hughes' house, George Chambers had spotted a strange-looking car which turned out to be stolen. The officers were concerned that it might contain a booby-trapped device and so they began evacuating houses nearby. The intention was to clear the immediate vicinity before calling in the army bomb disposal squad to examine the vehicle.

Suddenly the sound of heavy gunfire filled the air as Official IRA gunmen opened up from two separate firing positions. The police officers were totally unprepared for the onslaught and three of them, including George Chambers, fell to the ground hit in the first fusillade of shots.

As George Chambers lay there injured, one of the gunmen broke cover and ran forward until he stood directly over the constable. The IRA man continued firing into the officer's body from close range and then stole his Sten gun. It was only when the fourth policeman returned fire that the terrorists fled. George Chambers died at the scene and the killing sparked outrage and condemnation from many quarters, including many people on the Kilwilkie estate.

In Lurgan the murder of George Chambers became known as 'the shooting of Santa Claus'. A senior member of the Official IRA, which was on ceasefire at the time, carried out an investigation into the shooting. The officer's funeral took place a week before Christmas and he was buried at the Scarva Presbyterian burial ground in his native Bannbridge. Arrests soon followed and one man was sentenced to life imprisonment after being found guilty of murder. Two other men were convicted on firearms offences in connection with the same investigation.

That day had been one of the most violent in Northern Ireland for some time. A UDR man died in a hail of terrorist gunfire in Armagh and another member of the regiment was lucky to escape a murder bid in Derry. In Belfast, seven young men were shot in three separate incidents. Right across the Province, security forces were forced to deal with a spate of bombings and robberies as various terrorist organisations struggled to gain advantage.

It was around this time that Martin O'Hagan joined the Official IRA in Lurgan. Being naturally inquisitive, he had become interested in politics after watching television pictures of policemen battering civil rights demonstrators in the streets in Derry. Martin was a man of his time. He became influenced by the radical politics sweeping across Europe with the rise of student movements based in the universities, and in Ireland the Officials seemed to be the left-wing movement.

The eldest of six children, Owen Martin O'Hagan was born in Lurgan in 1950. Marty, as his friends called him, spent his early years in British Army camps in Germany. His father was a professional soldier and the O'Hagan family were entitled to family accommodation. But when he was four years old, his parents returned to Lurgan, where he grew up.

Marty's father hit on an idea which would soon provide his growing family with an above-average income in a town which had been blighted by unemployment and poor wages since its traditional linen industry all but collapsed many years before. The television industry was on the up and up and the retail sale of sets into the domestic market was about to take off. The training Marty's father had received during his army days stood him in good stead and he opened a soon-to-be-thriving TV and repair shop in Lurgan town centre. When Martin was of school-leaving age, he joined his father in the family business. Marty's job was to install aerials at the homes of customers who had either purchased or (more likely) rented a TV set from his father. A number of RUC officers working out of Lurgan police station even signed up as customers. Marty was a hard worker and the sight of him shimmying up a ladder onto a rooftop at speed was a fairly regular occurrence in the Lurgan of the 1960s.

Life was good for the O'Hagan family during that period. But with the onset of the Troubles, things were to change for the worse. Marty's parents parted and the family business closed when his father left for London. Marty's interest in radical left-wing republicanism, however, continued to grow and he took part in many protests and demonstrations. On one famous occasion, when he was 18, he travelled to Dublin to join in a protest against America's foreign policy regarding Vietnam. US President Richard Nixon was in town and so Martin and his friend Mairin de Burca, also a member of the Official republican movement, bought six eggs from a corner shop with the intention of throwing them at the famous visitor. The plan was to pitch the missiles and then take off at high speed on the back of Mairin's motor scooter. It didn't quite work out like that. The eggs were fired in Nixon's direction all right, but a member of An Garda Siochana was watching the entire incident and promptly arrested the republican protesters. When Marty and Mairin appeared in court, the judge appeared to have some sympathy with their views because he fined them just two pounds each before releasing them.

When the internment swoops were introduced, Marty was one of the first in the Lurgan area to be arrested and it was in the cages of Long Kesh that he embarked upon a programme of self-education – a dicipline he practised for the rest of his life. In Long Kesh, Marty came in contact with other republicans and he soon became immersed in the whole military structure of that time. Years later he used to laugh when he recalled that he and Jim Sullivan were the last Official republicans allowed to leave Long Kesh.

In 1973, he was convicted for arms possession offences and was jailed for seven years. This time Marty didn't find jail so romantic and passed his time studying at every opportunity. It was probably around this time that he decided paramilitarism – Official or otherwise – wasn't for him, because he retreated into himself and spent a lot of time on his own. By the time he was released from prison in 1978, Marty was a confirmed, if not committed, Marxist. But he was also totally opposed to any form of violence in pursuit of politics.

Although he had a wife and family to provide for, Marty embarked on an ambitious plan to build a new career. He decided he wanted to be a journalist. The odds were stacked against him, but determination was one of his greatest qualities and it wasn't long before work began to come his way. He could always be relied upon to deliver and editors got to know this. As a means of stabilising a regular form of income, he took a part-time job editing a community newspaper in the south Armagh village of Crossmaglen and he also worked on the prestigious Belfast-based journal *Fortnight*, which prided itself on providing a platform for political discourse. At *Fortnight*, Marty did everything. He wrote stories. He liaised with the printer. He delivered the magazine to the shops and he collected the money as well. Andy Pollak, a one-time *Fortnight* editor, says Marty walked into his office one day in 1982 and declared he wanted to be a journalist. Marty was, in the words of Pollak, 'the original muckraker'.

Later, Marty landed on his feet as far as his new-chosen career was concerned when sectarian squabbling erupted in the Tunnel district of Portadown. The Protestant citadel was only 11 miles from Lurgan and he knew most of the major players personally. When Peter Taylor, the well-known *Panorama* journalist and expert on Ulster's terror war, came to Portadown to make a TV programme, it was Marty he consulted before making a move.

A number of major newspaper editors began using Marty's copy, including Jim Campbell, the Northern Editor of the Dublin-based tabloid, the *Sunday World*, which enjoyed a massive circulation in Northern Ireland.

For many years, Campbell had been a thorn in the side of loyalist paramilitaries and he had written many exposés on the murderous activities of UVF killer Robin Jackson. Known as 'The Jackal', Jackson had been responsible for many shocking sectarian murders and was still deeply involved in paramilitary activity. But in 1984, Jackson hit back and arranged for a UVF killer gang to call at Campbell's north Belfast home. When the journalist went to the front door he was shot several times and critically injured. Only skilled emergency surgery saved Campbell's life.

During the time Campbell was recovering, Marty O'Hagan stepped up his *Sunday World* contributions and was eventually rewarded by being offered a position on the staff. All Marty's hard work had paid off. He was a great asset to the newspaper and covered a range of stories. 'Everything from showbiz to shock horror,' he often boasted.

For some time Marty had been aware that a new gang of UVF killers were about to spring into action in the sectarian hotbed of Mid-Ulster. They called themselves the 'Brat pack' and were led by Billy Wright, a complex character who mixed old-time religion and paramilitary violence with drug dealing.

Marty made it his life's work to expose Wright in the same way that his boss Jim Campbell had exposed Robin Jackson. Every week the *Sunday World* carried his stories about Wright's seedy activities. But around this time, Marty fell prey to a man who was a former RUC informant. The former police tout had been dumped by his handlers and had fallen out with them over money. As a means of getting his own back, he took to ringing Marty claiming to be a police officer. The anonymous caller fed Marty stories over the phone (they never met) alleging police collusion with loyalist paramilitaries. These stories appeared regularly in the *Sunday World*.

By coincidence, Ben Hamilton, a South African-born researcher for an independent TV company called Box Productions, arrived in Ulster looking for a story. He had been interested in a recent news story concerning undercover SAS activities which had ended in the death of a number of republicans. Unfortunately for Hamilton, John Ware from the BBC's *Panorama* programme beat him to it. Not wanting to return to London empty-handed, Hamilton began to trawl the newsrooms of Belfast looking for a story of interest and in the *Sunday World* office he found one. Using Marty's stories as a starting point, Hamilton began to research cases of alleged police collusion with a number of leading loyalist paramilitaries, including Billy Wright.

Hamilton's boss at Box Productions was Sean McPhilemy, a native of Castlederg, Co. Tyrone. He had gone to Queen's University in Belfast during the unrest of the late 1960s, where he became a member of the radical student group 'Peoples' Democracy' which included, among others, the former Mid-Ulster MP Bernadette Devlin. McPhilemy was convinced Hamilton was onto something and the end result was a TV documentary broadcast on Channel 4 which alleged senior unnamed RUC officers were involved in setting up Catholics for sectarian murder.

The day after the programme was broadcast, the RUC issued a strongly worded statement which amounted to a complete rebuttal of the programme content. Detective Superintendent Jimmy Nesbitt – the same officer who successfully solved the Shankill Butchers case – was asked to head up a team of inquiry into the matter.

Nesbitt was anxious to discover the identity of a man who had appeared on the programme in disguise. It was his contribution on which the collusion allegation was based. Jimmy Nesbitt eventually learned that the disguised man was Jim Sands, a contact of Marty O'Hagan who was a member of the Ulster Independence Movement, which enjoyed some support among hardline Protestants in mid-Ulster. During police questioning, Sands admitted his TV allegations were false. Police who interviewed Sands say he kept laughing at how ridiculous the whole thing had become.

Back in Portadown, however, Billy Wright did not consider the programme a laughing matter. He had already threatened Marty when he called at Wright's home. Wright lifted Marty by the throat and pushed him against his garden fence. This time Wright vowed to take revenge.

Wright persuaded his UVF friends in Belfast to plant a bomb in the *Sunday World* offices. Terrified staff were forced to jump over the device in order to escape. Van drivers and newsagents were threatened not to either distribute or sell the *Sunday World*.

The terror unnerved Jim Campbell, who began to suffer flashbacks of the time he was shot, and he left Belfast to live in the Republic. Marty's employers moved him to Cork for his own safety.

Things eventually settled down, however, and the paper began selling again. In the run up to the paramilitary ceasefires of 1994, Marty returned north to take up his old job on the northern edition. He settled in well and it wasn't long before he was bringing in a range of top-quality stories. But this time, under the new Northern Editor Jim McDowell, Marty was encouraged to take a more measured approach – if for no other reason than his own safety and the safety of his family and his work colleagues.

On 27 December 1997, Billy Wright, whom Marty had given the fitting nom de plume 'King Rat', was shot dead by the INLA as he sat in a minibus inside Maghaberry Prison where he was serving a sentence for issuing death threats. Many people in Northern Ireland both publicly and privately gloated over Wright's murder but Martin O'Hagan certainly wasn't one of them. He was appalled by violence.

Wright's death, as far as Marty was concerned, was just another sad tale in a sea of unnecessary sorrows. Henry McDonald, the *Observer*'s Ireland correspondent, maintains Marty O'Hagan's attitude to Billy Wright's murder reminded him of the time he met the *Sunday World* man at Belfast City Hall within hours of the Provisional IRA calling its 1994 'cessation of hostilities'. Paraphrasing his hero Karl Marx and being mindful of the ceasefire the Official IRA announced 22 years before, Marty said: 'Henry, the first time it was tragedy, the second time it's farce.'

By this time, life had changed for Marty. His three daughters were growing up and Marty and his wife Marie decided it was time to move from the house that had been their home in Lurgan since they first married. They bought a nice property on the outskirts of the town on the Tandragee Road. At the time, some of Marty's friends expressed concern that he could be placing himself in danger because the new house at Westfield Gardens was within spitting distance of the Mourneview Housing estate – home to some notorious paramilitary figures in the Loyalist Volunteer Force (LVF). The LVF was a dangerous collection of killers and drug dealers formed by Billy Wright after he quit the UVF because that organisation was 'too communist'. Marty refused to listen.

O'Hagan's working week started on a Tuesday morning when he entered the *Sunday World*'s Belfast office. From then, he went at it hell for leather, churning out stories until around 3.00 p.m. on Friday afternoon, when he would quietly slip out the door and head back to Lurgan.

Marty was a creature of habit and enjoyed nothing more than a Friday evening in his local bar, Fa' Joe's in Lurgan town centre. It was there that he met up with his old pals from yesteryear and over a bottle of Guinness, which is all he ever drank, they would reminisce about times that were long past. Generally, his wife Marie would arrive later and the pair would walk home together.

On Friday, 28 September 2001, Marie O'Hagan called into Fa' Joe's – the pub's real name is the Carnegie Bar – to enjoy a few drinks with her husband. Little did she realise it would be her last. Two weeks previously, as Marty and Marie walked home (a distance of around a mile), someone said something to Marty which uneased him. A loyalist he knew said: 'You've been clocked walking down here.'

Marty, assuming the man was warning him that it could be dangerous, said: 'Thanks for the tip-off.'

To which the loyalist barked: 'It's not a fucking tip-off!'

Two weeks later, on their journey home the O'Hagans passed the entrance to the Mourneview estate. Their house was within sight as they walked past an occupied car parked at the side of the road. The men in the car were members of the LVF and they had been waiting for Marty. One of their 'spotters', who had been in Fa' Joe's pub, had tipped them off that Marty and Marie were on their way.

In the back seat an LVF gunman cocked a 9mm Browning pistol and lowered the rear window. As the car moved off slowly, the gunman shot Martin O'Hagan three times in the back. Instinctively, Marty pushed Marie into a neighbour's hedge as the gunfire erupted. As he fell to the ground, the car containing the killer gang sped off.

Marty told his wife to call an ambulance. She rushed for help but when she returned seconds later Marty was dead. That second Marty became a murder milestone on a bloody road with no end in sight. He was the first, and so far the only, journalist to be murdered in Northern Ireland.

In a call to a Belfast newsroom, a group calling itself the Red Hand Defenders claimed responsibility for the killing, claiming he was shot for 'crimes against the loyalist people' – but everyone knew his killers belonged to the LVF.

There has been great speculation about why Marty O'Hagan was murdered, much of it nonsense. The most realistic reason to explain why the LVF chose to kill Marty was because they could. Marty, 51, was the journalist who first told the world about Billy Wright's murderous and drug dealing activities but, more than that, he was living on the LVF's doorstep.

Marty's friend Andy Pollak was right when he said Martin 'had a courage bordering recklessness'. In the end, it was probably that which made him the softest of targets for those whose only contribution to society is to inflict death and destruction.

Epilogue

John Tierney, a former Mayor of Derry and now a member of the Legislative Assembly at Stormont, has spent a lifetime in politics. He is on the socialist wing of the SDLP and is a popular figure in his native city. Tierney and his family live in William Street on the edge of the Bogside. The street was the scene of many riots in the early days of the Troubles and it was there, on 19 April 1969, that RUC officers charged into Sammy Devenney's home before beating him unconscious. Mr Devenney died three months later as a result of the injuries he sustained that day. He was an entirely innocent victim and no one was ever charged in connection with his death. Many people in Northern Ireland believe the incident marked the start of what we have come to call 'the Troubles' – an era of violence which was to last more than a quarter of a century and claim nearly three and a half thousand lives.

During an interview with the author in the members' tearoom at Stormont in the spring of 2002, John Tierney reflected on the Troubles. He spoke at length about the improved security situation in the wake of the paramilitary ceasefires and the political progress made as a result of the historic compromise enshrined in the Good Friday Agreement: 'I don't know how we came through the Troubles,' said Tierney as he drew heavily on a cigarette, 'however, I am certain of one thing: we could never go through it again.'

John Tierney's measured words speak volumes about the almost surreal nature of the Troubles. Men and women who had never before been involved in violence or crime of any kind perpetrated horrendous deeds on others they had never even met. The value of human life plummeted to an all-time low and, after a while, news reports of political murder in Northern Ireland rarely made national television news.

Maybe it's only with the benefit of hindsight that we can see that the warning signs were obvious long before the violence erupted. In the 1960s, unionism's refusal to adapt to a changed political climate created the conditions in which conspirators felt justified in resurrecting the UVF to oppose the reforms being proposed by the liberal wing of the Ulster Unionist Party. The murder of Peter Ward outside the Malvern Arms marked the culmination of a secretive plot that was always destined to end in death.

Retrospectively, Harold Wilson's Labour government of the 1960s must shoulder much of the blame for its refusal to enter the arena sooner. As early as 1965, Paul Rose, MP for Blackley, Manchester, had complained that there was something terminally wrong in the Northern Ireland body politic. In his role as chairman of the Campaign for Democracy in Ulster, Rose constantly warned government ministers about the dangers of ignoring unionist misrule. It could be argued that if the British had forced the unionists to grant Catholics in Northern Ireland the same rights as other citizens of the United Kingdom, then the Troubles may never have happened.

Unionism's violent response to the reasonable demands of the civil rights campaign ensured that 'physical force' republicanism, which was practically moribund, would be revitalised in the form of the Provisional IRA. From the beginning, the Provos were intent on a military adventure that stood little chance of success. Cathal Goulding, who took over as the IRA's chief-of-staff in 1962, had pointed out that republicans always seemed to want to start military campaigns with little thought of how it would end.

The story of nine-year-old Patrick Rooney – the first of 68 children to die in the Troubles – beggars belief. The youngster was killed in his own home by a bullet fired from an RUC machine gun on the first night of the Troubles. The policeman who fired the fatal shot may not have intentionally set out to kill anyone, but the rashness of his behaviour – firing wildly in a built-up Catholic area – meant it was destined to end in tragedy. At the time, some observers believed Patrick Rooney's death would bring the combatants to their senses. How wrong they were.

With the arrival of the British Army in Ulster the day after Patrick Rooney lost his life, a collective sigh of relief was heard in the Catholic community, as local people offered tea and sandwiches to the soldiers. However, the sight of 'their' army protecting people who they believed gave succour to the IRA put unionist noses out of joint and the IRA were also unhappy to see Irish people at ease with the British Army on the streets. The newly formed Provos had taken a decision to foist yet another military campaign on the people of the North, with the stated intention of bringing about a united Ireland. It also has to be said that, after a relatively short period, the behaviour of the army on the streets did little to endear them to the minority community.

The Provos had been in existence for 13 months before they managed to draw blood. Robert Curtis, a 20-year-old soldier in the Royal Artillery, was shot dead by IRA sniper Billy Reid, who was himself shot dead three months later. In the autumn of the same year, the Ulster Defence Association was formed and the stage was set for a slaughter frenzy that would last for three decades.

Standing alone, none of the murders or deaths covered in this book tells the story of the Troubles, but collectively they give a flavour of the ingredients that sparked and then ensured the Troubles continued.

When the IRA called a ceasefire in August 1994, republicans paraded up and down the Falls Road in a cavalcade of horn-blasting taxis with IRA supporters hanging out the windows waving tricolours. The ceasefire was not unexpected and very quickly Northern Ireland settled down to enjoy the peace. A plethora of bistros and wine bars sprung up in Belfast and a kind of 'normality' descended upon the city. However, unionists viewed the republican celebrations with caution. 'Has a secret deal been done behind our backs to sell out our British birthright?' they demanded to know. The reality was that there was no deal, but needless to say republicans did nothing to reassure unionist fears.

In the end, it was the actions of the much-maligned Special Branch and Anti-Racketeering Branch of the RUC that gradually closed down both republican and loyalist paramilitary murder machines. The Provos could have struggled on forever, but the campaign was going nowhere and they knew it.

The IRA's so-called 'Long War' became just another fact of life in Northern Ireland and everyone knew that, as long as the IRA maintained its campaign of violence, Protestant paramilitaries would happily carry out despicable deeds in response. Dead policemen or soldiers generally meant dead Catholics days later. As the Troubles became protracted, criminal cultures established themselves in both communities, which had previously been extremely law-abiding. These criminal empires, which range from drug dealing and tobacco and alcohol smuggling to drinking dens and extortion rackets, are still in place today. But with less resources having to be diverted to security, the RUC, and later its successor the Police Service of Northern Ireland, became more adept a counteracting paramilitary crime.

Throughout the Peace Process, the dynamic that drove it was the close cooperation of the British and Irish governments. This arrangement emerged in the dark days following the Shankill and Greysteel atrocities. It became obvious then that Northern Ireland could easily slip into a Beirut-type situation where paramilitary gangs held sway. When the IRA broke its ceasefire after 17 months by detonating a huge bomb at Canary Wharf in London's docklands, which claimed the lives of a cleaner and a newsagent, this dynamic, instead of disintegrating, intensified, and eventually the ceasefire was reinstated. Despite recurring periods of crisis, the imperfect peace we enjoy today seems to have taken root among the people of Northern Ireland, if not among the politicians. The Catholic community has accepted Northern Ireland as a political reality and is taking part in the institutions of government with some relish. A growing section of the Ulster Unionist Party appear frustrated at the continued existence of the IRA, which still controls a huge arsenal of weaponry, but, despite the occasional outbursts from its leader, Ian Paisley's DUP are taking part in the process of shared government.

Security experts believe paramilitary organisations – both republican and loyalist – will be part and parcel of Northern Irish life for many years to come. And the drip-feed campaign of both the Real IRA and the Continuity IRA still pose a real threat to political stability.

There can be no doubt that there was no justification for any of the paramilitary campaigns. Nationalist grievances, real or imagined, did not justify what the IRA did in the name of the Irish people. And the actions of Protestant paramilitaries – often encouraged by so-called democratic politicians – were equally reprehensible.

In the final sentences of his excellent book, *Faith of Our Fathers*, Maurice Goldring, the French academic, writes about justification of terrorism, which he condemns out of hand. Goldring states: ' I have written about Ireland in the past, and I have sometimes found good reasons for terrorism, particularly when it originated with a certain section of the population of Northern Ireland. I was wrong. I shall never again make the gift of a single "but" to the proponents of murderous folly.'

Maurice Goldring is right. There is no room in Ireland, north or south, for any more 'buts'.

Glossary

APPRENTICE BOYS OF DERRY: A Protestant male marching order which commemorates the siege of Derry of 1689 by marching round the walled city of Derry

ARD FHEIS: Irish Gaelic for an annual delegate conference – usually political

B SPECIALS: A part-time section of the RUC which was abolished in 1970. Catholic leaders claimed it operated in a sectarian manner

CESA: Catholic Ex-Servicemen's Association

DAIL EIREANN: Lower House of the Irish Parliament

DUP: Democratic Unionist Party, a hardline Protestant party led by Rev. Ian Paisley

FIANNA EIREANN: Youth section of the IRA

FIANNA FAIL: The largest party in the Irish Republic. It was founded by Éamon de Valera

FIANNA GAEL: The main opposition party in the Irish Republic

FREE DERRY CORNER: A place in the Bogside district of Derry which has become a tourist attraction

GARDA SIOCHANA: The unarmed police force of the Irish Republic

GOOD FRIDAY AGREEMENT: Also called the Belfast Agreement, signed in 1988. This deal was backed by both the British and Irish Parliaments and all parties in the North, with the exception of the DUP

GAA: Gaelic Athletic Association – an Irish sporting group which is organised throughout Ireland

INLA: Irish National Liberation Army – a military group which split from the Official IRA in 1974. It is the military wing of the Irish Republican Socialist Party

LONG KESH: A collection of ex-RAF Nissan huts which were turned into a prison following the introduction of internment in 1971

MAZE PRISON: This replaced Long Kesh as the largest prison for sentenced terrorists. It was the scene of the IRA hunger strikes of 1981, when 10 prisoners lost their lives

NICRA: Northern Ireland Civil Rights Association

OFFICIAL IRA: Originally the majority section when the IRA split in 1970. A left-wing group which called a ceasefire in 1972

ORANGE ORDER: A protestant male marching order, closely aligned to the Ulster Unionist Party

PAV: Protestant Action Volunteers

PEELER: A policeman

PROVISONAL IRA: The largest republican paramilitary group which was responsible for nearly 1,800 deaths in the conflict

PROVOS: Another name for the Provisional IRA

REAL IRA: A splinter group from the IRA composed of members who disagreed with the ceasefires of 1994 and 1997. The Real IRA was responsible for the Omagh bomb which, on the 15 August 1988, claimed the lives of 29 people, including the mother of unborn twins

RUC: The Royal Ulster Constablulary – the police force of Northern Ireland from 1922 until it was replaced by the Police Service of Northern Ireland in November 2001

SDLP: Social Democratic and Labour Party – the main moderate Catholic party in Northern Ireland

TAOISEACH: The Irish Prime Minister

TOUT: A slang word for a police informer

UCDC: Ulster Constitution Defence Committee

UDA: Ulster Defence Association – the largest Protestant paramilitary group. It is also known as the UFF – the Ulster Freedom Fighters

UDR: Ulster Defence Regiment – a regiment of the British Army which was set up following the disbandment of the B Specials. It was later incorporated into the Royal Irish Regiment

UPV: Ulster Protestant Volunteers

UUP: The Ulster Unionist Party – the largest unionist party in Northern Ireland

UVF: The Ulster Volunteer Force – the oldest loyalist paramilitary group

Notes

CHAPTER ONE

An account of the IRA raid on Brookeborough RUC station is carried in J. Boyer Bell's excellent and very detailed book, *The Secret Army* (Dublin, Poolbeg Press, 1970).

Interviews were carried out with a former RUC officer who was present in the police station during the attack and another former officer who at one time worked as a handler to the Special Branch agent George Poyntz.

The *Belfast Telegraph* at the time covered the raid and the inquests into the deaths of Sean South and Feargal O'Hanlon.

The Politics of Illusion: A Political History of the IRA by Henry Patterson (London, Serif, 1997) contains a number of interviews with Sean Garland.

CHAPTER TWO

A booklet entitled *Songs of the North*, which was published by Saor Ulaidh shortly after the Roslea attack, contains an article by the organisation's leader Liam Kelly. He details aspects of Connie Green's life, including his military record in the British Army during the Second World War.

Derry-based Irish language activist Proinsias O'Mianain, who was interned in the 1950s, was a great help in finding out about Green's early life. Paddy Joe McClean, who had been a member of Fianna Ulaidh, pointed me in the right direction.

A policeman who was on duty at the RUC roadblock when Constable John Hunter was killed at Jonesborough provided invaluable information about Hunter's life.

CHAPTER THREE

Roy Garland's book *Gusty Spence* (Belfast, Blackstaff Press, 2001) gives an account of the Malvern Arms shootings.

The *Belfast Telegraph*, the *Irish News* and the *Newsletter* covered the aftermath of the shootings and the trial of Spence and the others.

Barrister John Creaney, who was Junior Counsel in Spence's defence team, was a tremendous source, providing excellent analysis of the case.

Ed Moloney and Andy Pollak's book *Paisley* (Dublin, Poolbeg Press, 1986) provides an excellent insight into Ian Paisley's early life and first forays into the world of unionist politics.

UVF by Jim Cusack and Henry McDonald (Dublin, Poolbeg Press, 1997) is an important account of how this most deadly of paramilitary organisations works.

CHAPTER FOUR

Executed: Tom Williams and the IRA by Jim McVeigh (Belfast, Beyond the Pale Publications, 1999), with a foreword by Joe Cahill, gives a flavour of life inside the republican movement in the 1940s.

Another usual reference guide was Eamon Pheonix's *Northern Nationalism: Nationalist Politics, Partition and the Catholic Minority in Northern Ireland 1890–1940* (Belfast, Ulster Historical Foundation, 1994).

Man of War – Man of Peace: The Unauthorised Biography of Gerry Adams by David Sharrock and Mark Devonport (London, Pan Books, 1998) gives excellent information about the IRA response to Williams' execution.

Uinseann O Rathaille Mac Eoin, *The IRA in the Twilight Years 1923–48* (Dublin, Argenta Publications, 1997).

John Ellis, *Diary of a Hangman* (London, The True Crime Library).

CHAPTER FIVE

Ulster by the *Sunday Times* Insight team gave a great outline of the main ingredients which provoked the Troubles.

The Sparks That Lit The Bonfire – a BBC 2 *Timewatch* programme produced by Ken Kirby and edited by Nigel Rees provided valuable information on how the Irish government supplied money which found its way into the IRA's coffers.

Sean MacStiofain: Memoirs of a Revolutionary (Edinburgh, Gordon Cremonesi, 1975).

Eamonn McCann, *War and an Irish Town* (London, Penguin, 1974).

Rosita Sweetman, *On Our Knees: Ireland 1972* (London, Pan Books, 1972).

A number of interviews were carried out with former members of the IRA who were involved at the time the IRA split into the Provisionals and the Officials.

CHAPTER SIX
Eamon Mallie and Patrick Bishop, *The Provisional IRA* (London, Corgi, 1987).

Tim Pat Coogan, *The Troubles: Ireland's Ordeal 1966–1995 and the Search for Peace* (London, Hutchinson, 1995).

Peter Taylor, *Provos, The IRA and Sinn Fein* (London, Bloomsbury, 1997).

Adrian Guelke, *The Age of Terrorism* (London, I.B. Tauris Publishers, 1998).

Brendan O'Brien, *The Long War: The IRA and Sinn Fein 1985 to Today* (Dublin, The O'Brien Press, 1993).

CHAPTER SEVEN
In-depth interviews with a member of the IRA from the Belfast area, which had originally been conducted for the *Sunday World* newspaper, provided invaluable information about the murky world of informers, as did interviews with superspies Martin McGartland and Kevin Fulton.

Sean O'Callaghan, *The Informer* (London, Bantam Press, 1998).

Martin McGartland, *Fifty Dead Men Walking* (London, Blake Publishing, 1998).

Martin Dillon, *The Dirty War* (London, Hutchinson, 1988).

Former *Cook Report* producer Howard Foster provided detailed information about IRA informers.

Kevin Toolis, *Rebel Hearts: Journeys within the IRA's Soul* (New York, St Martin's Press, 1995).

CHAPTER EIGHT
Conversations with Robin Walsh, former BBC Controller Northern Ireland, gave me a fascinating insight into the shooting of Gunner Robert Curtis, the first British soldier to lose his life.

Ardoyne Community Project, Ardoyne, *The Untold Truth* (Beyond the Pale Publications).

Martin Dillon and Denis Lehane, *Political Murder in Northern Ireland* (London, Penguin, 1973).

Brendan O'Brien, *A Pocket History of the IRA* (Dublin, The O'Brien Press, 1997).

Toby Harnden, *Bandit Country: The IRA and South Armagh* (London, Hodder & Stoughton, 2000).

An interview with former Detective Superintendent Tim McGregor revealed that Jimmy 'Nailer' Clarke had been a long-term source of the RUC in Ardoyne.

Former Detective Sergeant Eamon Canavan provided valuable information on IRA gunman Paddy McAdorey.

Interview with former republican Peter McKenna.

CHAPTER NINE

Interview in Belfast with Joe Clarke, the youngest of the 'Hooded Men'.

Interview in Berragh, Co.Tyrone with Paddy Joe McClean, whose torture case was taken to the European Court of Human Rights.

Interview in Derry with Mickey Donnelly – one of the hooded men who was beaten up in his own home by Provos.

CHAPTER TEN

Tony Crowe in Derry provided background to the murder of Senator John Barnhill, the first political killing.

Interviews with former Official IRA members who provided information on the bombing of the Parachute Regiment's HQ at Aldershot.

Barrister John Creaney helped with background on the Marcus McCausland killing.

CHAPTER ELEVEN

Interview with Bernard Moane on the murder of his father.

Interview with former IRA man who took part in abduction of James McAvoy in Newry.

Interview with former IRA man about police informers in Derry.

Geoffrey Bell, *The Protestants of Ulster* (London, Pluto Press, 1976).

CHAPTER TWELVE

Details of Colm Carey's last hours were provided by Kevin 'Biggsy' Johnston, who drank wine with Carey prior to his murder. Johnston was interviewed on a number of occasions while on hunger strike outside Stormont.

Interviews with Willie Carlin in Newcastle and Ballymena on the killing of Joanne Mathers.

J. Boyer Bell, *The Irish Troubles: A Generation of Violence 1967–1992* (Dublin, Gill & Macmillan, 1993).

Liam Clarke, *Broadening The Battlefield* (Dublin, Gill & Macmillan, 1987).

Liam Clarke and Kathryn Johnston, *Martin McGuinness: From Guns to Government* (Edinburgh, Mainstream Publishing, 2001).

CHAPTER THIRTEEN

Gilbert Denton and Tony Fahy, *The Northern Ireland Land Boundary 1923–1992* (Belfast, Customs Office, 1993).

Conversations with John McCann, retired Assistant Collector, Belfast.

Eamon Collins, *Killing Rage* (London, Granta Books, 1997).

Thomas Hennessey, *A History of Northern Ireland, 1920–1996* (Dublin, Gill & Macmillan, 1997).

Interview with former Detective Superintendent Tim McGregor regarding Owen Connolly, whom he worked with before becoming a police officer.

CHAPTER FOURTEEN

Interview with Mickey Mooney's friend Dominic Thompson.

Interview with former Detective Superintendent Kevin Sheehy, a one-time head of the RUC Drugs Squad.

Jeremy Adams interviewed James 'Doc' Halliday for a BBC *Spotlight* programme.

Interview with Henry Robinson, who was in Crumlin Road Prison at the same time as Mickey Mooney.

CHAPTER FIFTEEN

A number of interviews were conducted with writer Martin Dillon, author of *The Shankill Butchers: A Case Study of Mass Murder* (London, Hutchinson, 1989)

Interviews with Detective Sergeant Philip 'Bogie' Boyd, who was a member of the RUC investigation team. It was Boyd who got a confession from Robert 'Basher' Bates.

Interview with a senior UVF figure who knew Lenny Murphy, the leader of the Butcher Gang.

Interview with TV journalist Clive Entwhistle of *The Cook Report*, who made an excellent programme exposing Jimmy Craig as an extortionist and thug.

Interviews with builders who had dealings with Jimmy Craig.

Peter Taylor, *Loyalists* (London, Bloomsbury, 1999).

CHAPTER SIXTEEN

Interviews with former Detective Sergeant Johnston Brown, who led the investigation into Johnny Adair and who investigated the murder of Noel Cardwell.

Interviews with a number of detectives based at Tennent Street, Belfast, about Adair's activities.

Details of why Adair was placed back in prison following his release were obtained from 'The Substantive Determination in the matter of John James Adair', compiled by the Sentence Review Commissioners.

Jonathan Stevenson, *We Wrecked The Place: Contemplating an End to the Northern Irish Troubles* (New York, The Free Press, 1996).

Steve Bruce, *The Red Hand* (Oxford, Oxford University Press, 1992).

CHAPTER SEVENTEEN

Discussions with Martin O'Hagan.

Interviews with former members of the Official IRA who were in prison with O'Hagan.

Discussions with journalists Liam Clarke and Barry Penrose regarding the Inner Force allegations of police collusion.

Article by journalist Susan McKay in the *Guardian* Weekend magazine, 2001.

Interviews with a number of former RUC officer who served in the Lurgan area during the 1970s.

Maurice Goldring, *Faith of Our Fathers* (Dublin, Repsol Publishing, 1982).

Index

LOST LIVES

The Stories of the Men, Women and Children who Died as a Result of the Northern Ireland Troubles

D. McKittrick, S. Kelters, B. Feeney and C. Thornton

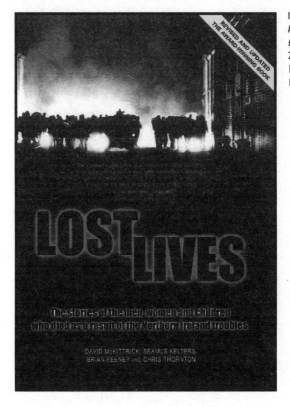

ISBN 1 84018 504 X
Available now
£30.00 (hardback)
246 x 156mm
1,648pp
1 x 16pp b/w

Lost Lives is the story of the Northern Ireland Troubles told as never before. All the casualties are here: the RUC officer, the IRA volunteer, the loyalist paramilitary, the Catholic mother, the Protestant worker, the new-born baby. Each account is impossible to ignore.

'In its encyclopaedic detail, in its towering integrity and in its moral compassion, it could be the most influential study of Irish history ever presented'
Irish Times

'. . . the most important and significant book of the year'
Independent on Sunday

THE BILLY BOY
The Life and Death of LVF Leader Billy Wright
Chris Anderson

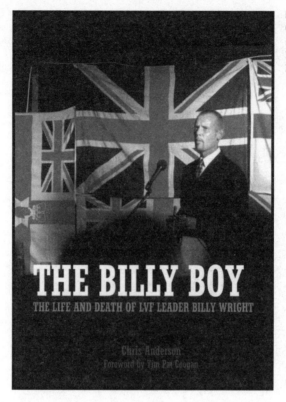

ISBN 1 84018 639 9
October 2002
£15.99 (hardback)
234 x 156mm
208pp
1 x 8pp colour

The Billy Boy tells the explosive story of Billy 'King Rat' Wright, the only loyalist paramilitary icon to emerge in over 30 years of bloodshed in Northern Ireland.

Revered and respected by loyalists, despised and feared by nationalists, Wright is reputed to have been involved in a number of sectarian murders before he himself was shot dead by republican gunmen inside the Maze Prison in 1997.

The book charts his chequered life as a loyalist paramilitary through to his controversial trial and subsequent imprisonment, and investigates the allegations of state collusion in his death. Terrifically gripping and often disturbing, *The Billy Boy* is an exhaustive account of a notorious Irish rebel, whose life and death were surrounded by controversy and political debate.

BREAKING THE BONDS
Making Peace in Northern Ireland
Fionnuala O Connor

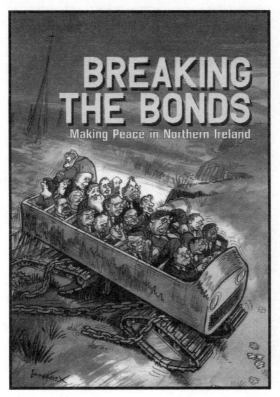

ISBN 1 84018 610 0
Available now
£9.99 (paperback)
234 x 156mm
288pp
b/w illustrations throughout

Award-winning writer and broadcaster Fionnuala O Connor charts Northern Ireland's path out of conflict, profiling leaders including Gerry Adams, David Trimble, John Hume; and others, including the Reverend Ian Paisley, who've harried and condemned the 'peace process'.

People in Northern Ireland watch their politicians with amazement and fury, and occasionally with affection and pride. O Connor portrays these men, and a few women, in the context of remarkable times, while the outstanding cartoonist Ian Knox catches those profiled as their acts and histories reveal them.

'A penetrating analysis of two communities in transition and a process still on trial'
Belfast Telegraph

RESEARCHING THE TROUBLES
Social Science Perspectives on the Northern Ireland Conflict
Edited by Owen Hargie and David Dickson

ISBN 1 84018 635 6
October 2002
£20.00 (hardback)
234 x 156mm
336pp

Researching the Troubles highlights how, for over 30 years, the seemingly irreconcilable division between the Catholic and Protestant communities in Northern Ireland has resulted in horrific violence and over 3,700 deaths. It brings together for the first time a number of the most prestigious research projects into cross-community conflict and reconciliation. The contributors are all well-known academics from across a broad spectrum of social sciences who provide a wealth of insight into the reasons for, effects of, and possible ways to ease the hostility. *Researching the Troubles* is an indispensable tome for those who wish to fully understand the ongoing conflict in Northern Ireland from every angle.